# New Worlds for Old

# NEW WORLDS FOR OLD

Reports from the New World and
their effect on the development of
social thought in Europe, 1500-1800

*William Brandon*

**OHIO UNIVERSITY PRESS**
*ATHENS, OHIO  LONDON*

**Library of Congress Cataloging-in-Publication Data**

Brandon, William.
  New worlds for old.

  Bibliography: p.
  1. America—Discovery and exploration.   2. Europe—Civilization—
American influences.   I. Title.
E121.B73  1986   303.4′827′04   85-25818
ISBN 0-8214-0818-6
ISBN 0-8214-0819-4 pbk.

*To Janey*
*and all futures*

# Contents

# Preface

It has been many times related that Europe found (or thought it found) a "golden world" in newly discovered America, promptly destroyed it, and stamped upon its remains the conquering culture of Western civilization.

The thesis of this book proposes that the New World insidiously engraved upon the Old World — especially via seventeenth- and eighteenth-century France — changes as profound in some respects as those suffered by the New, that garbled influences from the New World are in fact ascendant in certain noteworthy areas of social thought in our present world.

It has also been many times argued that the marvelous New World differences that sometimes seemed to European observers so golden were fictions anyway, invented from the Old World's rich imagination and racial memory.

The thesis herein proposes that the most significant of the marvelous differences recorded were indeed real, that the reports of European explorers, travelers, colonists were for the most part objectively factual, that the societies of the New World were for the most part built upon foundations basically and radically different from those of the Old.

This study suggests that the one greatest dividing difference fell in the attitude toward property, the usual Old World tendencies summed up in the word *dominium,* the New World's in the word *communitas;* that these two differing tendencies led on the one hand to preoccupation with business, competition, adversarianism, authoritarianism, and the ultimate act of dominium, total war — on the other hand to preoccupation with group relationships, lack of interest in the acquisition of property, and frequently a lack of central authority resulting in a seeming masterlessness.

It is further suggested that the conflict between these two strains of the Old World and the New, these two religions, these two ethics, these two visions of the purpose of life, of right behavior, has been an integral part of the chronic conflict between authoritarianism and liberalism that has burned at the core of Western history since the seventeenth century, a chronic conflict that shows signs of remaining, under other aliases, one of the central conflicts of the future.

# Acknowledgments

Most of the work on this book was carried out in France and England in a number of libraries and archives, principally in the Bibliothèque Nationale and the Archives de France in Paris and the British Library and the Cambridge University Library in England. I am glad of an opportunity to express my gratitude to the librarians, archivists, and staffs of these extraordinary institutions.

Numerous other institutions and individuals have been of endless help, far too many to list here, but I would like to note particular gratitude (which must not be taken as an indictment of their complicity in my controversial thesis) to my old and learned friends Wilbur Jacobs, Rodman Paul, Helene Harris, Terence Armstrong, Harry Porter, and the late Ray Billington; and it gives me special pleasure to add a special word of thanks to Carol and Ping Ferry, without whose continuing interest and support this long and difficult work would not have been possible. Finally and chiefly my thanks to Victoria Ginger for her invaluable assistance in discussions of the final version of the book and for her preparation of the index.

# Prologue

## 1. Rue Quincampoix

The rue Quincampoix, one of the oldest streets in Paris, was the scene of the brokerage office of John Law's business empire in 1719 and 1720 when his Mississippi Bubble added a new wrinkle to the basic pattern for the modern business world. The street — narrow, withered, grimy, gloomy — was just yesterday (it changed in the 1970s) the hunting ground of a particular type of prostitute, hard-jawed, leaden-eyed women who wear black leather miniskirts and steel-studded or bicycle-chain belts. The boulevard Sebastopol a short block away no doubt furnished much of their clientele, possibly from audiences at the particular type of film offered in abundance there: blood and torture, huge brutality, delectable rapine — violence of all the showier varieties. In 1719 when Monsieur John Law, or Monsieur Jean Lass as the French mispronounced his name, set up his stockjobbing shop there, the rue Quincampoix had been for centuries a center for various sorts of commercial enterprises, the rue des Lombards at the foot of the street having been named after the Italian moneylenders established there in the early 1300s following Philippe le Bel's expulsion of the Jews from Paris. Giovanni Boccaccio was born on the rue des Lombards in 1313, the result of an "adventure," as it is put by Jacques Hillairet in his *Connaissance du Vieux Paris*, of one of these Florentine "Lombards" with a Parisienne of those frolicsome days.

The quarter had also been noted for its *ribaudes*, medieval for whores, since at least the time of Saint Louis, when the vicinity of the nearby church of Saint Merri was designated one of the several localities in Paris specifically reserved for bordels, in an effort (vain) to limit their proliferation. The number of ribaudes was apparently always proverbial in Paris — by the fifteenth century there were five to six thousand who marched in their yearly procession honoring Saint Madeleine. "These women intoxicated with their bodies," said Saint Louis. Curés of Saint Merri were far from charmed, though, by their presence and agitated for years to have them expelled from the streets about Saint Merri's church and sepulcher, places of most venerable sanctification, Saint Merri (Médéric) having been one of the several saints bestowed on Paris in the seventh century, some of whose tombs, such as those of Saint Merri and

Saint Josse, have lain within shouting distance of each other ever since, so does the neighborhood reek of ancient days. But the ribaudes stayed, supported by the commercial leaders of the quarter, who said they were good for business.

I'm trying to show that the rue Quincampoix is a miniature relief map of a very considerable slice of history, gullied and peaked with the mysteries and miseries and mayhems, the agonies and anxieties and ex- ultations of a long, unbroken, and vehement human presence, with John Law's Mississippi Company very possibly the most lasting cut of all through this vast reach of time. If Monsieur Law's business estab- lishment there did not give birth to the whole of modern finance (as Jacques Perret asserts in a recent guidebook — *Paris Tel Qu'on l'Aime* — adding that even the French Revolution found roots therein as well), it may at least have occupied an identifiable place in these large begin- nings, a place conspicuous both then and now: a popular song of 1720 maintained that "a sweet sojourn in Quincampoix" was a thousand times to be preferred to any isle of Cythera, while a recent serious study finds John Law's "experiment . . . at the origin of certain profound and durable evolutions and mutations."

I walk through the rue Quincampoix now and then on my way to the Archives Nationales where I work occasionally with documents con- cerning American Indian history — colonial or precolonial encounters between Europeans and Indians. American Indian history, an element in the Mississippi Company's raw material — the thought has occurred to me many times. Actual American trade was not of much importance in John Law's operations, real or projected, but his dream of world trade owed much to the popular vision of a treasure-trove America, a vision in which there was much reality — America having already poured into Europe more gold and silver than the Old World had seen in all its pre- vious history. And a treasure house tended by the most easily plunder- able people the Old World had ever met (the trademark of the Compag- nie d'Occident, forerunner of Law's eventual Compagnie des Indes, pictured American Indians offering, with most joyous cordiality, a horn of plenty). Law's efforts to found a system of broad popular credit using in part the psychological leverage of this bright vision made him, in the words of the Socialist historian Louis Blanc, a "collectivist pioneer" struggling on behalf of the public, the people, against the privileged owners of "dead riches."

The pattern of those New World encounters, the behavior of the American participants — what those eccentric natives of the New World did for their own eccentric reasons — figured in the creation not only of the Mississippi Company but also of how many other post-Columbian creations great and small? How many new patterns, new designs and combinations, how many varied new worlds, were brought into being by collision with the New World and its peculiar people? The action itself of those encounters, the sinuous process of American Indian behavior in itself, is woven into how many of the multiple strands making up the pattern of our world of today?

Some of the most interesting and consequential of these possible strands are involved with the development of our present idea of liberty, liberty for all, popular liberty. Talk and thought of popular liberty appear to be everywhere in our modern world, markedly more so than in antiquity or in medieval times; this generalized and widespread interest in a generalized popular liberty appears to be a particular product of our age, an interest still oddly unsure of itself when it comes to specific definition, composed of assorted notions of liberty and equality that, separately, appear to be vague and contradictory in the extreme. A French parliamentary commission held lengthy hearings in 1976 and 1977 on the subject of what exactly liberty might be; the testimony (of which more later) from experts in many diverse fields was exceedingly diverse, quite often squarely at odds.

It has seemed to me, looking at this tangled question from the perspective of American Indian history, that descriptions of the American Indian world published in Europe during the several hundred years of early modern European history, from the Renaissance to the nineteenth century, may well have had something to do with the formation of certain key aspects of our complex present day conceptions of liberty.

## 2. Thesis

I offer here the proposition that in its collision with the New World the Old World did not escape unscathed — on the contrary it will be argued that the Old World was subtly infected by reports from the New to the point that tangled New World influences appear to be dominant in certain of our own social ideas today.

One of these is in the idea of liberty. Evidence will be presented that our current idea of liberty developed much of its modern sense in Europe and America in the three centuries following European contact with the New World. It will be suggested that the special nature of life and society in the New World as reported by European explorers, travelers, soldiers, colonists, missionaries, during those several hundred years was a factor of some importance in this development.

These reports on the New World headlined notions of liberty, a popular liberty involving elements of equality and masterlessness, that may really have been in a fairly literal sense new notions for Europe. These same reports gave persistent emphasis over a long period of time to fundamental differences between the Old World and the New in habits of thought concerning property, politics, inequality, and authority.

If the Western world's concept of liberty did indeed change following contact with the New World, it would seem not unreasonable that the concept thus altered may owe something to these New World reports.

I will propose on similar grounds that further altered concepts revealing New World influences have likewise already been accepted in our current attitudes and that the conflict between still further New World influence and Old World resistance is at the root of certain tensions critical to the basic structure of our own New World of today.

# I

# *The Aliens*

## 1. The Discovery of Utopia

European historians customarily fix the dividing point between the Middle Ages and modern European history at the discovery of America, a convenient central peg for the turbulent procession of events usually referred to as the Renaissance. The earth is still trembling beneath our feet from the effects of this great reorientation (if the sometimes disputed term *Renaissance* may be thus reconstrued), this wheel and turn of history that in the course of a century or two, among a worldful of other momentous developments, brought into being the modern nation states of Europe and set them in motion toward the succeeding centuries of accelerated growth, trade, war, conquest — of European expansion over the whole earth.

No doubt the pattern of forces there at work contained threads from all the preceding epochs of the Old World past, from China with its generous gifts including gunpowder and printing, from all the sciences of Arabia, as well as from the then newly excavated glories of ancient Greece and Rome and from the subsequent less glorious but uproariously tumultuous career of Europe itself. But did some threads also lead in from the New World, from the New World people then coming into contact, for the first time, with the Old?

The New World as a colonial treasure house has for a long while been recognized as one of the principal factors in the "rise of modern capitalism" and the emergence of the modern world, among a number of somewhat less obvious political and economic developments in which "the opportunities and the challenges represented by the New World . . . helped to shape and transform" the Old. The New World as a background for an image of paradise in the European mind has been sometimes advanced as another significant factor and will be discussed at some length later in this study.

But could the New World have been not only a passive resource but an active participant? Not only silver ingots and gold moidores and cargoes of oiled furs and an inviting scene for the white man's creative imagination but also actual societies of strange people, their own attitudes, their own dreams and ambitions and fears and wishes, their own actions playing a genuine historic role? Could the ways of life of these newfound American people, ways of living no doubt stemming from all the preceding epochs of *their* long past, constitute in themselves some of those lines of force leading into the intricate present?

A life lived free of toil and tyranny, free of masters, free of greed and the struggle for gain, became so much the key picture presented by the first historian of the New World, Peter Martyr of Anghiera, that his English translator summed it up in the repeated word *liberty*. Their "aunciente libertie" (says this translator, Richard Eden, writing in the 1550s) had made the New World people "most happye of all men." They were living in the golden age, wrote Peter Martyr (and explained Richard Eden, "of the whiche owlde wryters speake so much: wherin men lyved simply and innocentlye") without even weights and measures to cause disputes, free of lawsuits and law enforcement, free of calumniating judges and the resultant learned professions of craft and deceit, free of books, free of the pernicious presence of deadly money, content only to satisfy nature — and, added Richard Eden to his translation, incapable of servitude, having "been ever soo used to live at libertie, in play and pastyme."

Italian by origin, Renaissance humanist by trade, in a position of some authority and influence at the Spanish court (a favorite of Queen Isabella's and a sometime ambassador for the Spanish crown), Peter Martyr assigned himself the task of collecting the fullest information available on the newly discovered lands beyond the western seas, "these marvelous new things" compared to which (as Eden's pre-Elizabethan phrasing put it) "what so ever from the begynnynge of the worlde hath byn doone or wrytten to this day, to my judgment seemeth but lyttle . . ."

Beginning with Columbus, whom he interviewed a number of times, Martyr questioned the returned explorers, encouraged them in making systematic and objective observations of the new people and the new land, talked via interpreters to Indians brought to Spain, and served as a general clearing house for information on the great discovery. He was made a member of the Council of the Indies and was by far its best historian. He recorded hearsay as hearsay (such as the island of Amazons) and primary data as primary data (such as the first American Indian vocabulary to appear in Europe, the brief list of Taino words — starting with *canoa* meaning "a barke or boate" — gathered from the little group of New World people brought to Seville by Columbus on the return from his first voyage). His considerable learning apparently gave him doubts from the outset that Columbus had merely sailed to India; he wrote in a letter of October 1493 that "the hidden half of the globe is brought to light . . ."

He continued his history, presented for the most part as collections of newsletters to friends and patrons in Italy, until his death in 1526. Its later stages suffered from overburden and the snarls of conquistadorian politics but with his early work, suggest modern anthropologists, modern anthropology began.

"Come therefore," Eden has him say in his translation of Martyr's dedication, "and embrase this new worlde."

Among the people there, he wrote, "Myne and Thyne (the seedes of all myscheefe) have no place . . ." (In his original Latin, "necque meum aut tuum, malorum omnie semina . . .") Land was held in common, as free to all as the sunlight or the sea, "in open gardens, not intrenched with dykes, dyvyded with hedges, or defended with waules. They deal trewely one with another, without lawes, without bookes, and without Judges." They even lived without toil, he was informed, so bounteous was their fair country and so innocent their wants, in their "free kynde of life" that was "given to Idlenes and playe."

These lines are taken from the Richard Eden translation of Peter Martyr's first collection, or "Decade," as he termed it (each such gathering — there were eight Decades ultimately — was to contain ten "books"). The First Decade was printed in an Italian version in 1504 and 1507, in its original Latin in 1511, and in Latin together with later Decades in various subsequent reprintings during the 1500s. Selections from several of the Decades appeared in France in 1532 (apparently made for the instruction of the children of François I), and further Italian extracts in 1534. The Richard Eden translation, published in 1555, was of the first four Decades only, together with translations of various other narratives of exploration and colonization; a slightly enlarged edition of the Eden volume was published in 1577, and several later English editions on into the early 1600s.

Columbus's first report on his discovery, a letter written on shipboard in February 1493 while on his way home from the first voyage, was printed in Spanish that same year and went through nine editions in Latin translation before the end of 1494. A translation into Italian verse — the news magazine of the time, sixty-eight stanzas' worth, meant to be sung in the streets — sold out three editions before the end of 1493. A German translation and another Spanish edition appeared in 1497 — in all, some seventeen editions were produced between 1493 and 1498. Amerigo Vespucci's several letters, from the reasonably authentic to the gloriously garbled, enjoyed almost innumerable early editions, the best known (usually spoken of under the title *Mundus Novus*) having been put into Latin from Vespucci's original Italian and going through fifteen editions from 1503 to 1507 while being translated into five languages for numerous further imprints. A French version of a couple of Vespucci letters mixed well and highly seasoned with added fiction appeared in Paris in 1505 and racked up literally dozens of new editions and reimpressions during the next fifty years.

The great popular interest in these first publications on the New World centered, as Samuel Eliot Morison remarks in his biography of Columbus, on the people, the naked, timorous, generous natives living, so it seemed, in a veritable Garden of Eden. Wars and contentions existed between their "nations" — as said Peter Martyr, "ambition and the desire to rule trouble even them." But, wrote Columbus in his letter-report, "they are artless and generous with what they have to such a degree as no one would believe who has not seen it. Of anything they have, if it be asked for, they never say no, but do rather invite the person to accept it, and show as much lovingness as though their hearts went with it." In his Journal entry for Christmas Day 1492, Columbus declared with some solemnity that in all the world "I do not believe there is a better people or a better country; they love their neighbors as themselves" and was moved to add that "they have the softest and gentlest speech in the world and are always laughing."

Tales of rivulets of gold, gold considered valueless by the Indos unless, as Eden's Peter Martyr puts it, "the hande of the artificer hathe fashioned it in any coomely fourme," also attracted notice to be sure, as did tales of the serpents in the Garden — the fearsome cannibals; but even these things drew only second billing, and of such stately issues as trade routes to India (state secrets for the great, and then as now dull reading) there was scarcely any mention at all. In recounting Columbus's first landing on the South American coast (1498), Peter Martyr speaks of the ferocity of the people there, who killed several members of later expeditions, but this mention is buried (in fact rather apologetically buried, introduced by "It must be admitted . . .") beneath the headline news of Columbus's reception with enthusiasm and "gaiety" by an innumerable throng, at that time "kind and hospitable," and by the attitude of the natives toward the "Indian pearls" they had in abundance: "In twisting up their lips and gesturing with their hands they seemed to say that among them pearls were of insignificant account." (The wording here is rendered from a modern French translation; Eden has their "scornful giestures" indicating "that they nothing esteemed pearls.") The admission of ferocity, and a report of dangerous animals

— lions, tigers, crocodiles — in the mountains of the interior, is followed immediately by a stout qualification from the good Martyr who points out that he speaks here only of the mainland and not of the islands: "Everything in the isles breathes a perfect gentleness, except that is for certain men, of whom we have already spoken, the Caribs or Cannibals, who have a hunger for human flesh." Peter Martyr himself went to Madrid to "examine" the captured Caribs brought back on Columbus's second voyage; his reaction as given by Eden: "There is no man able to behowlde them, but he shall feel his bowelles grate with a certen horroure," so "infernal and repugnant" the aspect "nature and their own cruel character" lent to them. But the mainland too had its supernal glories: Martyr later mentions Columbus's theory that in the great mountains of the mainland interior may be the site of the terrestial paradise, much speculated upon by medieval geographers: "He eventually convinced himself of this."

A site for another sort of earthly paradise was suggested to Thomas More by the first descriptions of this genuinely new New World: he placed therein his *Utopia*, from whose previously undiscovered bourn a traveler has just returned its wonders to relate. His bustling republic, with its scrupulously organized and vigilantly enforced equality, is scarcely a copy of any American society alive or dead; but among its sources (so often noted) from Plato and the primitive Christian church and similar models from antiquity evidence can be found of other sources (not so often noted) from early accounts of New World people. Several such possible sources are discussed in the exhaustive edition of *Utopia* published as volume 4 of the Yale University Saint Thomas More Project; J. H. Hexter in the Introduction to this volume presents in particular certain passages from the letters of Amerigo Vespucci as "decisive" ("together Plato and Vespucci freed More's fancy"), passages speaking of American natives living together in perfect equality, each his own master, sharing everything in common, without private property, despising pearls and gold. Sidney Lee came many years ago to the even more single-track conclusion that *Utopia* owed its "foundation" to the "letters of Amerigo Vespucci . . ."

Possibly the only Catholic saint whose name is also said to be inscribed in Red Square as a hero of the Russian revolution, More is considered by Marxist commentators an essential link between classical thought and modern socialism. The "point of great originality in his thought" in the words of the Introduction to the edition of *Utopia* in the series Les Classiques du Peuple is the economic structure given to Utopia, where the Utopians were free of the corrupting use of money and all wealth belonged to all, where there was no private property and none of the mechanism "as complicated as vicious" (as the translation used by the Classiques du Peuple edition has More put it) necessary to the "principle of thine and mine."

These ideas were plentifully present not only in the published letters of Vespucci but in other widely circulated early reports on the New World. Perhaps they were present as well, maybe with embellishments, in sailors' yarns current at the time in Antwerp, where More conceived the notion for his explosive little book and where "at least five printings of American tracts had taken place . . . between 1493 and the time of More's visit."

Published reports and subsequently printed sailors' yarns both make much of the American disregard for what Europeans regarded as riches, akin, maybe, to such touches in *Utopia* as pearls being only playthings for little children and gold being used to make slave collars and chamber pots — this last calling forth in an early edition of the book a jubilant marginal notation thought to be by Erasmus: "O magnificam auri contumelian" (O magnificent mockery of gold).

Other commentators have carried the radical equality of *Utopia* rather beyond a link with modern socialism, as with the Hexter Introduction to the Yale volume finding More's thought oriented "not toward the past but toward the future" and quoting Tawney's *Equality* to the effect that the class struggle is not at all unavoidable but the "creation, not of nature, but of social convention . . . Men have given one stamp to their institutions; they can give another."

Not only is America directly present in *Utopia* (although not by name, the name at that time still only slowly coming into use following its introduction by Waldseemüller in 1507) — the narrator, Raphael, voyages thence with Amerigo Vespucci to begin his journey to Utopia — but there is collateral evidence that the New World was prominent in More's personal world at the time. In real life his own brother-in-law, John Rastell, one of the first Englishmen to be bitten by the America bug, sailed off for the sparkling New World with the intention of making "a voyage of discovery to the New Found Lands" in 1517, the year following *Utopia*'s first publication. (Unfortunately his "kaytyffe" crew would go no farther than Ireland but his son John, More's nephew, gave the dream another go in 1536, joining with "divers others of good worship, desirous to see the strange things of the world" in an expedition that won through to Newfoundland, disaster, cannibalism, piracy — and immortality in Hakluyt's *Principall Navigations*.)

*Utopia*, enthusiastically boomed by the intellectual avant-garde of the day under the generalship of More's old pal and mentor, the great Erasmus, who himself participated in editing the best early edition

(Basle, 1518), was an instant classic. Guillaume Budé, kingpin of the "New Learning" in France, contributed an introductory letter to an edition done almost immediately in Paris (1517); and, following a German translation of the Second Book only in 1524 and an Italian translation of the same portion in 1548, the first complete translation from Latin into a modern tongue was in French, by "Maitre jehan le blond," published in Paris in 1550. An early fan of the book was the writer called by Sidney Lee in his *French Renaissance in England* (1910) the "most advanced thinker of the early days of the French Renaissance" — François Rabelais, who adopted Utopia as his, and Pantagruel's, standard of the ideal state and sent Pantagruel on a voyage thither, using geography phantasmagorified from Peter Martyr and, some say, from conversations with Jacques Cartier and the master transatlantic pilot Jean Fonteneau. *Utopia* has continued to inspire daydreams ever since and remains a solid seller to the present moment. A recent Penguin edition, using a new translation by Paul Turner, enjoyed ten reprintings in the first ten years or so following its original printing in 1965. More than this, the book and its fissionable chain of ideas remain of moment to contemporary thought, as is clear from the Introduction to the Classiques du Peuple edition, which also stresses specifically those points closest in relationship to reports of More's day on the aboriginal American world.

Beyond even this, the book still bears a message of hope to the people of an almost but never quite hopelessly imperfect world. A nineteenth-century French translation by Victor Stouvenel was used for the Classiques du Peuple edition, and this same Stouvenel translation has in another of its recent editions an Introduction by Jean-Robert Delahaut that is worth a longish look in the context of *Utopia*'s continued relevance to hope. It gives a picture of Europe in More's time, in the midst of a conflict between the growing royal powers and the declining feudal system, with France and England and Italy (where five states had absorbed most of the others) at various stages along the road toward centralization, a road littered with the debris of wars civil and international and countless crimes and assassinations, while in Germany there still remained "a mosaic of five or six hundred little states . . . principalities lay and ecclesiastical, electorates, duchies, margravates, palatinates, free cities or seigneuries . . ." and everywhere the rivalries of princes and the constantly shifting power play alliances provoked further continual wars. "The life of the people was nothing. Of their happiness there was no question. Of their liberty one did not even speak . . . It was in this climate of injustice and hate, nearly three centuries before 1789, that Thomas Morus dreamed of equality, of liberty and of justice . . . still today no more than a dream . . . But man has a need to

dream . . . As he has a need to hope . . ." The Introduction was
signed at "Brussels, 21 July 1944."

The Garden of Eden strain continued to run strong in the flood of
New World descriptions that followed on the heels of Peter Martyr, even
as such high civilizations as those of Mexico and Peru floated, like cities
out of a golden dream indeed, into the European ken. The Spanish historian José de Acosta, writing in the 1580s after a number of years in the
New World, chiefly in Peru: "Surely the Greeks and the Romans, if they
had known the Republics of the Mexicans and the Incas, would have
greatly esteemed their laws and governments. We today only enter there
by the sword, giving them no heed, no hearing, no more consideration
than a venison taken in the forest . . . Men more profound and diligent, who have penetrated the secrets of their customs and their ancient
government, have an entirely different opinion, and marvel at the order
and reason that existed among them."

Part of Acosta's purpose in his *History* was to demonstrate that the
people of America were truly rational human beings in spite of their
strangenesses and that "they erre in their opinion, which holde the Indians to want iudgement." In this argument he was even capable of finding some of their strange ways superior to the ways of Europeans: speaking of the light and winsome airs of the New World climate, but with the
theme of the Americans' famous indifference to money underlying his
thought, Acosta writes that if Europeans could conquer their greed for
wealth, they too "could no doubt live very well and happily in the Indies. For what poets sing of the Elysian Fields . . . or Plato recounts, or
avers, of his Isle of Atlantis, men could in fact find in these lands, if with
a generous spirit they would master their avarice for money rather than
remain slaves to it as they now are."

Geoffroy Atkinson, a specialist in the "geographical" literature of
this period in France, cites a long list of French language works of the
sixteenth century that dwell largely on the accepted "fact" that a land
enjoying a real live Golden Age has been discovered in America. Great
names joined this chorus of revelation, as in a little book in French based
on a few pages from the famous Cardinal Pietro Bembo's history of Venice, with a ring already familiar: the people of the isles of the New World
"for the most part live a life of the age of gold, they don't know what it is
to set up boundaries and distinguish possessions. They have no lawsuits,
no law, no books of writing, no merchandise . . ." The same familiar
ring was sounded in works by one of the best-known mapmakers of the
epoch, Jodocus Hondius: "The people of this Country are content with
the bounty of nature, neither doe they know what belongs to mine, or
thine, or money, but have all things in common, even as nature bestow-

eth the light of the Sunne and water on all men equally; therefore their Gardens are open and unfenced, and nature teacheth them that which is right without lawes." Authors of general histories copied the news one from another, sometimes shining it up a bit on the way, as authors of general histories sometimes do. Typical is Jean Macer, summing up the New World: "Those who live there exceed and excel all other peoples in kindness, warmth and humanity . . . For it is unheard of that anyone is ever in any way ill-treated among them. Justice, nursing mother of all other virtues, is followed there . . ." Vespucci's more or less corrupt letters might have furnished a model for this passage, as in a French edition of 1556, "the people are very human, warm, friendly, ill-treating no one."

But Atkinson directs special attention to on-the-spot observers who are under no illusion in regard to wholesale American saintliness and yet can discern a veritable innocence of Eden behind the barbaric reality. The Jesuit missionary Father Manuel Nobrega, for example, Superior at Bahia in Brazil, in letters of 1552 and 1553 first describes the bloody wars of vengeance and the execution of captives, with attendant cannibalism, that he has witnessed "among this people worse than brutal," but then expands on the ownership of goods in common, the lack of interest in amassing riches, the generosity and kindness shown "to all the Christians who come to their houses . . . Wherever we went we were benignly received . . . Veritably I believe there are no people in all the world more disposed to receive the holy faith and the sweet yoke of the evangel than these . . . for you can paint on the heart of this people at your pleasure as on a clean sheet of paper." The Calvinist parson Jean de Léry, in Brazil in the 1550s, came to know well the "savages" and found plenty to complain about but, for all that, found Europeans "far behind the humanity of these people, whom nevertheless we call barbarians . . ." After his return to France, Léry wrote that "although I have always loved and continue to love my country . . . I often regret that I am not still among the Savages, where (as I have amply shown in this history) I met more sincere honesty than among many here."

The new idea of total liberty retained a leading place in these accounts. Léry, from personal observation: ". . . they have neither kings nor princes, and consequently each is more or less as much a great lord as the other." Macer, drawing conclusions from what he had heard and read: "They do not recognize a King or any superior, and will not subject themselves to the orders of anyone. Each there is King, master and Lord." Acosta, one of the best-informed Americanists of his time: "A number of the peoples and nations of the Indies have never suffered Kings nor Lords of an absolute and sovereign sort. They live in common

*13*

and create and ordain certain Captains and Princes for certain occasions only, during which time they obey their rule. Afterward, these leaders return to their ordinary status. The greatest part of the New World governs itself in this fashion . . ."

Response in French thought to such reports as these was early and notable and continued to constitute the most noteworthy of such currents in Europe — even during the first generation after 1492 Paris held the leading place in publication of "Americana" — although the actual beginning of official French interest in America came quite late. French (and English) interest in the New World was directed first (aside, naturally, from convenient piracy on Spanish ships) toward the newfound lands to the north that were to become Newfoundland and Canada. France formally entered the New World action with the voyage of Verrazzano, sailing in the employ of François I in 1524 and getting the first look of record at the entire Atlantic coast from the Carolinas to Nova Scotia. The Grand Bank fishing southeast of Newfoundland had become big business, unofficially, well before that time for the French seafaring provinces of Normandy, Brittany, Saintonge, Guienne, whose ships were at the teeming Grand Bank fishing ground very soon after (if not before) its discovery by John Cabot became general knowledge in 1499, certainly by as early as 1504.

Sir Thomas More's adventurous brother-in-law John Rastell, still seeing New World visions, wrote *circa* 1519 (published a few years later) a playlet propagandizing for transatlantic colonization in which he stated that Frenchmen and other foreigners "yerely of fyshe there they layde / Above an c. sayle" and records show sizable fleets Newfoundland bound from Rouen, Dieppe, Saint Malo, and La Rochelle, sixty such ships sailing in one day in 1542. When Jacques Cartier discovered the Gulf of Saint Lawrence in 1534, he discovered also a La Rochelle fishing vessel there ahead of him. These fishing crews pulled ashore for a little casual trading, or a little piracy, up and down the New World coasts for many a mile. After Cartier's search for the fabulous kingdom of Saguenay dissolved in empty league on league of the black north woods of Canada (leaving as its only legacy a French proverb for worthlessness: "Un diamant de Canada"), a large share of French attention, official and unofficial (and some English mercantile attention), turned more and more toward Brazil, source of the valuable dyewood ("brazilwood") purloined as treasure cargoes by far-ranging ships of all nationalities nibbling, in defiance of Spanish and Portuguese protests, at the forbidden American shores.

William Hawkins, father of Sir John Hawkins, brought home to England in 1530 a "savage king" from Brazil to meet King Henry VIII,

who with "all the Nobilitie did not a little marveile . . ." New World
people, a little group of "savages" from (perhaps) Newfoundland, had
appeared in Rouen in 1509, and Cartier's kidnaped Huron chief Donnacona cut a sensational swath at the court of François I in the 1530s and
influenced French policy with his stories of rich Saguenay; but when
Rouen staged a royal fete in 1550, it was a "Fête Brésilienne" complete
with more than two-score Tupinambas brought from Brazil on special
package tour for the occasion to whom were added some 250 Norman
sailors disguised as "brésiliens" which is to say unclothed, stained
brown, and decorated with feathers. A Tupi village was built and the
indigenes, real and facsimile, entertained with sham battles and hunts,
dances, Tupi songs and poems, and romantic sea-borne tall tales. Henri
II was present with all his court, including the queen, Catherine de'
Medici, the eight-year-old Mary Stuart (future Queen of Scots), be-
trothed to the dauphin, and — the real center of all eyes — Madame la
duchesse de Valentinois, Diane de Poitiers, the king's mistress, fifty years
old and more radiant than ever after a lovers' quarrel that had kept the
court agog for a month and left her still the ruler of the king and ergo of
France. (The quarrel concerned Mary Stuart's governess, the beauteous
Lady Fleming, who had — "God be thanked" — become pregnant by
the king and was rapturously declaring to anyone who would listen that
she found the royal blood within her a "sweeter and more savory liquor"
than any ordinary variety.)

The court ladies bravely survived the sight of so much nudity, Tupi
poetry became the rage of fashion, and the extravaganza succeeded in its
real purpose, which was to sway royal favor in behalf of Rouen's brazilwood business. Five years later a French colony was founded in Brazil,
six hundred settlers under the command of Nicolas Durand, chevalier de
Villegagnon.

Pierre de Ronsard, the most admired poet of his time in Europe — an
opinion in which he himself heartily concurred ("Je suis Ronsard, et
cela te suffice!") — spoke of this expedition in a poem of the mid-1550s,
"Discours contre Fortune," imploring "the learned Villegagnon" not to
think of "civilizing" these fortunate people of America "who know not
the names . . . / of Senate or King" but "are their own only masters . . ." He then repainted even more glowingly than his predecessors
a picture of the New World as a land of liberty, where the earth like the
air belonged to all in common and where wealth, like the water of a river,
was shared by all; where there were none of the "lawsuits engendered by
the words Thine and Mine." Leave these people alone in their freedom
and tranquility, he begs ("I pray thee . . . if pity can move thee"); do
not lock to their necks the strangling yoke of servitude, bringing them

under under the cruel authority of a tyrant or judge or a strange set of laws. "They live now in their golden age . . . / Live, happy people, free of care and troubles, / Live joyously, I would that I could live as well."

These lines have been much quoted but I think it might be worthwhile to look over as a whole the poem containing them. It's a long poem, nearly 450 lines, addressed to "Odet de Colligny, Cardinal de Chastillon," opening with the line "C'est a vous, mon Odet, à qui je me veux plaindre," and using the first dozen lines or so for a graceful and fulsome tribute to Coligny, his "most perfect" patron. He then complains of Fortune, utterly wicked, constantly inconstant, most worthy of her personification as a woman, and for the next fifty or sixty lines describes her power and the way his patron, the puissant cardinal, has sheltered him from her attacks — but it is precisely this protection that has been his downfall, since it has given him a vainglorious sense of security and permitted selfish ambition to gain entrance into his heart. For more than a hundred lines he tells how contented he had been with only his poetry and what successes it had achieved — he was the first to conduct the Muses from Greece to France, the first to make the Greek and Roman poets speak in French, until there was no educated Frenchman who did not honor his songs — but after becoming infected with ambition he was no longer satisfied with the solitude of study and learning but "burned with desire to amass and to possess" and dreamed of fat bishoprics, priories, and abbeys.

His Muses, very properly outraged, have therefore beseeched Fortune to punish him; this mighty goddess enters the poem at about line 200 and after summoning all her thousand servants selects Ill Luck to seek out Ronsard and dwell in him, since which time all has gone most hopelessly wrong.

Now (by line 325) Ronsard dreams of traveling, in a vain attempt to escape, perhaps to Italy, or even with the Villegagnon expedition to America. Here, at about line 340, commences his parenthetical plea to the French colonists in Brazil to spare the New World people the cruel destiny under which the Old World lives; for if you teach them to divide the earth in private ownership they will then turn to making war to enlarge their lands, trials at law will come into being, friendship will go by the board, and grasping ambition will come to torment them as it torments us poor denizens of the Old World, who have all too much justification to be miserable under its rule.

There follow fifty lines or so of conclusion, begging his patron to continue his patience and support in spite of all these fantasies the poet would never have uttered were his soul not so unwell, and the unhappy poem is ended.

The main line of the piece is not a complaint against fortune, as the title claims, but a lament over the way of life Ronsard has adopted, transforming himself into a besotted courtier haunting the palace of the Louvre, dreaming of receiving royal benefactions, when he used to wander so happily by woods and streams, drinking from springs with his hands for a cup, wanting nothing but the endless delight of making up his songs.

Moralizing on the virtues of the sweet and simple life had been a favorite plot line of poesy under many skies and a special favorite in the Middle Ages, but here Ronsard adds something new, in fact two somethings new: he links the theme to liberty and equality and communal ownership of property, and he attaches it to a real world of real living people rather than to a dream world of allegory or myth.

In a poem written a few years earlier he had located some of the same qualities in a land left only imaginary, "Les Isles Fortunées" (the title, a name descended from myth, although sometimes applied to the Canaries), where "avarice has not/Bounded the fields" and where the people are free of any fear

> of falling under the hand
> Of a harsh Senate, or an inhuman Prince . . .
> There justice is not depraved by gold,
> Nor the sad law engraved on brass,
> Nor do Senates or evil people
> Disturb the repose of those fields . . .

But by now this particular land of Cockaigne has moved into the factual world, to Villegagnon's Amérique, where, the poem tells us, such a totally different mode of life actually exists. Real but alas inaccessible for the poet possessed by the Old World: "I would that I could live as well" — but he couldn't.

Ronsard got his fat abbey, his town house in Paris, and his priory, where he dragged away his dying years, a deaf and splenetic old man, out of favor at court and everywhere else, including with himself. He exulted "with ferocity" over the defeat, some dozen years after the "Discours Contre Fortune," of his once most perfect patron, who had chosen the wrong side in the religious wars.

"Les Isles Fortunées" was dedicated to Marc Antoine de Muret, a professor at Bordeaux, whose most famous student, Michel Eyquem de Montaigne, published in various of his essays in the 1580s what have become the most quoted remarks of his century on the New World people. "Our world has just found another . . . no less extensive, fruitful, and peopled than itself" (from "Des Coches") where the people "newly

issued from the hand of God" ("Des Cannibales") live in freedom
"without rule . . . without ruler" ("Apologie de Raymond Sebond")
obeying only the laws of a benevolent nature that supports them like a
"nursing mother" ("Des Coches").

They are evidently not inferior to us in wit and just reasoning, he
wrote in "Des Coches," and the "astounding magnificence of the cities
of Cusco and Mexico" and the beauty of their works in many arts show
that they need cede us nothing in industry, while "as for devotion, obser-
vance of justice, goodness, liberality, loyalty, frankness, it has served us
well that they outdo us in these things; they are lost by having such an
advantage."

Reflecting (thinking particularly of the Peruvians and Mexicans) on
that "untameable ardor with which so many thousands of men, women
and children . . . had fought for the defence of their gods and their
liberty, their great-hearted determination in suffering all difficulties and
extremities, unto death, rather than submit to the domination of those
who had so shamefully deceived them, and others choosing to die from
hunger, being captured, before accepting food from enemies so vilely
victorious" Montaigne finds himself thinking that no nobler a people
had ever fallen to Alexander or to the ancient Greeks and Romans; and
what a marvel it might have been if instead of attacking them with inhuman cruelty for the purpose of base commercial profit, "we" (the Europeans) had met them with a fraternal and intelligent friendship, what
a society of genuine virtue might have been created, those "souls so new"
of the New World having "for the most part such splendid natural
commencement." He wrote in "Apologie," in line with a tradition followed by innumerable later writers, "Those who return from this new
world, discovered in our parents' time by the Spanish, can testify to us
how these nations, without judges and without laws, live more legiti-
mately and more orderly than our own, where there are more officers and
laws than anyone and anything else."

His best-known essay on the New World people, "Des Cannibales,"
dealing principally with Villegagnon's Brazilians, finds them "still
commanded by the laws of nature" in a fashion so direct that he wishes
Plato and Lycurgus could have known of them, for it seems to him their
society surpasses not only what poetry has painted of the Golden Age but
also what philosophy has been able to imagine in trying to conceive of a
truly happy human condition. Philosophers (he is referring to Plato's
*Republic*) have never dreamed of an innocence so pure and direct as that
we actually witness there.

"It is a nation, would I answer *Plato*," so reads "Des Cannibales" in
its first English translation (1603) — and subsequently follows almost

word for word, it will be noticed, certain of the points made in Peter Martyr's "Decades" of so many years before — "that hath no kinde of traffike, no knowledge of Letters, no intelligence of numbers, no name of magistrate, nor of politike superioritie; no use of service, of riches or of povertie; no contracts, no successions, no partitions, no occupation but idle [modern French scholarship makes the meaning of this phrase 'no occupation but what is agreeable'] . . . no use of wine, corne, or mettle. The very words that import lying, falshood, treason, dissimulations, covetousness, envie, detractions, and pardon, were never heard of amongst them."

Shakespeare, in writing *The Tempest*, took for the play's framework the Bermuda shipwreck of some Virginia-bound colonists in 1609, twisted the monster Caliban's name from an anagram of "canibal" (the play is filled, incidentally, with personages — from Caliban to Ariel — longing only to be free), and in act 2, scene 1, gave the honest old counselor Gonzalo a speech on the ideal commonwealth that, as has been often remarked upon, included word for word various of Montaigne's (and ergo of Peter Martyr's) above phrases:

I' the commonwealth I would by contraries
Execute all things: for no kind of traffic
Would I admit; no name of magistrate;
Letters should not be known; no use of service,
Of riches, or of poverty; no contracts,
Successions; bound of land, tilth, vineyard, none;
No use of metal, corn, or wine, or oil;
No occupation; all men idle, all;
And women too; but innocent and pure;
No sovereignty . . .

# 2. The Golden Screen: Strophe

The dream of a golden world is apparently as old as humanity, or at any rate the Old World variety of humanity. From the Garden of Eden to the newest five-year plan of the latest dictatorship it seems to have been always with us. The Romans made a father-god — his children Jupiter, Juno, Neptune and Pluto — of Saturnus, a mythical king of Italy supposed to have introduced agriculture and the affiliated arts of civilization, and called his reign the Golden Age. Herodotus found the distant Scythians examples (on occasion) of a primitive golden world, as did Tacitus the virtuous Germans, and as various other classic writers found various other sufficiently faraway peoples, such as the Aethiopians or the Brahmins.

The common folk of the Middle Ages imagined the Land of Cockaigne, with houses made of sugar and spice, and contented pigs running about offering the contented people free flitches of bacon, while the erudite imagined the earthly paradise, described in the fifth century by Avitus (Bishop of Vienne in South Gaul, not the briefly enthroned Emperor of the West of the same name and period) as lying "Beyond the Indies where the world begins and where (they say) earth and sky meet," a walled grove peopled by angels, where there is no freezing winter and no burning summer but a mild eternal spring; no blustering winds, no cloudy skies, no rain, "plants are content with their natural dew," all always green and yet flowering, and fruit ripening every month; lilies never wither, nor do violets; "Autumn with its fruits and spring with its flowers fill the whole year."

The earthly paradise was eventually placed by Richard Eden "in the East side of Afrike," in the country of the legendary Christian king Prester John, disagreeing with Martyr's report of Columbus's expert opinion. His view, as Eden recorded it for Hakluyt, was followed not only by Peter Heylin in his *Cosmography* of 1652, who named the precise location (on the summit of a lofty "Mount Amara") but also by Milton in *Paradise Lost*, where it is noted (IV, 281-2) that "Mount *Amara*" in Abyssinia is "by some suppos'd/True Paradise."

The ancient and medieval poets and geographers and historians who dreamed these dreams borrowed liberally, if not literally, from each other, whether describing the strange races of other lands or times — headless people or people with only one eye or only one leg, or who lived birdlike in trees, or Amazons or centaurs — or listing the virtues of an austere primitive life. There is evidence that even Tacitus simply copied some Greek statements about Scythians to apply to his Germans. "Evidently differences among barbarians [writes a modern anthropologist] were not considered important enough to require accurate reporting . . . The result was the development of a series of ethnographic commonplaces such as that barbarians use neither images nor temples in their worship; that they live by war and pillage; that they do not appreciate the value of precious metals; and so forth."

It has been suggested that the existence of this conventional model of primitive people, a classical "noble savage" inhabiting a classical golden world, renders suspect the accounts of New World explorers, who may have been copying the classic model in their minds rather than reporting what they actually saw. The world they described, according to this supposition, was that of a European dream that touched only haphazardly the American reality. Numerous pre-Columbian remarks on primitive people have been turned up that show similarities in certain respects — such as communal ownership — to numerous New World reports, beginning with Homer, who speaks of the Scythians who possessed all things in common (although his "above all, their wives and children," is not in the usual New World vein). But to assume from the existence of such occasional similarities that a New World explorer's report of common ownership may derive as much from Homer or from some other classical model as from his own observation may remain debatable.

The total of works mentioning an idea of noble savagery that appeared in the two thousand years before Columbus is not large — "the few writers of Classical Antiquity who took an interest in anthropological comparison are conspicuous exceptions . . ." Specialists on the subject have collected a total of some sixty-five citations from some four dozen pre-New World authorities on the "Noble Savage in Antiquity." The qualitative no doubt far exceeds quantitative indications, and the sixteenth- or seventeenth- or eighteenth-century European in America was certainly encumbered by his origins (classical and otherwise) as are all of us. The problem is a serious one and will be discussed at length later (VI, 1, The Golden Screen: Antistrophe). It will suffice at present to say that I think the suggestion of classical preconceptions seriously deforming the American reality for European observers has been exaggerated.

Nevertheless, certain phrases from the most widely reprinted or the most trustworthy early European observers do indeed echo certain of the golden phrases referred to above on lost Paradises: some versions of the letters of Amerigo Vespucci recall Avitus and company in describing the New World as "exceedingly temperate and fertile, and marvelously pleasant and delectable . . . The trees and the fruits grow of themselves, with no help from the hand of man . . . if there is any terrestrial paradise in the world, it is certainly not far from this country . . . In this land the sky is almost never cloudy but all year long the weather is fine and serene: it is true that sometimes dew falls, but lightly and without forming rain" And José de Acosta: " . . . one doesn't know what winter is, which freezes by its cold, nor summer, which wearies with its heat . . . one scarcely needs a different set of apparel all year long" And various ancient notions of the golden world and of outlandish peoples were unquestionably present in many of the New World yarns. André Thévet, a great liar (and even recognized as such in his own day, an unusual tribute) but all the same a great traveler who had been in person, if but as fleetingly as possible, to Villegagnon's Brazil, was far from alone in

speaking (in 1557) of the New World's Amazons; and Donnacona, undeniably authentic voice of the New World, the Huron elder kidnaped by
Jacques Cartier, was said to have enthralled the court of François I with
tales of such plinyesque monsters as unipeds, not to mention a marvelous race of people unprovided with anuses, over there someplace in the
Canadian unknown.

Seneca, the most "extreme" primitivist of classic times, eulogized (in
*Epistulae morales*, XC) the state of nature in terms notably similar to
those of Montaigne as well as to much New World comment: the first
peoples, fresh from the gods, sharing the good gifts of nature in common
— what generation of men was ever happier than these? — before avarice, craving to sequestrate, broke in upon this best of all conditions,
introduced poverty and lost all by wanting too much. (Seneca's picture
became notably dissimilar to comment on New World liberty and equality when his first men chose a ruler, submitting themselves to him for "it
is the way of nature to make the inferior subject to the superior.") Seneca
also quotes Virgil on this happy time in an excerpt (*Georgics* I, 125 ff.)
that might seem to cast Martyr's shadow before —

No ploughman tilled the ground,
No fence dividing field from field was found;
When to the common store all gains were brought
And earth gave freely goods which none had sought.

The cited poem, though, is not lamenting a lost paradise, as a modern
reader could suppose from the quoted excerpt, but is recalling the "heavy
sluggishness" of pre-agricultural life before Jove "sharpened men's
wits" by forcing them to learn the art of farming, an allusion Virgil's
contemporaries could have been expected to grasp as quickly as a modern reader a reference to Hamlet's resolution. The poem was generally
regarded as one of Virgil's finest works and was accordingly well known
in his time.

Any debts to classical tradition notwithstanding, the Renaissance
brought a "fundamental change," first with a realization of true cultural
differences between the people of the present and the people of the past
and then with the objective observation of different contemporary peoples in "the records of early Portuguese and Spanish exploration . . ."
Peter Martyr was the commanding figure here, his work largely responsible for the fact that the literature of sixteenth-century Europe provides
"better and more detailed information on New World cultures than on
those in other parts of the world which the Europeans were exploring
at that time."

Rather the same conclusion was reached by Geoffroy Atkinson, who found in his extensive studies of sixteenth-century works on the New World numerous objective passages in which actual observation was evidently more important than any preoccupation with literary convention. But for Atkinson the significant feature of these accounts, as has been mentioned, is the insistent presentation of "the Golden Age that had been *verified* overseas" (his emphasis), not an exercise of imagination or misty memory of legend but real, live, positively existing, in effective operation at this very moment. The force and frequency of this statement of apparent fact accumulated considerable early weight, Atkinson contends, pointing out that this actual golden world was well established for Brazil, from writings of Peter Martyr, Vespucci, et al, for more than fifty years before Léry's authoritative work on the region of the Villegagnon colony and Montaigne's subsequent essays. This asserted reality of a contemporary Eden raised many grave problems — theological, social, political — even though they were a long while coming clearly into view.

For me the crucial point in all this is the entrance of the idea of liberty in accounts of the New World's golden world. Pre-Columbian references to the Golden Age usually described a lotus land where there was a lake of stew (and of whiskey too) and the hens laid soft-boiled eggs, or extolled the benefits of a simple primitive life of austerity, sometimes (although by no means always) instancing a happy state of equality accompanying communal ownership of property, but not often instancing a happy state of kinglessness, masterlessness, of liberty for all — instancing much more typically the "just" rule of a "good" king.

With the discovery of America liberty, masterlessness, each person as much a great lord as the other, became a leading item, accompanied by an increased emphasis on the absence of the principle of thine and mine. By the beginning of the seventeenth century this news had traveled from mere tales of voyages into the sober precincts of the first treatise to make use of the term "political economy" — Montchrestien (1615): "They are truly Barbarians and Savages, but otherwise quite fortunately endowed, as far as nature is concerned, and of ways perfectly proper to receive the form of true virtue . . . They are of rather subtle intelligence, but ignorant of our arts, whether of war or of peace. They hold that the earth belongs to no individual, any more than the light of the sun . . . They give freely of what they have and want to be treated with the same liberality by others . . ." And with a true political economist's twist: "They are born totally free and therefore are little given to work."

It would appear that a new capital city, Liberty, had already by this early date been added to the traditional map of the golden world.

At the same time the literature dealing with such pleasant worlds was more or less suddenly multiplied at a ratio of something like a hundred to one, and more important still we see the finest minds of their time, Ronsard, Montaigne, Shakespeare, concerning themselves with this range of thought.

Gilbert Chinard, the most assiduous of students of New World influence on Old World thought, writes that for the early explorers who, with the old myth of the Golden Age in their minds, saw a land fabulously rich, furnishing without toil delicious fruits, peopled by gentle and happy savages apparently free of oppression and never suspecting that elsewhere (such as in Europe) masses of human beings lived in misery, "the terrestrial Paradise became something tangible and present" and from this moment on "the essential traits of the American mirage were fixed." A sort of crystalization began that was to place America in the popular imagination as "the land of plenty and the land of liberty" that it was to remain for centuries of immigrants.

If Peter Martyr and the explorers he inspired did in fact bring something new in the way of objective reporting, one of the most consequential products of this newness may well have been a new idea of liberty.

But not, even so, disentangled from the rest of the golden dream, which has clung like a penumbra to the idea of liberty ever since — for what was it, what is it, in reality, the dream of a golden world? A dream of the past, or of a world still to come? Or if, as said Plotinus, "All that is Yonder is also Here," then perhaps "The golden age that a blind superstition had placed in our past (or in our future)," suggests a modern ethnologist, underlining the words, "is *within us.*" Or it was and still is, so holds some contemporary thought, really a dream of the abstract objective the world was lived for, a vision of the end for which the rest was spent, of what was to come in fact when the world ended, and even those "who denied the hereafter and all its transcendentalism, such as Hegel, Comte, Marx and Nietzsche, prophesied nevertheless the arrival of that golden age which would give a sense to history . . ."

# 3. The Invention of Liberty

A few years ago Jean Starobinski wrote the text to a handsome picture book called *The Invention of Liberty*, and placed the event in the eighteenth century, an impression generally prevailing in France. But G. C. Lichtenberg wrote (in *Reflections*) in the 1790s, from the vantage point of the very top of that century, "How did mankind ever come by the idea of liberty? What a grand thought it was!"

Its cries and tossing placards fill the street under my window on occasional weekend evenings in the Paris spring. Were marchers for liberty a feature of the Paris of Louis the Fat, of Philip the Fair, even of the revolutionary Cabochards? Not so the chroniclers could notice it (the Cabochian Ordinance of 1413 demanded government efficiency not democracy, say the historians). When did these shouts for liberty, liberty for all, first sound on the European scene? Out of what nowhere into what here?

We have seen the subject getting some noteworthy (and New World-related) attention in the sixteenth century. F. W. Maitland, the historian of the laws of England, found that the English philosophers of the seventeenth century developed an "obsession" with liberty, but in examining this obsession Maitland could not locate its historical "foundation," after concluding that neither the Puritans nor the classic Greeks could fill the bill as instigators, although adding that it is "not until a late period in the history of men that the idea . . . arises."

Lord Acton, after the better part of a lifetime spent in research on a projected history of liberty he never got around to writing ("the greatest book never written," said a Cambridge wit), came to believe — this was in the late nineteenth century — there was no "practical" liberty to speak of before "100 years ago. Never till then had men sought liberty knowing what they sought" "Very little practical liberty of old" appears in various wordings repeatedly in his notes, and he quotes with approval the religious historian William Mitchell Ramsay: "The widest democracy of ancient times was a narrow oligarchy in comparison with our modern states."

Isaiah Berlin, in his *Four Essays on Liberty*, writes of today's idea of liberty (as "absence of obstacles not merely to my actual, but to my potential choices"), that he can not find "convincing evidence of any clear formulation of it in the ancient world" and that it "is an interesting, but perhaps irrelevant, historical question at what date, and in what circumstances, the notion of individual liberty in this sense . . . first became explicit in the West." (He does suggest that it might be "the late product of a capitalist civilization . . .")

The liberty that raised an inspiring and sometimes beautiful voice among the ancients was as a rule the corporate expression of a class or party, a people or a state. It was in essence a feature of the transfer of power from a "wicked" ruling apparatus to a "good" one. (Tom Paine referred to precisely this long tradition by writing that the causes of the American Revolution were — and he underlined the word — "*different* . . . Here the value and quality of liberty . . . were known" and the Americans "had no particular family to set up or pull down.") The transfer of power, from "wicked" to "good" rulers, is revealed in the several centuries of Greek history preceding Alexander as a constant fluctuation: kingship cut down by the aristocracy (Aristophanes' "Knights"); the aristocrats, grown great with increased land ownership and wealth, toppled by a demagogue with the support of the oppressed poor; the demagogue, become a tyrant, again overthrown by the aristocrats; and so ad finem, while the city-states likewise were devoted to endless schemes and wars of conquest against each other, all aiming of course for a transfer or consolidation of power into the hands of the "good" state or party or ruler. Political liberty in the ancient world, as at Athens in the best days of Pericles or at Rome in the republic, or even as idealized by Aristotle or Plato, says Acton, was never more than "partial and insincere." (It should be remembered that both Plato and Aristotle, while supporting representational political liberty for the full-fledged citizens who composed the state, were heartily opposed to the sort of mob rule they thought of as "democracy.")

The prevailing idea of liberty in classical antiquity reflected this picture of a liberty naturally confined within a framework of self-interest — as was for that matter the storied Athenian patriotism, which was not at all impugned, in the mind of the time, by the actions of various Athenian leaders, such as Themistocles or Alcibiades, in going over to the enemy when their self-interest seemed to make such a move imperative.

Liberty's noble expression at Athens against Persian overlordship spared little concern for such cities as Naxos or Thasos, crushed under harsh Athenian subjection, or for the helots of Sparta, held, with the occasional help of Athenian military cooperation, in a cruel serfdom. The love of actual personal freedom feelingly recorded in an age when defeat in war could mean literal iron-collared enslavement was not balanced by a fellow feeling for vanquished people brought home as slaves. On the contrary, the people of Paphlagonia, a country repeatedly plundered by Athenian slave raiders, were proverbial objects of derision and ridicule (as Cleon a "Paphlagonian" for Aristophanes).

An *ex parte* view of liberty was, not surprisingly, still more clearly evident in Rome; the Roman streets ran copiously with blood more than once to prove it, and its most eloquent spokesman, Cicero, was butchered like a beef — and his head and hands nailed to the rostrum he had so often so magnificently graced as speaker — as reward for his conception of the permissible limits of liberty, which is to say for his partisanship, for his ardent labors on behalf of a liberty seen as a handmaiden to the transfer (or retention) of power.

The anarchy of feudalism and the rise of medieval urbanism, with crown and church, city corporation, seigneuries clerical and secular, guilds and soldiery, all in conflict, maintained or if anything strengthened this view of liberty as lying only in the path of one's partisan interest. The path of intellectual liberty was more usually concerned with the group liberty of cult, as in the long struggle of the Cathares in France or the contentions of any number of lesser known medieval "heresies," or with theological definition, as in Boethius' great final section (*De Consolatione Philosophiae*, V) on the liberty of the Christian soul, the question of free will versus predestination that occupied European thought for many generations (and still occupies a prominent sector philosophiae). The path of physical liberty was apparently most often financial, as in the many instances of riot and revolt with taxes or profit at their mainspring. The most explosive social upheaval in the history of Florence, the revolt in 1378 of the *ciompi*, the impoverished woolen workers, failed in the long run because of the lack of what we could now call solidarity between the ciompi and their presumed allies in the lesser guilds, particularly the class of small shopkeepers. "Neither in the fourteenth nor in any later century have the small bourgeoisie and the industrial workers found it easy to merge their interests" and the key word is "interests." "We will overthrow the city," said a ciompi speaker, "we will kill and despoil the rich who have despised us; we will become masters of the city; we will govern it as we wish, and we will be rich." The cities of Lombardy changed often enough "their masters" after the decline of feudalism but did not "rouse themselves for liberty," wrote P.-J. Proudhon; the "social economy" repeatedly changed its forms but never its basic relationships. The independence fought for in the thirteenth century by the universities of Paris, Oxford, and Bologna was perhaps "equivocal," says a medievalist, in its distinction between liberty and privilege (the universities won with papal support, the desired privileges, but at the cost of becoming, to a certain degree, "agents of the pontificate").

An echo of political liberty reentered the king-ridden Western world in the thirteenth century with the reappearance, via Arabic and Jewish scholarship, of Aristotle's *Politics*. Rendered meet to the ears of Christians by Aquinas and Dante and John of Paris, it attained with the fourteenth-century commentators Marsilius and Bartolus what has been called an early expression of "populist" theory — political power seen as deriving "upward" from the citizens rather than "downward" from the ruler.

The concrete idea of liberty per se to complement this echo of political abstraction, the simplistic idea of liberty as in the New World reports, liberty for all, bosslessness for all, liberty for others as well as for oneself, this idea so universally acclaimed in the militant liberalism of the nineteenth and twentieth centuries seems to have appeared only rarely and superficially, so far as I can find, before the sixteenth century. The necessity, the beneficence, of a hierarchy of power, is drawn in Dante's illustration (*Il Convivio*, IV, 4) of a perfect government — an emperor of the world; or in Shakespeare's own vehement statement of the necessity of hierarchy to sustain order, in Ulysses' comments on "Degree" — comments that were "commonplaces" at the time — in *Troilus and Cressida*. In a world so utterly owned by bosses of one kind or another, where to be a "masterless man" was to be an outlaw, the idea of bosslessness was obviously too absurd even to occur elsewhere than in the lunatic fringes, a madness obviously too dangerous to find a serious hearing in responsible and solid intellects, all solidly in agreement that O, when Degree is shak'd/ . . . The enterprize is sicke . . .

# 4. New Hierarchies for Old

The leading minds of the sixteenth century, the biggest of big guns for shelling the old soil of Europe with new ideas, obviously knew not what they did in lavishing their encomia on the reported New World liberty. Ronsard, Montaigne, Peter Martyr were not by any means revolutionaries. Clearly, although they gave resounding expression to the subversive new idea of simple liberty, they did not associate it with themselves or their own world.

"If I might have been among those nations that are said to live still under the sweet liberty of the first laws of nature, I assure you that I would very willingly paint myself all over and go naked," wrote Montaigne, in the Preface to his Essays. I don't think it questions his sincerity to note that he had not the slightest intention of going to America and doing so. The sweet liberty was, perhaps, real enough as idea but as distant as another planet from his own real life. Like Ronsard he was speaking of something in a zoo. Both were suspending reality in the interest of contemplating a curiosity, as medieval and Renaissance farmers evidently suspended the reality of their own experience with animals in accepting the nonsense tales of contemporary bestiaries, interesting curiosities that might have a moral to make and might even be true — someplace — as the authors claimed, but that could scarcely have anything to do with one's own real world.

C. S. Lewis in his lectures on medieval literature published as *The Discarded Image* (1964) speaks of the great thirteenth-century map of the world in Hereford cathedral that shows, among other fantasies (such as the earthly paradise), England and Scotland as separate islands, an error many of the map's admirers must have been aware of from its first appearance. Evidently the map was regarded as something quite apart from reality, perhaps, Lewis suggests, simply as "a rich jewel embodying the noble art of cosmography," a description that could fit quite a bit of early geographical writing about the New World.

The progress of libertarian ideas in the Renaissance is as well foughten a field as any in history, with the date, or even the century, of the advent of free thought in France still one of its contested issues. In Italy such innovators as Biondo Flavio and Lorenzo Valla did their principal work in the first half of the fifteenth century; their creation of an excessive interest in pre-Christian antiquity entrained a subtle lessening of interest in Christian faith, subtly encouraging in turn a liberated spirit of speculation and even (with such as Paolo del Pozzo Toscanelli) scientific inquiry; the idea of a universal religion of which Christianity was only a variant was established in Italy by Marsilio Ficino and Giovanni Pico della Mirandola well before the end of the 1400s. Printing, introduced in Italy from Germany in 1464, helped spread new ideas and old writings almost, one could fairly say, like wildfire: two towns in Italy (Rome and Venice) had printing presses in 1470; 73 by 1500, the majority of their output classical Latin and Greek.

If actual free thought, in the sense of free from any serious religious restriction, free to go even as far as atheism, was really only a "myth" for France before the seventeenth century, as some recent scholarship maintains, it is nevertheless evident that disciples of the "New Learning" in both France and England were extraordinarily receptive to new ideas at a very early period in the sixteenth century, in fact almost from the moment of Charles VIII's return to France from his Italian expedition in 1496 "bringing the Renaissance in his saddlebags." He brought also the Greek scholar Janus Lascaris, teacher of Guillaume Budé; even Erasmus came to Paris as a student for several years at the turn of the century before going on to Italy. The cult of antiquity was as rapidly planted in France as printing — presses sprang up as if in the wake of a Cadmus literally sowing words for dragons' teeth: more than a hundred printing establishments operated in France before 1500.

A passion for antiquity naturally became suspect to defenders of the status quo. Rabelais as a student monk in 1532 found himself in grave trouble when a search of his room turned up books in Greek, his Franciscan order having a prejudice against the study of Greek as inclining to revolt and heresy. Rabelais fled, and it took the help of the august Budé and the intercession of the pope, Clement VII, to get him out of his classical hot water.

Riotous ways, rightly or wrongly, were frequently charged against these dangerous Greek scholars, as witness (and from a fellow-Greek) Rabelais' epitaph written by Ronsard, perhaps meant seriously, perhaps not: "splattering in wine like a frog in mud." A printer of *Gargantua*, and printer also of condemned works of Erasmus as well as author of a great "etymological" Latin dictionary, Etienne Dolet, drew upon himself the special hostility of important persons and members of Parlement by bold words spoken (when he was twenty-five years old or so) on behalf of protesting students. This was in 1534 and was the beginning of Dolet's long series of difficulties with established authority — although all he wanted, he wrote, was that he might be allowed to "live in peace,/ And my study in liberty pursue." One of his difficulties in pursuing this tranquil end was a murder, for which he was pardoned by François I, the pardon celebrated at a dinner attended by stars of the New Learning from Budé to Clement Marot and Rabelais.

Printing itself attracted official displeasure with the "Affair of the Placards" (1535) when printed posters denying the verity of the Mass appeared overnight on Paris walls and doorways. Numbers of more or less suspect persons were investigated (put to the "question") and executed, and the king, François I, struck logically at the root of the trouble with an edict banishing printing altogether. The Parlement of Paris balked at this, however, and a compromise was reached requiring royal permission for each publication in the future, a requirement which continued in force in France until the Revolution two hundred and fifty years later.

The new ideas of the New Learning turned, for the most part, through a sphere with religion as its axis and with reforms moral and pedagogical embraced in its circumference. This spirit, questioning some of the basic assumptions of the corrupt times, burning to see a new order grounded on classical philosophy and the original teachings of Christ replace the old order become rotten with injustice, was bulwarked with citations from Cicero and Seneca, Plato and Aristotle, Sallust and Plutarch and pantheons more of classical authority in attacks on despotism and in tracts supporting the right of a people to limit the power of a monarch or even depose — or even assassinate — a wicked ruler. The tone of violence in these works took a great leap upward upon the outbreak of the religious wars, and in France turned for a time, after the St. Bartholomew's Eve Massacre, to overt advocacy of sedition and revolution.

The pamphlet *Le Tigre* of 1560 was wholly classical in form, being composed in imitation of Cicero's first denunciation of Catiline, but so daring in content, a savage and personal attack on the leaders of the Catholic party, the powerful Guise family, that "if the gallant author could have been apprehended," wrote Brantôme in *Les Dames Galantes*, "should he have had a hundred thousand lives he would have lost them all" (the gallant author was at the time unknown, and outraged authority settled for hanging a printer in whose house had been found a copy of the pamphlet). The author, François Hotman, a Huguenot professor of law at Bourges, escaped to Geneva after the massacres following St. Bartholomew's Eve, where he published (1573) an indictment of Charles IX arguing that he should be deposed for his crimes, and the historical treatise *Francogallia*, arguing that historically French kings were subject to the people, to whom alone "belongs the right to elect and depose kings." Jean Bodin, distinguished for the epoch in not being a religious controversialist, drew a fundamental line between society and the state in *De la République* (1576): society founded on the family, the state on organized force. An absolutist the most absolute, Bodin considered a hereditary and authoritarian monarchy infinitely preferable to republicanism, and private property indispensable to good order and discipline. His work became a basic text in political theory in England. Philippe de Mornay, seigneur du Plessis-Marly, under the pen name Stephanus Junius Brutus, wrote shortly after the St. Bartholomew's but did not publish until five years later his *Vindiciae contra Tyrannos*, holding that government was a contract between God, king, and people to uphold the "true religion" and that the people have a duty to depose, through properly organized parliaments, a wicked king — an extremely influential work, particularly so in England. In Scotland George Buchanan, a teacher of Montaigne, of Mary of Scotland and her son who was to become James I of England, produced in 1579 *De iure regni apud Scotos* which found a king subject to laws enacted by the people through their legitimate representatives, and held that it was just to resist or even put to death a tyrannical ruler.

Theodore Beza, Calvin's successor as Moderator of the Company of Pastors at Geneva, authored anonymously in 1574 *Du Droit des Magistrats* justifying revolt against a tyrant under the leadership of the properly authorized magistrates, or at least "the healthier part of them." Beza also preached in his commentaries on the Psalms that God would permit resistance to an unjust king — particularly with Psalm 109, which he offered the embattled Huguenots (who already had the habit, in Shakespeare's phrase, of "singing psalms to hornpipes") as a veritable war song of "holy indignation" against a king who "When he shall be judged, let him be condemned . . ."

The Huguenot justification of resistance to royal absolutism in the name of religion was turned against them by Catholic writers in attacking monarchs opposed, or thought to be opposed, to their cause, most famous of these the Spanish historian Juan de Mariana, whose *De rege et regis institutione* (1599) seemed to praise the assassination of Henri III of France ten years before and was blamed for inciting the assassination of Henri IV some ten years later.

The principle of a hierarchy of power was not, however, seriously challenged by these various statements, fiery though many of them were. The system of Degree remained pretty much unshak'd. It was not the rule of kings that was questioned but only its abuse. Liberty of opinion remained proper only for one's own party — for the opposition it was license, if not heresy or sacrilege or treason. François Hotman did a quick change and defended the power of the king when the king became his preferred candidate, Henry of Navarre. Catholic pamphleteers who had supported the royal power in France became partisans of popular sovereignty after Henri III's attack on the Catholic League. Peasants in Swabia and Franconia, inspired by Luther's daring opposition to duly constituted authority, revolted and issued a genuinely revolutionary manifesto; they were repudiated by Luther ("You assert that no one is to be the serf of anyone else . . . This article . . . proposes robbery, for it suggests that every man should take his body away from his lord, even though his body is the lord's property. . . . This article would make all men equal, and turn the spiritual kingdom of Christ into a worldly, external kingdom; and that is impossible. A worldly kingdom cannot exist without an inequality of persons, some being free, some imprisoned, some lords, some subjects, etc.") and duly crushed (an estimated one hundred thousand peasants slain) by more or less properly constituted authority. Anabaptists in Thuringia (perhaps not unaware of Thomas More's *Utopia*) announced a program as communistic as religious; their leader was put to death and their lunatic reputation turned serious men of state against them for years to come — Beza wrote in *Du Droit des Magistrats* that he prayed no one would assume he favored in the slightest "these maddened Anabaptists and other seditious and mutinous persons, who on the contrary I believe deserve the hatred of all mankind . . ."

## 5. *Contr'un*

Early in this period, though, there were two works that received serious attention and yet were truly radical in that they questioned the total idea of Degree and even the system of kingship itself. One was More's *Utopia*, already mentioned. The other was Etienne de La Boétie's brief essay entitled *Discours de la servitude volontaire, ou Contr'un. Contr'un* is a direct attack on kingship, not simply on a wicked or tyrannical king but on the basic idea, the principle, the system of one man ruling over a whole people. It was not transfer of power from one group (however bad) to another group (however good) that La Boétie advocated, but the abolition of power itself. Riot and revolution were quite unnecessary. The people were so much stronger than the one man, the ruler, that clearly they served him only voluntarily; in fact (says the author) the people seemed so willing to be serfs that one might think they had not lost their liberty but won their enslavement. All that was needed was for the people simply to resolve to serve no longer, and on the instant they would be free. La Boétie doesn't urge any violence whatever, not even the slightest shove to the monolithic monster, but only to stop sustaining it, "and you will see it, like a great colossus from which the base has been removed, crash and shatter of its own weight."

Nature, says *Contr'un*, has meant all men to be brothers, and all men to be free. If we lived according to the rights nature has granted us "we would be obedient to our parents, subject to reason, and serfs to no one." The very beasts "would cry out to men, if men were not too deaf to hear, VIVE LIBERTÉ!"

*Contr'un* thus takes a position contra *any* master, any infringement of liberty, and constitutes therefore a genuine break with the traditional Old World view of liberty, which was typically contra *them*, the other party, the rival contestants for power.

The essay was circulated in manuscript among the Huguenots as the religious wars got under way (La Boétie himself was a Catholic), and after its first (and by no means authorized) publication in mutilated form in the 1570s was used by various different groups as antiroyalist propaganda, not, however, with very great effect, possibly for the precise reason that it did not attack a specific ruling group nor demand a transfer of power to a new specific group. It has attracted more attention in certain later periods, the time of the Revolution, for example, and the present day.

Its first publication was not until several years after La Boétie's death, and the exact date of its composition has remained a matter of some dispute. La Boétie was the great friend of Montaigne, the inspiration for Montaigne's famous essay on friendship, and Montaigne said, after La Boétie's death when the piece was being put to (a particularly unwelcome) political use, that *Contr'un* had been written during its author's schoolboy years, a mere schoolroom exercise on a very ordinary subject hashed over a thousand times in previous books. There was never a more law-abiding citizen, Montaigne wrote (*Essays*, Book I, Chapter 27), nor one more hostile to civil discord and disruptive new ideas.

The most usual supposition has it that *Contr'un* was written in 1548 in reaction to the bloody troubles in Guienne, La Boétie's home province, where the imposition of the salt tax (the gabelle) had triggered a revolt that had been put down with great cruelty by the Constable of France, Anne de Montmorency. At this date La Boétie was eighteen years old, Montaigne fifteen, and though Montaigne may have read *Contr'un* at about that time, as it went from hand to hand in manuscript among "persons of discernment," he did not meet La Boétie until some ten years later. Montaigne afterward set the date of composition a couple of years earlier still, perhaps to wipe out once and for all any political motivation whatever, claiming La Boétie had written it when he was sixteen and that it had been suggested by a reading of Plutarch. Such early dates don't jibe, however, with a mention in the essay of Ronsard and his fellow poets Baif and Du Bellay, of the group that came to be called the Pléiade, and their achievements in "advancing so well our language" — their manifesto on the virtue of French translation of the ancients dating from only 1549, and their first poetic successes principally from the early 1550s. La Boétie also speaks of "la veine de notre Ronsarde, en sa Franciade," which was not published until years later, although the prologue was read before Henri II by Lancelot de Carle (La Boétie's wife was a de Carle) in 1550 or 1551. Some editors of La Boétie have gotten around these difficulties by wondering if the reference to Ronsard and friends may not have been added at a later rewriting, La Boétie perhaps having become acquainted with Ronsard and friends later on while a student at Orléans, where La Boétie received a degree in law in 1553. But this of course would open the door to any other point in the essay — such as its extreme views on liberty — having also been added at a later (and thus presumably more mature) rewriting.

Montaigne did not mean to impugn La Boétie's sincerity or his brilliance — far from it; he regarded La Boétie as "the greatest man of our century" — but simply to deny him any intent of becoming a public agitator, a revolutionary, and to counter the unwelcome political use of his essay.

Montaigne had decided against publishing *Contr'un* in a posthumous volume of La Boétie's works (principally translations and poems) he put together in 1570: "I have used all I could . . . except a Discours de la servitude volontaire, & some memoires on our troubles over the Edict of January, 1562 — as to these two latter pieces I found them of a fashion too fragile and delicate to be abandoned to the violent and stormy air of these unpleasant times" Apparently, though, he did intend to publish *Contr'un* later, when the times were more settled. But the times did not settle and the Huguenots beat him to it and, in effect, stole the piece (for the moment) for Calvinism.

A recent study suggests *Contr'un* as the germ of Montaigne's "Des

Cannibales" and as the inspiration and planned centerpiece for Montaigne's whole first book, for which Montaigne "reluctantly" substituted La Boétie's twenty-nine sonnets forming "chapter 29, 28 chapters before, 28 after . . ." According to this analysis, La Boétie was to Montaigne not only his great friend but a companion in exile, for Montaigne saw himself as a man of classic times exiled in sixteenth-century France; and still another exile the Brazilian Indian, one of those American "savages" in whom are "alive and vigorous the true and most useful and natural of virtues," met by Montaigne at Rouen in 1562 and quoted at length in "Des Cannibales."

"There is therefore in the middle of the first book the portrait of three brothers in exile: La Boétie in the center — beside him Montaigne and the Cannibal. These three exiles form a chain linking the two happy and virtuous societies . . . antiquity, where it was necessary to search back to the golden age for happiness, and Eldorado . . ." La Boétie thus came (for Montaigne) from "other centuries or other continents. His 'imagination' would have been perfectly at home not only among the Greeks or the Romans but also in the life of these new Indies . . ."

The best testimony to the striking originality of *Contr'un* is given by those among its editors, not motivated by any personal sense of loss or disappointment as was Montaigne, who turn the essay every way but loose in trying to prove it really doesn't exist. Possibly the best of these editors, for this purpose, is Paul Bonnefon, writing from the dawn of the top-hatted "Belle Epoque" in his Introduction to *Etienne de La Boétie, Oeuvres Complètes* (Paris 1892).

Above all, says Bonnefon, *Contr'un* is a work of youth — and it is certainly true that everything in La Boétie's life including his death at the age of thirty-three breathes of youth. The essay is also, Bonnefon points out, a Renaissance work, La Boétie having, like so many of his contemporaries, given himself "with a thoughtless imprudence" to a feverish study of antique letters. "For, like them, he never dreamed that in stirring these ashes of the past he might stir up trouble in the present. The young man had no intention of attacking the established order of things." He was simply expressing his youthful love of humanity and of liberty, liberty in its most classic sense, sweet liberty opposed to tyranny, but in his youthful zeal (and lack of political experience, the editor adds) he was carried beyond the harmonious classical resolution of this struggle: the tyrant driven out and a good ruler installed in his place. Instead, he asked the people to overturn all rule altogether. "After having failed to distinguish between legitimate authority and illicit authority, and having attacked the principle of authority itself, La Boétie outlines for us a naive illusion. He seems to believe that man could live in a state of nature, without society and without government, and would have us believe that this situation could be a happy one for humanity. A puerile dream, although presented with an infectious eloquence."

*Contr'un* is, I think, one of the first clear statements of the ideal of masterlessness that seems to be basic to modern notions of liberty. All citations in the piece are classical — he goes beyond his antique models only in his solution, as More went beyond the limited communism of Plato in applying it to an entire people and recommending it for the entire world. There is nothing in his essay to indicate La Boétie had ever heard of the New World and the reports of the liberty there. Nothing, that is, except the similarity of ideas. Perhaps La Boétie, while a student at Orléans, came across the same New World ecstasies that Ronsard plucked out of the air of the same time and place. Or perhaps not — perhaps La Boétie's unique voice was entirely out of his own head, a true doppelgänger in the world of thought. *Contr'un* "is an isolated effort," and so it was, whatever its origins.

It is interesting that the two genuinely revolutionary works of the sixteenth century, those of More and La Boétie, both came before the religious wars set fire to revolt — and repression — all over Europe. It is as if, once swords were really drawn, the urgency of an actual battle for power would no longer permit such idle luxuries as visions of actual liberty and equality. Seen in this light, possibly the religious wars set back true libertarian thought in Europe for a hundred years.

It is particularly interesting — poignant might be a better word — that Montaigne, when he wanted to evoke an idealized liberty that he could praise in his own voice, could only call on the curiosity in a zoo that was the New World rather than on the liberty become so uncomfortably close to home, dreamed by his beloved friend.

# 6. Neither King nor Lord

The sort of generally admirable verdict on the New World's people that has been presented thus far was not by any means unanimous, even though "enthusiastic descriptions of the Good Savage" were "much more numerous" during the several generations of early contacts than the "exceptional" texts which "spoke of the inhabitants of the New World as 'brute beasts.' " But there were plenty of the latter even so, that pictured the native Americans as truly savage, barely distinguishable from wild animals. Many of the earliest reports, coming from the Antilles and the South American coast, featured sensational tales of cannibalism. Others dwelt largely on such competing thrills as nudity and red-hot sex, in which the lovely naked women ("quite beautiful and with well-made bodies") were so "insatiably voluptuous" that a man went in literal risk of a fate worse than death, the women giving their presumably helpless male victims "the juice of certain herbs" or applying venomous insects to inflate, or overinflate, the penis, which they would then assault most cruelly, all this resulting in some poor devils' "losing the virile member, and also the testicles." The authority here is none other than America's somewhat questionable (alas) godfather, Amerigo Vespucci, who also states, as a "marvel worthy of admiration," that the women's breasts and "shameful parts" were always in appearance those of virgins, in spite of childbearing and their aforesaid unflinching dedication to carnal pursuits. They also, he added, usually live to be a hundred and fifty years old.

The South Americans ate human flesh, said one of Vespucci's frequently reprinted and immensely popular even though (or perhaps because) distorted letters, "the father the son or the son the father." He knew one man who boasted of having eaten more than three hundred persons, and "I have seen a man eat his children and wife." In a town where he resided for some "twenty-seven days" he saw human bodies hung up by the heels as butchers hang up beeves. Speaking of the "warm friendship" with which they were usually welcomed everywhere, and which usually included the pressing gift of a daughter "that we should sleep with her" he interrupts to remark that "they eat all their enemies that they kill or take, as well females as males, with so much barbarity that it is a brutal thing to mention, how much more to see it, as has happened to me an infinite number of times." Then, with a return to the principal theme, recounting a stopover in a certain village: "Here they offered their wives to us, and we were unable to defend ourselves from them."

André Thévet, a later sixteenth-century "geographical" writer of much influence, although (or perhaps because), as previously mentioned, a great liar, describes the Brazilians as "living like irrational beasts, just as nature has produced them, eating roots, going naked," except where the Christians have been able, little by little, to replace this brutish state with a more civil and humane fashion of life. He related that these "cruel and inhuman" people take more pleasure in their cannibal feasts "than we do with mutton" and pictures them tearing the body to pieces and washing the male children in the blood, adding that the women commonly got the entrails to eat.

Villegagnon wrote (in a letter to John Calvin, who had been his fellow student at the University of Paris) shortly after arriving at his colony in Brazil, that the natives were "so different from us" in every respect, so distant from "all proper behavior and humanity" that he really sometimes thought "we have fallen among beasts wearing human faces."

Similar observations were common, even in reports by witnesses otherwise full of praise for some aspects of the American way of life, such as Jean de Léry speaking of their slave women (war captives they had bought) as poor "wretches" who could be constrained to wear clothes only by much whipping — and even then did not have sense enough to wear them so they covered the parts that (to the Christians) were indecent. Elsewhere, however, Léry maintains that the Brazilians were superior in "discourse" to most European peasants and indeed to some other Europeans who believed themselves well educated in this respect. Even Thévet found that his brute-beast Americans kept promises, did not steal from one another (although would if they could from Christians), and were exceedingly charitable and fair, "more so I would say than one finds among Christians." And Villegagnon's exemplary behavior toward the Indians living near his colony might indicate that he eventually found them sufficiently human — the Portuguese governor in Brazil reported that Villegagnon was excessively liberal in dealing with the natives and observed such strict justice that he would hang one of his own people for committing a wrong against the Indians, and was therefore feared by his colonists "but adored by the natives. He has taught them the use of arms, and as the tribe with which he is allied is very numerous and one of the bravest, he could become very redoubtable."

But all these counter attractions, cannibalism, nudity, even sex, could not match the theme of liberty and equality in capturing the interest of the leading minds of Europe — and perhaps still more to the point, most of the New World reports, no matter how hostile toward the American people, found occasion to speak of their extraordinary liberty — "led only by their own lusts and sensuality," as said in 1609 an indignant English pastor. The Vespucci letter quoted above puts it that the inhabitants of this country "have neither King, nor Prince, nor Lord, each is the master of himself." Another version of the same letter, regarded as more accurate, makes this line "They live amongst themselves without a king or ruler, each man being his own master" and emphasizes elsewhere the same point: " . . . nor do they obey anyone, but live in freedom . . . They have neither king nor lord . . . Neither the mother nor the father chastise their children, and it is wonderful that we never saw a quarrel among them . . . They have none of the riches which are looked upon as such in our Europe and in other parts . . ." The so-called Bartolozzi Letter, believed to be a thoroughly authentic version of Vespucci's letter of 1502, written after his return from his first Brazilian voyage, uses its only exclamation mark for the passage, "no private property, because everything is common . . . no boundaries . . . and no king! They obey nobody, each is lord unto himself . . ."

This same letter says (probably speaking of the Guarani), "the more astonishing thing about their wars and cruelty is that we could find no reason for them, since they have no property or lords or kings or desire for plunder, or lust to rule, which seems to me to be the causes of wars and of disorder." André Thévet, speaking of war among the "Sauvages," says that since among them each is as much a great lord as the other and that among them there are no riches, "their motive for war is certainly ill-founded, solely from desire for some vengeance, without any other reason, quite as among brute beasts . . ." The "Amériques," he writes, trouble themselves with no other ambition than tending their gardens.

Thévet was a Franciscan friar who was financed during fifteen years of travel, most of which was in the Near East, by Charles de Guise, Cardinal of Lorraine, head of the Guise family and of the Catholic party in France. He stayed as short a time as possible at the Villegagnon colony in Brazil, arriving in November 1555 and leaving by the first available boat early the following year, and got most of his American information from reading and hearsay, although he implied repeatedly that he was reporting as an eyewitness, whether speaking of Peru or Florida or Canada. Atkinson lists a number of contemporaries who questioned his veracity; and said Urbain Chauveton of a typical Thévet passage, "as many faults and falsenesses as words." Or confesses a nineteenth-century defender, "This bungler of a Thévet put so little order in his work that he was able to recount the same things twice in the same chapter with different figures." But Thévet was also an able politician (he blandly accused his accusers of plagiarism), with influence in the best of places: Ronsard and friends prefaced his work with the floweriest of odes, and he was ultimately honored by the position of Royal Cosmographer. Vespucci, a Florentine businessman associated with the Medici interests in Seville, participated actively and personally in several New World ventures. Majority opinion today among historians, while recognizing the great influence of his published letters and the ethnographic value of certain passages therein, reduces his supposed four voyages to two or possibly three and rules out the claim that he was the first European to strike the American mainland, a claim roundly lambasted in his own day by Bartolomé de Las Casas, a notable authority on such matters. Vespucci, though, also wound up with a top official position, that of chief pilot of Spain. As he was apparently the earliest master of sharp business practices to exploit the new world that was to bear his name, the naming might seem a particularly felicitous happenchance.

It is, I think, all the more impressive if such writers, in giving prominence to the new ideas of equality and liberty in the New World, were finding these ideas as much in the general fund of travelers' talk of their time as in their own personal but limited experience.

Some such casual references sometimes appear in circumstances most wonderfully intricate with morals historical and psychological to be drawn in all directions — for instance, a garbled and largely fanciful account dealing with French efforts to establish a colony in the region of coastal South Carolina and Florida in the 1560s speaks of arriving in a flotilla of galleys at the "Isle of Florida" where the hundreds of galley slaves (convicts) are temporarily liberated. But the galley slaves are seduced by the natives with talk of the "great liberty" they could have in the native American world, and conspire with the "sauvages" to attack the "captains and governors" and are perforce returned to their chains; they had intended to join with the native women "to live in the greatest abomination an Epicurean life . . . without God, without faith, without law . . ." There was in the factual story of the Ribaut-Laudonniere colony at Fort Caroline in the 1560s a "sedition" against Laudonniere, and he himself was held in chains for some days; Ribaut did arrive with two "roberges" (rowbarges, an especially stable sort of galley), and Laudonniere made use of other galleys and "galiotes." The reaction of the "savages" to the chains, hangings, and violent civil strife of their odd new neighbors may have played a part in the subsequent politics of the region, along with the blundering diplomacy of both the French and Spanish in establishing Indian alliances. (The French outblundered the Spanish and were eventually defeated.) The author of the galley slave scenario also describes, among the Floridian fauna, a great flying lizard which strews the roads with half-devoured human victims, a veritable alligator perhaps lurking someplace in its origin, as were the veritable chains in the murky origin of his account of the galley slaves' revolt — and evidently prominent in the sailors' talk that filled his ears that notorious "great liberty," so wonderfully unhampered by laws of God or man.

One of the relatively few New World works of note that did not point up these new ideas of freedom and equality was a history by Francisco López de Gómara (published in Spain in 1552; in France, as *Histoire Générale des Indes*, 1568). Gómara never saw the New World but seems to have made much use of information supplied by Hernando Cortez, conqueror of Mexico: it was charged at the time that Gómara was primarily a publicist and apologist for Cortez. His work contains some of the most violent anti-Indian statements of the century. Peter Martyr's Seventh *Decade*, published in 1530, printed a petition to the Council of the Indies by the survivors of native attacks on a New World monastery urging enslavement of all Indians. Martyr joined to this a number of pointed comments on Spanish rapacity and avarice although he acceded, after much pious doubt, in the council's decision to accept the petition. Gómara reprinted the petition without any such countering comments, and it was from Gómara's publication that the accusations in the petition, usually accepted as stating established facts, reached most European readers. The petition accused Indians in general of eating human flesh, of sodomy (a favorite charge for religious polemicists), of going naked, of shamelessness, of beardlessness, of being no better than beasts and living without any justice whatever; of being ignorant, stupid, insensate, of paying no attention to the truth unless it was to their profit, of being thieves, liars, traitorous, cruel, vindictive; of inconstancy, ingratitude, drunkenness, frivolity, with no obedience or manners and no capacity to grasp any teaching; of having little judgment and no faith and no public order; of being magicians and sorcerers and cowards, as timid as rabbits, as dirty as pigs; of eating lice, spiders, and raw worms; of having no "piety" toward their sick, abandoning them at the hour of death: "to sum up, I say that God never created a nation so full of vice and so lacking in any virtue."

And yet it was anti-American Gómara who most "stimulated the reflection" of pro-American Montaigne in regard to the New World, especially for the essay "Des Coches" — a stimulus to indignation. "So many cities destroyed, so many nations exterminated, so many millions of people put to the sword, and the richest and fairest part of the world overthrown for the commerce of pearls and peppers: vile victories . . ." said Montaigne of the New World conquest Gómara so fulsomely praised.

Gómara's apologia was not only rather crassly overdone, but was heavily outnumbered by works speaking with some sympathy if not favor if not admiration for the vanquished Indians. During the religious wars these reports on the butchered New World took on occasional political coloring in attacking the Spaniards, the Spanish being the leaders and financial backers of the Catholic forces in Europe. The noble savage even appeared in person in one of the French publications of this paper war, an anonymous pamphlet of 1596 entitled *Harangue d'un Cacique Indien*, the Indian chief, the speaker, warning the French of Spanish tyranny in rousing oratical periods and quotations from Virgil (in Latin), and including a thumbnail sketch of New World history: "of five or six million that we were, scarcely six thousand are living today, his [the Spaniard's] cruelty having put the most to the sword, his avarice having buried others alive in the mines . . . his inhumanity having led a million to die by their own hands rather than fall into his. And those who still remain prefer to drag out their lives in the desert among wild beasts rather than suffer without hope under the yoke of these Tigers."

The best known of these defenses of the Americans and denunciations of the Spaniards were by Bartolomé de Las Casas, whose *Tyrannies et Cruautés des Espagnols* appeared in French in 1579; and in translations into Latin and French that appeared in 1578-79 by Urbain Chauveton of Hierosme Benzoni's (originally Italian, 1565) *Histoire Nouvelle du Nouveau Monde*, a work that lost none of its critical passion in translation, or in the copious prefaces and notes and appendices added by the translator. Chauveton was a zealously partisan Protestant, his notes apparently "designed to fan French anti-Spanish sentiment, and . . . revive French interest in colonial expansion" in keeping with Huguenot strategy at the time. Avarice, says Benzoni/Chauveton, is the idol of the Christians while the Indians are neither avaricious nor rich, there being nothing they hold more in contempt than gold and silver. From avarice the Spaniards desecrated the "singular gift of God" that was the New World, bringing about revolts and mass suicides of the Indian people "who would rather die by their own hand than live under the mastery of the Spaniard." Gómara is singled out for specific criticism in this work, for writing from hearsay (Benzoni had spent fourteen years in America), and bringing "charges against the poor Indians of things they have never imagined, while always praising the Spaniards and dissimulating their misdeeds."

Villegagnon, Thévet, Léry, and numbers of "cosmographers" were all available to Montaigne, but the only such book he cites as a reference work for the ideas favorable to Indians expressed in "Des Cannibales" is this translation by Chauveton. His best source of information, Montaigne writes, was in talking to a man "I had for a long time with me . . . who had lived ten or twelve years in that other world . . ."

Some authors of anti-American works proceeded with rather more guile than Gómara, the most successful of these Francisco de Vitoria who to this day enjoys a reputation as an earnest defender of the Indians, justified if one is careful not to read too far in his work. There is an apparently sincere solicitude for the poor barbarians ("this suspect Vitorian solicitude for primitive peoples and for their mines") concluding with the regretful judgment that their conquest is legitimate, for while these people are not completely incapable they differ very little from the mentally retarded and do not appear capable of administering a "properly humane and politic republic," possessing "neither adequate laws nor magistrates, and not even being capable of governing their families."

Cardinal Garcia Loaysa, confessor of Charles V and presiding officer of the Council of the Indies, held as his opinion (having been told that some Indians thought the Ave Maria was something to eat) that the New World people were not capable of learning the holy faith ("no more than parrots"), and Juan Gines de Sepúlveda answered Las Casas' example of the magnificent architecture of ancient Mexico by pointing out "that bees and spiders could produce artefacts that no man could imitate."

Even Gómara turned to rather more subtlety (for Gómara) in discussing the final decision of the emperor not to regard the Indians as (officially) a people to be enslaved; this "liberation" of the Indians was being faithfully observed, said Gómara (which was very far indeed from the truth), and even though God had not sent these poor wretches this servitude and labor except as punishment for their wickedness, slavery being recognized as the mark of sin by "the holy Doctors Augustine and Chrysostom," nevertheless the ordinance of liberation reflected the greatest glory on the clemency of the king, for it was "just that men born free should not be slaves of other persons" — not even such people as these, whose freedom had been a captivity by the devil.

Las Casas' arguments were simpler, and reached with utter directness a very different conclusion: "Are they not men? Then by what right do you butcher those who are living peacefully in their homes?" He took these phrases, he tells us, from a sermon preached by another Dominican at Santo Domingo in 1511, the year before Las Casas was ordained. The main line followed by Las Casas and the other Spaniards of his time (there were many) who shared his opinion that "mankind is one" and that "the law of nations and natural law apply to Christian and gentile alike, and to all people of any sect, law, condition, or color without any distinction whatsoever" and that, in sum, "all the peoples of the world are men" (the basic source of his position, found, says Las Casas, in Cicero, Libro I), became the foundation of modern international law, holding that treaties must be honored even between peoples of opposing faith and customs.

Along with the denunciations or vindications of the conquering Spaniards there ran the insistent theme that the golden world had been no sooner found than destroyed. The Spaniards fell upon these "lambs so gentle," the Americans, wrote Las Casas, and in only forty years had wrought such destruction, by slaughter, anguish, afflictions and torments never before invented, that "of the more than three million" persons making up the aboriginal population of Hispaniola there were not now (1540s) two hundred remaining. Benzoni, writing a few years later (mid-1550s), said of Hispaniola that "out of the two millions of original inhabitants, through the number of suicides and other deaths, occasioned by the oppressive labour and cruelties imposed by the Spaniards, there are not a hundred and fifty now to be found" and a similar fate had befallen, he said, the natives of Cuba, Jamaica, Puerto Rico, and other places in the region. Motolinia, usually a defender of the Spaniards and their conquests, wrote (*c.* 1541) that the bodies of those killed by forced labor at Oaxaca covered the earth for a mile around and the sky was dark with scavenging birds, while to count the dead in the lands of the Caribbean was to count the drops of rain or the sand in the sea. Las Casas speaks elsewhere of what was perhaps the chief cause of the incredible mortality among the Indians, unchecked epidemics of Old World diseases against which the New World people had no immunity, saying of the terrible culminating Hispaniola epidemic, "I do not believe that 1000 souls can have escaped from this misery, out of the immensity of people our own eyes had once seen living in this island."

The point, the overwhelming fact noticed by nearly all who wrote of the New World in this period, was that the Golden Age, so miraculously real at the opening of the sixteenth century, had vanished well before the century's close, vanished at the Old World's touch.

In the meantime the idea of popular liberty, liberty for all — not an element in the ancient tradition of the golden world but very much an element of the New World image — retreated like the New World people from the Old World's deadly contact and became still more straitly identified with "unspoiled," indeed "untouched," American Indians. Where the Old World installed itself, liberty died; where the New World remained new, liberty still lived. Such seems to have been the most typical pattern of notions making up that New World image at the close of its first hundred years.

The *History* by José de Acosta cited earlier, based on seventeen years in America, mostly in Peru, and making use of information provided by officials of longer New World experience still, summed up the various American political structures in three categories: absolute monarchies, government by a group of leaders in a sort of senate, and those peoples who (in a passage previously quoted) "suffer" no permanent rule whatever but select temporary "Captains and Princes" only when occasion demands, the greater part of the New World being governed in this latter manner. The same categories appeared a few years later in an 800-page geographical compendium by Jodocus Hondius, but with their distribution seemingly rearranged, the first two apparently limited to the Old World, and the third, entire liberty, apparently occupying the entire New World: "One sees also what diversity exists among peoples dissimilar in color, condition, sense, reason . . . One sees how different are their governments and sovereignties, some preferring the government of a sole King, others to be governed by a number of leaders, and still others requiring entire liberty, and owning all things in common after the manner of those who lived in the golden age of which the Poets speak. This is still seen in usage among the nations which inhabit the new lands, where the Indians, with an unprecedented obstinacy, have fought for their liberty . . ."

# II

# The New World: Vision and Reality

## 1. Vision

Myth or reality, something in the American way of life convinced a great many observers that they were seeing a marvel even more marvelous than Vespucci's ageless women and even more worthy of admiration, a world of genuine equality and freedom in actual existence.

Present opinion, supported by painstaking studies of all available evidence, historical and archaeological and ethnological, finds some social stratification an integral part of nearly all aboriginal American societies. The Arawakan people of the Caribbean, for example, the area of first European contact, gave great respect to their community leaders, and in fact the same accounts that ecstasized over the perfect freedom and equality of these naked islanders sometimes ecstasized also over the august presence of these leaders, men and women, apparently unaware of setting afoot any contradiction. Peter Martyr accompanies his picture of American Indian liberty with "they gathered by signs and by conjectures that the islanders were governed by kings" and "There is but one king for the whole of the island [Puerto Rico], and he is reverently obeyed." Numerous other accounts of the New World spoke (unlike Vespucci) of Indian kings and queens — more or less in the same breath with enthusiastic descriptions of New World liberty.

Where then were the vaunted freedom and equality?

It is difficult of course, if not impossible, to deal with such questions in reference to "the New World" as a whole. At least as great a variety existed among societies of the New World as in the Old, and one can scarcely speak of these two vast tapestries of contrasting time and space as two entities each neatly all of a piece. And yet some basic traits may be submitted, in a very general way, for each.

New World stratification appears to have been founded most often not on property relationships as in customary Old World structures but on religious or kin-group arrangements, with the leaders spokesmen for their social groups rather than rulers. Most often, rule seems to have been managed by clan and council, the political structure that of a society rather than a state in the apt distinction of some modern ethnologists. Equality and liberty are in European thinking frequently suspected of being antithetical — although the English historian A. F. Pollard argued that there "is only one solution to the problem of liberty, and it lies in equality" and was warmly seconded in this opinion by R. H. Tawney in *Equality* (1931) — while in Indian America liberty and equality evidently contrived to give at least the occasional appearance of living together compatibly, which might tell us something. Repeated emphasis in the early literature on the absence of thine and mine could indicate that a difference in attitude toward property might have had a bearing on an impression of classlessness. The usual American attitude tending toward the use of property in common was in flagrant opposition to the general European tradition of competition to acquire private property, and thus (as in Utopia) the familiar machinery required to enforce the principle of thine and mine — courts, lawsuits, money, boundaries, police — was for the most part either rare or absent in the New World, as for so long so many reports agreed. Some such possibilities may underlie at least some of the elements that made up the Old World's vision of American freedom.

But the Old World's vision is easier to document than the New World reality. Painstaking study of all available evidence notwithstanding, present opinion finds much terrain still under dispute, including an uncomfortable number of key points. This is especially true for various regions in Mesoamerica (land of Aztec and Maya and, after the Caribbean, a region of very early European penetration) where the data are extremely complex and are by no means always given the same interpretation by all students.

Most early Spanish reports on the Aztecs pictured (even while the European vision of the New World continued to glow so ardently of freedom) a rigorous monarchy supported by the "nobles" of a sort of feudal aristocracy, the "emperor" enjoying a regal state more absolute than that of any king in Europe. This view of Aztec political structure persisted until the mid-nineteenth century, when it was attacked by the American anthropologist Lewis Henry Morgan who wrote, "All the grand terminology of the Old World, created under despotic and monarchical institutions . . . to decorate particular men and classes of men, has been lavished . . . upon plain Indian sachems and war-chiefs, without perceiving that thereby the poor Indian was grievously wronged, for he had not invented such institutions nor formed such a society as these terms imply."

Morgan criticized particularly the writings of the American historian H. H. Bancroft, who answered with the impressive list of his sources (sometimes, unfortunately, accompanied by comments none too accurate); but a series of anthropological studies had been published in the meantime by Adolph F. A. Bandelier supporting Morgan, treating in detail of Aztec military organizations, land tenure, and governmental structure. These studies appeared to abolish concepts of kingship, feudal aristocracy, and especially private ownership of real estate among the Aztecs.

Their conclusions were reexamined and generally confirmed by a leading anthropologist in 1916 and remained pretty much accepted until recent years, when with works such as Eric R. Wolf, *Sons of the Shaking Earth* (1959) and Michael D. Coe, *Mexico* (1962), the trend of interpretation was again reversed, to lay stress on military authoritarianism and the likelihood of inherited rank, accompanied by expressions of anthropological astonishment "that such false conclusions could have been arrived at as those of Morgan and Bandelier which were in vogue during the first quarter of this century."

Kings and nobles have since returned to much of the archaeological literature as unabashedly European as they were in the early Spanish chronicles. Some current interpretations present blood lines for certain Mesoamerican high-caste families with as rigorous a studbook as any in Europe, from which it might be supposed that the people of ancient Mexico could have understood quite well Lady Fleming's effusion on the friande liquor of blood royal. Majority opinion seems now to settle for "little doubt that the Aztec state was a rigidly class-structured system."

## 2. Reality

Controversy continues, both direct ("a bias toward totalitarian interpretation," wrote John Collier in a review of the above work by Wolf) and indirect, in interpretations underlining what seem to be family group building blocks in Mesoamerican social organizations; but the most serious obstacle to this present reactionary trend in interpretation appears to be a parallel trend resisting all efforts, from whatever direction, to express Indian history in European terms. This development, which may turn out to be of considerable importance, turns to study of Indian thought — in effect, the structural alphabet of the Indian mind — in the hope of establishing non-European communication contacts and points of view that may be more in harmony with the reality of the Indian past.

This approach has, for the Aztecs and neighboring societies in south-central Mexico, given particular attention to purely literary sources, such as those surveyed in the works of Angel Maria Garibay K. (*Historia de la Literatura Nahuatl*, 1953-54) and Miguel Leon-Portilla (*Aztec Thought and Culture*, 1963), resulting in a concentration on religion and the religious functions of political officials, and on the complexity of the religio-political edifices thus erected, where religious ceremony and mythic representation are inextricably intertwined with the "real" world, where religion "intervened" in all activities, including activities we do not now think of as related to religious sentiment, in politics and commerce, in the purpose of each individual life and the purpose of the community as a whole, there being "not a single act, of public or private life," uninvaded by religion.

The essence of this search for Indian meanings and values in order to make Indian reality accessible lies in the stress placed on the fundamental difference of the Indian world, a difference so irreconcilable it can be seen, really, only through different eyes.

Well in advance of this present trend, the archaeologist George C. Vaillant argued that the "downfall of the Aztecs cannot be explained in terms of European history, and the standard reasons give a false picture. Moctezuma, singled out by European authors as a weak and vacillating monarch, was a tribal leader devoid of the constitutional rights of a European sovereign. His empire is also a European creation, since it consisted, in reality, of communities sufficiently intimidated to pay tribute, but in no wise bound to Aztec governmental conventions." Vaillant speaks explicitly of liberty, or rather its absence, in ancient Mexico, where "freedom of thought, individual liberty, personal fortunes were non-existent" but an Aztec "would have been horrified at the naked isolation of an individual's life in our western world."

Aztec social organization was based on the group, possibly a kin group, known as the *calpulli*, made up of several hundred or even several thousand persons — perhaps combined from still smaller groups known as *tequitanos* that might have been clan groups or extended families. There were, according to most estimates, twenty *calpullec* in the great city of Tenochtitlan, the Aztec Mexico City, although a recent study of settlement patterns suggests more than sixty; all larger social groupings — towns, cities, nations — says the same study, were "growths from this pattern." This basic social unit, the calpulli, operated in educational, political, economic areas as well as in the all-embracing area of religion. The several dozen calpullec were organized into four principal groups or quarters (as was the universe, according to Mesoamerican cosmogony), and a council of "speakers," one elected from each calpulli, chose four principal speakers to preside over these four quarters, who then elected as "revered speaker" the official usually called by the chroniclers the "king" or the "emperor." This appointment was for life (although an unsatisfactory appointee could be removed by the council) and was usually made from the same lineage, and the revered speaker received more than royal, rather a godly, reverence.

The revered speaker is thought to have represented, among the Aztecs, in his religious manifestation, the god Quetzalcoatl. Another official, thought by some students to have been second in rank in Tenochtitlan, represented the earth goddess Cihuacoatl. The two "functioned necessarily as a team, sharing equal powers." Together they personified the dualism of the spirit (Quetzalcoatl) and the flesh (Cihuacoatl), the dualism of religious mysticism and workaday reality, the dualism, perhaps, of the double government — one government (Quetzalcoatl) to deal with matters outside the community and the other (Cihuacoatl) to deal with matters inside the community, a double administration frequently encountered in Indian administrative organization, a dual organization exemplifying a theory of reciprocity "as soundly based as the theory of gravity." The revered speaker embodied, for the outside world, all the authority of his people, while the Cihuacoatl saw to the machinery of the actual operation of the community, an operation that must have been quite complex for the great city of Tenochtitlan, with a population variously estimated at from 60,000 to some 300,000 (London in the early sixteenth century had an estimated population of 120,000).

Both these leading officials appear to have been dependent on the consent of the council for actual authority as rulers. The most famous, the most powerful "king" in southern mid-Mexico at the time of the Aztec rise to power, Tezozomoc of the city of Azcapotzalco, died of disappointment (so they say — at the age of 106) because his council overruled his wish on a crucial decision. Moctezuma was, according to some accounts, stoned to death by his own people when the Spanish forced him to urge publicly a course of action in opposition to the popular will.

Among the multitudinous religious observances of the Aztecs, several of which involved human sacrifices, there was one particularly dramatic ceremony dedicated to the god Tezcatlipoca. The most perfect youth among the war captives destined for sacrifice was selected to impersonate the god for an entire year. He was taught all the proper graces (says the sixteenth-century *Florentine Codex*), how to handle the flute and the tobacco pipe, how to "converse well." He was given a retinue of servants and companions, and four chosen women as wives. He was attired in the

greatest splendor and magnificence — adorned by Moctezuma himself
with the costliest of cloaks, jewels, golden bracelets, "princely sandals
with ocelot-skin ears." Wherever he appeared he was

    much honored

    honored as our lord
    treated by all as our lord the great god
    entreated with sighs for favors

    before him the people bowed and
    kissed with reverence the earth . . .

For one year he lived thus
    he went about playing music
    following whatever way he wished
    by day or by night

Then at the end of the year, at the festival of the great god Tezcatlipoca,
he climbed alone "of his own free will" the pyramid to his death, throw-
ing away step by step the gorgeous possessions that had been so temporarily his, until at the summit

        nothing
  was left to him nothing

  and there
  at the summit of the temple steps
  the priests fell upon him

    they threw him on his back upon
    the stone

        they cut open his breast tore out
        his heart and raised it to the sun
        in offering

        later his severed head was
        impaled upon the skull rack . . .

For whoever rejoices in possessions and
prosperity
sweet things and riches
ends in nothing and in misery . . .

The point, repeatedly stated in ancient Mexican literature, was the
elusive nature of ownership, the impossibility, precisely, of possession
of things. Says one of the sixty songs attributed to Nezahualcoyotl,
"king," of the city of Texcoco,

That great man that great conqueror Tezozomoc
(at the age of a hundred years)
his palaces and gardens surely so one thought
would last forever
but now already are dry and ruined
as everything must end in death
as all life is illusion and deception in the end . . .

Or another:

The riches of this world are only lent to us

the things that are so good to enjoy
we do not own . . .

none of these beautiful things can we keep for more
than an hour

one thing alone we can own forever
the memory of the just
the remembrance of a good act
the good remembrance of a just man

this one thing alone will never be taken away from us

will never die

The theme was *live!* Live correctly, live for living, live the right way,
and above all waste no anxiety on possessions, on acquisition, a precept
squarely opposed to the European ethic of acquisition for the sake of
acquisition. A foreigner might have taken the condemned youth of the

Tezcatlipoca ceremony for the "emperor" himself, judging by his raiment and the veneration of the populace. He was in fact a living sermon, walking the streets each day among the people, on the insubstantiality of power and glory and possession of good things. It is hard to imagine a Renaissance European playing the role so submissively — all his models of correct behavior, all his "instincts," would have impelled him to escape, taking along his riches and one (only one, for the sake of propriety) of his women, for the traditional Old World ending: "and they lived happily ever after." For in the Old World mind there was no ending to the happiness of possession; one lived happily *ever* after.

As a rule in Indian America a man owned his weapons and tools; a woman owned her household utensils; both, together with relatives, might own a hunting territory or fishing place. In some cases an individual could own such nonmaterial property as a particular song or ritual, and certain officials might possess accouterments of office or sectarian treasures (perhaps of considerable intrinsic value) rather as a Christian priest might possess, during his tenure, his church and its furnishings. Land was usually owned by a group, usually, among the Aztecs, by religious or political or military establishments or most commonly by the calpulli, which parcelled out its use among its members. Exceptionally some lands among the Aztecs seem (on the evidence of post-Spanish land claims by descendants) to have been held by outstanding individuals or their families, political and religious officials or persons of extraordinary merit, the *pipiltin*, often translated as "nobles," although it does not appear this could have involved ownership European-style, with the right to sell such property whenever or to whomever one wished or in fact the right to sell it at all. Exceptionally also, some families seem to have held a favored position in the distribution of communally owned lands or their produce — in a number of places in Mexico such primacy seems to have accompanied claimed descent from the Toltecs, the conquerors and builders of the tenth and eleventh centuries, before the appearance of the Aztecs. Even to this day a tradition of the caciquedom and its perquisites residing in a specific family has been documented for villages remote from modern political power centers.

The calpullec, in addition to owning and administering real estate, might operate markets of their own as well as their own plazas or "civic centers" under their own local religious, political, and military officials (with sometimes these varying functions combined in the same persons), the calpullec thus controlling most of the sources of real wealth, "the things that are so good to enjoy" of all kinds.

Agricultural labor in Mesoamerica — in Mesoamerica man's work, not woman's — has been seen by some students, basing their interpretation on the ceremonial calendar, as occupying a working period of one hundred days a year, and as being so much bound up with religious ritual that to a European it may not have been always recognizable as work. There was in any case enough time left over from work of any kind for general participation in the rest of the ceremonial year, a participation not only literally endless but endlessly active, in which the people took part, as says the *Florentine Codex,* "jostling, howling, roaring. They made the dust rise; they caused the ground to smoke. Like people possessed, they stamped upon the earth." Slavery existed in Mexico as it did in a number of New World regions, often (although not always) confined to war captives, but there is little mention in the early contact literature of regular forced labor as an aboriginal condition anywhere. The spectacularly high death toll from enforced "service" under the Spaniards might be in itself an indication that the obligation of incessant toil from dawn till dark, the perfectly normal lot of European peasants, was to American Indians a murderously unfamiliar experience.

A standard situation of the average common man working and living with and for his cooperative group, his community in the fullest sense, might reasonably have made for a life of less tension than that resulting from the competitive individual behavior of the Old World, possibly therefore giving an impression of a life "freer" than its European counterpart.

The Aztecs' opposite numbers in South America, the people known to us as the Incas, may have come nearer than any other New World society to breaking out of the trance of religious preoccupation to become an actual state in the European, even in the modern, sense of the word. Their wars of conquest approached true war and true conquest, their empire was true empire, their "king," although usually elected by the council from a "royal" lineage comprising hundreds of candidates, approached true kingship. Their wealth was unequaled; the virgin looting by the Spaniards yielded three times or more the amount taken from the Aztecs. Their rigid stratification into classes, all under the closest discipline, was unmatched. Post-Conquest Indian memories of Inca life give a glimpse of farm labor under a compulsion only very thinly disguised, in speaking of farmers, cultivating the Inca's land, being ordered by the overseers to "maintain a tidy appearance, sing and dance, and at the end shout 'Hailli,' our cry of victory." But even in the centralized and authoritarian, if not totalitarian, Inca world social organization was founded also on a community group, perhaps of related families, the *ayllu*; the country was divided into four quarters, the chief officials of which formed a council of state; and religion permeated all life, all thought.

The Maya societies encountered by the Spanish — a dozen or more separate little chieftainships — were a distant echo of the great Maya Classic Age of a thousand years before or of its later post-Classic renascence. But it is possible dregs from that long past that had produced one of the foremost civilizations anywhere in the ancient world still played some part in sixteenth-century life. Interpretation of that long past has been undergoing a sea of changes also. A generation ago the archaeologist Sylvanus Griswold Morley wrote, in *The Ancient Maya* (1946), that the six hundred years of the Classic Age gave little evidence of strong governments, strong rulers, or warfare. But more recently several specific dynasties of strong rulers have been proposed from studies of tombs and inscriptions, and human sacrifice and war have been given somewhat more emphasis. Both such varying interpretations might of course be correct — the number and variety of Classic Age "cities" could account for a considerable variety in ways of life and belief, and the centuries of time involved could encompass considerable change. There is evidence that militarism and human sacrifice grew more plentiful in the last three centuries of the Classic period, along with heightened influences from mid-Mexico, according to the eminent Mayanist J. Eric S. Thompson in his *Rise and Fall of Maya Civilization* (1954). Conceivably the suggested dynasties of strong rulers, also dating from the Late Classic, were another feature of this alien domination from central Mexico, which in its total effect may have had something to do with the eventual, and still puzzling, collapse of Maya Classic civilization. Morley and Thompson, however, have left conflicting legacies as to the dating of the Classic collapse and the transition to the Postclassic period, a still unresolved controversy that overshadows all such conclusions on the chronology of events in that time. Maya chronology in general is troubled by the fact that the complex problem of correlating the Maya and Christian calendars is also still unresolved, the two most acceptable correlations being some 260 years apart in the Classic period.

Domination and invasion from central (Toltec) Mexico became much more pronounced in the several centuries of the Maya Postclassic beginning in the tenth century, resulting in a world of exceptional complexity, in which particularly the "division of authority was complicated," although rule by a "joint government" could be discerned for Mayapan, largest and last of the Postclassic Maya centers. Mayapan was destroyed by civil war in the fifteenth century.

Such are some current notions of various elements underlying the Inca, Aztec, and Maya realities, customary examples of the most highly organized peoples in the hemisphere. Room can be found in even these superstratified societies, as has been seen, for impressions of cooperative rather than competitive endeavor seeming comparatively "free." One might suppose that most other societies in Indian America, being less highly organized, were likely to appear more "democratic" and more freely cooperative still. This may have been generally the case. The most conspicuous exceptions, the rank-conscious and wealth-conscious societies of the Northwest Coast, and the Natchez of the lower Mississippi Valley with an ironbound class system that might have been dreamed up by Jonathan Swift — these most notable exceptions were not really known to Europeans until the eighteenth and nineteenth centuries.

There were, in the New World's wonderful variety, societies composed only of loosely associated family groups (although even here a yearly cycle of all-pervasive religion was available); others were under the dictatorial authority of one or several powerful persons or families (individual success as a warrior or priest was most often the key to such power, but even here the self-made man was likely to bring his kin group or social group along with him); still others were under the authority of one or several powerful organizations, most commonly perhaps religious or military organizations; others were administered by directorates drawn from the entire community. Preferment or precedence in the performance of ceremonies may have been one of the more frequent causes of social conflict — an issue in *The Delight-Makers*, Bandelier's novel of ancient Pueblo life — but even here a conflict, a struggle, a motivation of the group.

The Pueblo peoples of the Southwest of the present United States (met by the Spanish in the 1540s) might be considered in some respects at an opposite pole from the Aztecs. Their village governments were (and some still are) intricately coordinated, delicately balanced, so subtle in their operation that they are still not fully understood by non-Pueblos, so thoroughly interwoven with religion they are described in some textbooks as theocracies, and yet so resolutely democratic that outward signs of rank are practically nonexistent. Most other Indian societies may have fallen someplace between the Pueblos and the Aztecs in this regard, with clan leaders, councillors, priests, spokesmen and notables of various sorts exhibiting outward semblance of authority to some degree between very ostentatiously or not at all — but the authority founded, in the majority of cases, on social groupings oriented toward kinship or religion. Said Robert H. Lowie in his classic *Primitive Society* (1920), " . . . in general the absence of central authority is one of the most impressive features of North American society."

The one most evident, most striking sameness underpinning the great majority of the New World's variety of peoples may well have been the devotion to religion. "In comparison with Whites in the United States today," says a current anthropological text, "the Indians were at least ten times as religious." Probably an understatement, but here again — here especially — no comparison with European terms can be very satisfactory.

The Indian world in general, in more or less all its great variety, made religion its fundamental — insofar as possible its only — business. Everywhere, from the simplest hunting societies to the great civilizations, religion seems to have been the one constant access to life, the one great force in behavior.

To the first foreigners (from the distant planet that was Europe) this might well have appeared to be a preoccupation with idle play taken seriously (in truth a free kynde of lyfe gyven to Idlenes and playe — early reports of this intense concern with religion filtered back to Montaigne as the delightful news that the Indians "spend the whole day in dancing" — or, a hundred years later, Dryden: "Guiltless men, that danced away their time,/ Fresh as their groves and happy as their clime"); hours or days spent in making, in precisely the right way, gewgaws of feather and fur, what seemed to be toys of twig or stone, what seemed to be carnal masks and ribald holiday costumes; weeks devoted to "singing up the corn"; days or weeks, or a lifetime, spent in learning songs and performing them, and sometimes everyone dropping all serious practical activity to celebrate en masse some perfectly ordinary event of life — birth or death, puberty or marriage, planting, harvesting, hunting, feasting, the new moon and the full moon, the rising sun and the setting sun, the progress of the summer sun and the winter sun toward the solstices, the recurrent march of the morning star and the evening star, rain and snow and dew and croaking frogs and leaping deer and birds floating in the wind. In this eternal celebration may have resided an aspect (more or less masked) of forced labor, for participation in ritual and ceremony seems often to have been obligatory, but Europeans may not have noticed this, while noting the apparent rarity of imposed tribute, military service, obviously forced labor, law courts, police.

The tax, the tribute, of this strange world was likely to be of the spirit rather than the sweat of the brow; or, as mentioned, work may often have been veiled in ceremony. The descendants of the Quiché Maya, for example, marked the new year, the first movement of the sun after the winter solstice, by a ritual journey from east to west, imitating the movement of the sun and a similar journey of one of the pairs of twin gods important in their theogony, a journey that concluded with a ritual clearing of brush from certain designated fields and the burning of the brush in a ceremonial new fire — but this was also the start of the planting season, and the fields so cleared were to become the year's new fields of maize. Life was for living, as said Nezahualcoyotl, and the world lived hand in hand with it in an endless sacred rite. "See the new mysterious morning," sang a Pawnee hymn, "something marvelous and sacred though it happens every day . . ."

# 3. The Difference Itself

Other samenesses must have been apparent from earliest meetings here and there — the strange unanimity rule, for instance, in operation among the Aztecs as among the Pueblos and many others, requiring the council to appear to be unanimous in every decision (every decision being simply a matter of following the right way as ordained by the gods, obviously it could not be reduced to a mere matter of secular politics, of majority vote). Or there was the dualism previously spoken of, so prevalent in religion as well as in politics, evident in many ways, among others by the division of a community or social group into halves (moities, in the terminology of the anthropologists), the Summer People and the Winter People or the Peace People and the War People or some such designations, a further example of the reciprocating engine, so to speak, of dual organization, for turn and turn-about direction of ceremonies or municipal administration; or evident as well in the factionalism that was apparently a basic element in the construction of most New World societies and that could combine with the element of reciprocation to create the two governments balanced one against the other, one the government "inside the walls," the other "outside the walls," in a system reported for tiny Pueblo villages as well as for the immense city of Tenochtitlan.

But undoubtedly more striking than evidence of underlying samenesses among various societies in the Indian world were, for Europeans, the evidences on every hand of radical differences from Old World ways, differences profound and differences ostensibly superficial but bizarre. One such instance among many was the custom of meeting after an absence with weeping, tears meant for the warmest and most joyous of greetings, "weeping in welcome," said Léry, a custom reported from the Atlantic coast of South America in the early 1500s, in the ancient traditions of the Highland Maya of Guatemala, from Texas in the 1530s (where Alvar Nuñez Cabeza de Vaca described it, "They have a custom when they meet, or from time to time when they visit, of remaining half an hour before they speak, weeping"), from the Carolina coast in the 1560s, from the Mississippi River in the 1680s, and by numerous later observers among the Iroquois, where it had become a formal ceremony, one of the most beautiful in American Indian literature, the welcoming rites of the Condoling Council. What was the origin of this, what was the meaning? It remains inexplicable still. Or the universal hospitality, most amazing to a European because it was fearless, mentioned by practically everyone from the earliest meetings (Vespucci in South America, 1502: "many of them swam out to receive us . . . with as much confidence as if we had been friends for years . . ." Jacques Cartier, 1535, in Canada: "five men . . . who as freely and familiarly came to our boats without any fear, as if we had ever been brought up together . . . one of them took our captain in his arms, and carried him on shore . . ." and the terrifying army of Francisco Vasquez de Coronado, hundreds of men in metal armor riding strange gigantic beasts that were horses and mules, meeting on the great plains of the American West in 1541 the buffalo-hunting people who were to become centuries later the Apaches, and who greeted the fearsome strangers with perfect, and perfectly fearless, friendship).

It seems reasonable that some of these differences: religion rather than business as the principal business; living to live rather than to get; belonging rather than belongings as a reigning value; apparent rarity of enforced service civil or military and the apparently frivolous nature of much religious service tending to disguise the possibility that it may have been enforced; group ownership of land and wealth, and consequent tendencies toward individual cooperation rather than competition, and apparent rarity of the police and lawsuits necessary to regulate individual possession; dualism and institutionalized factionalism with consequent tendencies toward reciprocating government, toward a world in balance between two opposing forces, whether the world of thought and the spirit or the world of practical politics, rather than the Old World compulsion toward one party rule, insofar as possible, whether in religion or politics — it seems not unreasonable that various of these differences, noted in a thousand varied manifestations, may have suggested some of the golden-world comments in early New World accounts.

The great thing, really, was the total difference itself, so multifeatured. The total picture of this difference, as with so many of the points touched upon in this broad survey, has long been a subject of lively (in fact sometimes acrimonious) debate among the experts. From the beginning there has been a more or less automatic supposition by some students that of course the Indian world had to be some sort of offshoot of the Old World — twisted and deformed perhaps but certainly an offshoot all the same. It was proposed on early acquaintance that American Indians were descendants of the Lost Tribes of Israel, and sometimes proposed later on that they were really Phoenicians or Egyptians or refugees from a sunken continent such as the sci-fi land of Mu. More recently it has been proposed that New World civilizations grew from Asian influences transported across the Pacific during several thousand pre-Columbian years. There are bits of evidence, particularly similarities in art motifs, for most of these suggestions, but the technical differences between the two worlds are so vast that the majority of specialists still see American societies as pretty much American creations. The further assumption that the New World was in reality only an infant Old World, was what the Old World itself had been in a "primitive" stage, is necessarily associated with this long-standing polemic over Old World influences on the development of American civilizations (these matters will be taken up in more detail in VI: Myth and Reality). The developing American world undoubtedly passed through sets of transitions similar in various general respects to the Old World's, but — if the argument for a basically different world continues to hold its ground — some basic differences obviously must have intruded someplace along the line.

Its exact dimensions notwithstanding, this gulf of difference between the two worlds, Old and New, the difference itself, within which, in the swirling mists of which, could be discerned all manner of contrasts, giving rise to all manner of marvels in the reports, the difference itself may have been the one principal feature to strike European observers. Whether they interpreted it correctly or not, whether to this day it is correctly interpreted, is perhaps less important than simply recognizing the fact of the enormous, subtle, profound, very possibly all but bottomless, all but unbridgeable, difference.

# III

# The Old World:
# Time of Change

## 1. La Maube

Ronsard and friends reside today in Paris on a little bust at the northeast corner of the grounds of the Collège de France, rue des Ecoles. Ronsard is the bust, wearing, from discoloration in the stone, a droll black-dyed little pointed beard that gives him a splendidly dandified air. The names of his friends of the Pléiade are inscribed around the base. A block west and on the opposite side of the street, Place Paul-Painlevé, Montaigne in a stone ruff turns his back on the medieval Musée de Cluny and raises his quizzical gaze to the Sorbonne. A couple of blocks to the eastward is the Place Maubert, where Etienne Dolet was hanged one August day in 1546, August 3, his birthday, so they say, *aetat* thirty-nine, and then together with his dangerously learned books was publicly burned to ashes. The gibbet may have come to him as a relief, after some two years in the dread prison of the Conciergerie, and after a night, specifically prescribed by his sentence for his last night on earth, of being put to "la question extraordinaire" in the torture chamber beneath the Conciergerie's massive Tour Bonbec. Dolet's crime was specifically heresy, the indictment brought on the wording of a translation of Plato (in fact on the translation of a single word), but his entire brief career was in conflict with established authority, printing condemned books, ignoring orders and ordinances secular and churchly: his real crime was an insistence on not only thinking but speaking freely. Therefore the sentence also ordered that if Dolet caused any "scandal or blasphemy" at the time of execution his tongue was to be cut out and he was to be burned alive: thus he had to make public recantation of the sins he was supposed to have committed and had to make it loud and clear. When he at first mumbled the demanded response the hangman told him, it seems with some sympathy, that he must say it clearly "or you know what I must do." The sentence may have reflected merely the normal ferocity of the law, especially when dealing with a defiance of authority, or it may have reflected the personal vindictiveness of the functionaries of that authority in at last getting Dolet securely in their grasp — he had been pardoned and sprung from the Conciergerie more than once in the past by François I, but now François had just died and a reactionary administration was taking power and all the joys of vengeance that went with it.

The Place Maubert was the heart of the student quarter, occupying the traditional site where open-air lectures had been given to students in the Middle Ages; Albertus Magnus lectured there in the thirteenth century and the Place bears (so some say) his name, Maitre Albert, worn down to Maubert. With this cultural background it had naturally become a favorite location for executions of persons more or less in the intellectual trades who betrayed too much interest in the new learning or the new religion or other matters that might gravitate toward free thinking. It was here, a few years before Dolet's death, that intellectuals involved (or accused of being involved) in the "Affair of the Placards" — printers, lawyers, booksellers — were burned alive, and it was here, a few years after Dolet's death, that the printer, Martin Lhomme, in whose house outraged authority had found a copy of the pamphlet *Le Tigre*, was hanged.

The city of Paris put up a monument to Dolet in 1889. I walked over to the Place Maubert a few years ago to look at it and found it missing. The plinth was there, with appropriate inscriptions, and seated at its base with his bottle of wine an old bum, of which the Place Maubert ("La Maube," they called it, wearing down Maitre Albert still a bit more) used to have a steady supply, but no statue. I asked the clochard what had happened to the statue. He made an effort to focus his eyes upward and said, "Statue? There is no statue, M'sieu'." "There was once a statue," I said. "The inscription here says so." "The inscription," said the old bum severely, trying to focus his eyes on me, "lies. There is no statue, M'sieu'." "The inscription says there was a statue erected here in 1889," I said. "Whenever that was, I was here," the old bum said. "I've been right here for a hundred years. There is no statue here, M'sieu'." "It was a statue to Etienne Dolet," I said. "He was hanged for being a free man." "I'm a free man," the old bum said, and gave me a cunning wink and said, "but they won't hang me." The statue (I learned later) had been taken away by the Germans in World War II for military purposes.

During the time I was first working on this book the empty plinth was surrounded by a works project, upset pigeons in residence on it, an islet in a sea of progress, by dozens. The old bum was long gone but on balmy evenings the Dolet monument (or what was left of it) was the occasional gathering place for little groups of hippies, who seemed, with their idly strumming guitars, far removed from anybody's agony, from any battleground. What were they doing there, what were they doing anywhere with their idle lives?

Pondering felicity, man, an American voice told me.

## 2. Serfdom and Soldiery

Toward the close of the seventeenth century occurred the two hundredth anniversary, widely uncelebrated, of Columbus' first landfall in the New World. During that two hundred years many thousands of Europeans — explorers, colonists, soldiers, traders, missionaries, fishing crews, miners, filles de joie, trappers and tramps, pirates and other commercial travelers — had come in contact with the New World's native societies, and many hundreds of these had published reports, letters, accounts of all sorts dealing with the peoples of America. During all this time, as the world of the American "savages" became continually better known in Europe, the two principal strains continued in published accounts of treating the Americans either as brute beasts or as, if not noble, at least praiseworthy citizens of societies founded on nature's own good laws.

The latter of these two themes continued to hold the lead in France, as shown by both Chinard and Atkinson in their previously mentioned detailed studies of the French literature on America during this period.

Some of the work in this latter strain had as its main objective a critique of the Old World, and some of the work in the former strain had as its real objective a justification of misdeeds in America committed by Old World entrepreneurs, commercial or religious.

But in the majority of these writings, of whatever varying strain, the subject of New World liberty remained fairly constant as a leading item. Typical examples: the Tupinamba of Brazil, wrote a Capucin missionary in 1611 (a hundred years after Vespucci and Peter Martyr), lived "continually in joy, in leisure, in contentment, without care or worry . . . and without oppression" while another Franciscan writing at the same period of the Hurons of Canada describes their life: "The men hunt, fish, go to war or to trade, make their houses or canoes or the tools proper to that work; the rest of the time, to tell the truth, they pass in idleness, playing, sleeping, singing, dancing, smoking, or feasting" and concludes that they have "a better government than ours, because each of them has more liberty than a European and knows no other master than himself . . ." and said a Jesuit of the 1650s, of the people of the Caribbean Islands and the nearby South American coast, "To tell the truth, the Savages have no civil rule, each does as he likes . . . no one has any superiority, or is subservient to another . . ."

These references were so commonplace that their import as radical criticism of Old World ways must have been perceived only subliminally. No one had yet made the great (and risky) leap of bringing the idea of New World liberty to the Old World as a realistic political possibility for the peoples of Europe.

However, the lesser but still noteworthy leap of transferring the idea of the liberty of the New World peoples to Old World colonists, once they were settled in the liberating New World air, was accomplished at this time by some of the publicists for New World colonies who now began to appear.

Marc Lescarbot, a Paris lawyer who accompanied Samuel de Champlain on one of his colonizing voyages to spend a year in Canada (1606), became France's best known early traveling salesman of colonialism, selling in his writings a Canada drawn as a land of prosperity and bliss ("contentment prepares itself for those who will live in New France . . . in New France will be restored the golden age"), and where, "above all, everyone could live in liberty."

Colonizing became something of a rage in both France and England as the seventeenth century got under way, encouraged as much by conditions at home as by the overblown promotional publicity ("rivers run with milk for you"). Michael Drayton's *Ode to the Virginian Voyage*, probably written to recruit volunteers for the 1606 expedition that founded Jamestown, promised that in "VIRGINIA,/ Earth's onely Paradise" you would reap from the "Fruitfullest Soyle,/ Without your Toyle,/ Three harvests more,/ All greater than your Wish" and find that there "the Golden Age,/ Still Nature's Lawes doth give . . ." Colonial press agents great and small glorified the rich New World, "the treasurie" of "this Nymph" Virginia "testified by the many and continuall presents of a temperate Clymate, fruitfull Soile, fresh and faire streames, sweet and wholesome Ayre," (Samuel Purchas, 1613) or pointed to still other possible rewards if the treasure didn't happen to work out, as a satirical verse history of Paris for the mid-1600s mentioned that one can earn a respectable "hundred and fifty thousand a year" out there by trading in slaves, or Hakluyt (1587) reminded "the Right Worthie and Honorable Gentleman Sir Walter Ralegh knight" of the likelihood that "her Majestie, which hath Christened and given the name to your Virginea, if neede require, will deal after the manner of honorable godmothers . . ." The English divine, Reverend William Morrell, who was present at the founding of the Massachusetts Bay Colony in 1623, was essentially an advertising man tubthumping for prospective colonists ("The fruitfull and well watered earth doth glad all hearts . . . / And yeelds an hundred fold for one . . . / . . . O happie Planter if you knew the height / Of Planters honours where ther's such delight . . .") Morrell shared the low opinion of Indians that was more common among the English than among the French but even so, in his verse description of New England (published in both Latin and English), he noted that "the aged Widow and the Orphanes all, / Their Kings maintain, and strangers when they call" and, ill-according though it may be with the previous mention of Kings, "They keepe just promise, and love equitie . . ."

Paris celebrities such as the poet Paul Scarron and the sex symbol of the time, Ninon de Lenclos, talked in 1651 of leading a colonial expedition to the Antilles; Scarron had just married a teen-age girl who had spent a year or two of her childhood in the New World, on the island of Martinique (she was known to her friends as la jeune Indienne), Françoise d'Aubigné, the future Madame de Maintenon. "There," he wrote, perhaps quoting his young bride, "it's springtime all year round / . . . Each month . . . gives fruit all at the same time ripe, green, and freshly sprouting . . ." An expedition that really did part the next year for Guiana, seven hundred men and seven dozen girls, created something of a sensation in Paris and Rouen, where the emigrants, who expected to find in the New World (said a disgruntled priest who accompanied them) "all sorts of wealth without turning a hand at work" drank up and gambled away the advances in goods and equipment they had received from the colonizing company. When these colonists later ran into armed conflict with the natives of the promised land across the sea, the same caustic priest, the Curé Biet, said they had robbed and mistreated the Indians but that what ultimately aroused the "savages" to violent resistance was the threat presented by the colony's presence to the "entire liberty" the Indians had previously enjoyed in their life of "brute beasts."

One of the century's most-quoted statements on the liberty of New World peoples was from another missionary writing in the tropics, the Révérend Père Du Tertre, in this case speaking of the Caribs of the island of Saint Christophe in the Caribbean: "the Savages of these Isles are the most content, the happiest, the least addicted to vice, the most sociable, the least false and the least tormented by sickness of all the nations of the world. Because they are such as nature produced them, that is to say of a great simplicity and natural naiveté: they are all equal, without anyone recognizing any sort of superiority or any sort of servitude . . . Neither is richer nor poorer than his companion . . . They have no police among them: they live, all, at liberty; they drink and eat when they are hungry or thirsty, they work and rest when they please . . ."

With all this, however, Du Tertre included a bow to the brute-beast gallery, writing that the Indians were brought up "more as brute beasts than as reasonable men; because they learn neither civility, nor honor, not even to say good day or good evening, nor to thank those who give them pleasure . . . They have no shame of their nudity, they belch, fart, and perform all other natural necessities without any circumspection . . ."

Whether of the brute-beast school or the noble-savage school, most of the French missionaries seem to have fallen into an odd contradiction that Chinard discusses at some length — "nearly all the missionaries" of both Canada and the Caribbean assert that the Indians are the most barbarous and inhuman of peoples, and then show us in their accounts just the opposite, what "commences as an indictment finishes with a dithyramb." Or again, "After having announced that they're going to make us shiver in exposing the impiety of the savages, they finish with a eulogy exalting these fine people, who, to believe them, their [religious] indifference apart, had all the rarest virtues."

Chinard finds the explanation of this apparently unconscious contradiction in the fact that the Indians are obdurate in refusing Christianity — or rather that while they allow themselves to be converted "with docility, they return with equal ease to their primitive paganism." For the zealous missionaries no "true virtue could exist outside the church." Thus the apparent excellence in the lives of New World people may have (subconsciously) assumed the character of an exotic phenomenon quite apart from the only admissible real excellence, which was Christian excellence — and undeniably attached to the demonic reality of their most unchristian souls. Possibly, if this is so, the idea of New World liberty as an element of a barbarism so inaccessible and exotic and even in some sense sacrilegious as far as "civilized" Old World society was concerned, could have reinforced in the European mind during these years a subconscious blockade more or less religious in nature against any idea of New World liberty as a veritable political possibility for Old World peoples.

Some, such as Du Tertre, come near to dispensing with this contradiction in finding so much of the world of the "savages" genuinely superior to that of "civilization," regardless of religious persuasion. Some went even further, wondering if the lack of shame at their nakedness, if their virtues so innocent in the bosom of nature, could conceivably mean that the Indians were somehow free of the guilt of original sin. Chinard cites, among several who ventured to raise this question, Father Pelleprat in Guiana: ". . . these people live in a marvelous innocence, and one would say to look at them that they had not sinned in Adam, like other men . . ." This touched on a theological question of infinite seriousness, one that "smelled terribly of the stake," in Chinard's phrase, and it may be some indication of their belief in the veracity of their own testimony that these earnest missionaries did not refrain from invading such fearful territory.

The reports and letters (and colonial sales pitches) of Jesuit missionaries published in France over many years were the seventeenth century's most influential missionary accounts. They assumed during the reign of Louis XIV (who favored the Jesuits with such loyalty that, so rumor had it, he eventually joined the order himself) something of the status of official documents. The abundant information on New World peoples in the Jesuit letters from America, especially from Canada (although all but drowned under many and many a page of mellifluous piety), information particularly concerning various Iroquoian groups, is an invaluable foundation for the ethnography of the Northeast. The Jesuit letter-writers recognized, as did many other observers, faults and vices of all sorts among the Indians, and ascribed most of these, as did many other accounts, to contact with evil Europeans. (Some of the Jesuits' enemies, religious and political, said they were due to contact with the Jesuits.) They encountered repeatedly the Indian intransigence in regard to conversion, or rather the ease at bland backsliding, and ascribed it, as did many others, to the work of the devil, who of course fought tooth and nail, or perhaps better put fang and claw, to retain his heathen domain — some of the missionaries had joined combat with him, so they said, in person. They speak with feeling and authority of the hardships and privations of Indian life and give agonizing pictures of the Indian torture of captives the missionaries witnessed and sometimes experienced. But again and again they conclude with an open admiration of these people "so taken with liberty," as Chinard sums up his general impression of these volumes.

We must not let everyone know how good it can be in the horrors of these forests, says the account of 1635, how much of heaven's light can shine in the deep shadows of this barbarism, or we would have so many people coming here we wouldn't have room for them. The account of the following year, both of these in the *Relation* of the R. P. Paul Lejeune, adds in the same vein, "and now we see a great number of very honorable persons land here every year, who come to cast themselves into our great woods as if into the bosom of peace, in order to live here with more piety, more freedom and liberty . . . Would to God that souls enamored of peace could see how sweet is life remote from the gehenna of a thousand superfluous compliments, of the tyranny of lawsuits, of the ravages of war, and of an infinite number of other savage beasts that we do not encounter in our forests."

"We see in the savages the beautiful remnants of a human nature entirely corrupted among civilized peoples," says a letter from a missionary of the 1690s, two long generations later. "To live in common without lawsuits, to content one's self with little without avarice, to be assiduous at work, and the most hospitable, affable, liberal, moderate imaginable in their discourse: in short, all our fathers and Frenchmen who have frequented the savages affirm that life among them passes more pleasantly than among us."

A recent study of the literature of seventeenth-century Canada, speaking of the "greater measure of liberty and equality in Amerindian life," cites a non-clerical report from the same period that rings the same by now so-familiar changes: No extortion of taxes, no lawsuits, no masters, no beggars, "not so much as an inkling of covetousness, which things should make us blush with shame. No distinction of estates among them, and they consider men only by the actions they accomplish."

Indian freedom in regard to property was used by English divines associated with the Virginia Company to justify seizing Indian lands (It is a sin in man *not* to take the land "out of the hands of beasts and brutish savages"), with the neat twist added (both these moral passages from the Reverend Robert Gray, 1609): "There is not *meum* and *tuum* amongst them. So that if the whole land should be taken from them, there is not a man that can complain of any particular wrong done unto him." Another English parson (Purchas, 1625) developed the even more ingenious argument that by holding no *mine* and *thine* the American natives defied the Eighth Commandment ("Thou shalt not steal") — since "stealing in properest sense cannot bee, if there be no proprietie [property]." They were therefore the wickedest of thieves, "theeves in divinitie" who would rob the sacred Decalogue itself. Lescarbot advanced an equally pious argument in explaining that the earth belongs to the children of God, a property right in which the unchristian Indians (for all his admiration of them as counterparts of classic Greeks) clearly miss out. Where property or religion or other such urgent reminders of self interest were not present, accounts by laymen could, and many did, mount to still rarer rhapsodic heights in regard to the freedom and other storied goodnesses of Indian life, especially before the appearance of Europeans, "when there was a much greater number of Savages than at present: they lived without care" — this from Nicolas Denys, best informed of all early authorities on the Micmac people of Nova Scotia and environs, with whom he lived and worked from the 1630s to *circa* 1671. "The law that they then observed was to do nothing to another that they wouldn't want done unto them . . . they all lived in fellowship, they refused nothing one to the other . . . they lived in purity . . ."

It is worth repeating that accounts which spoke of Indian life as anything but good, and many did, nevertheless found frequent occasion to mention, even if with disapprobation, New World liberty.

The realistic narrative by one of the survivors of La Salle's last expedition (1684-1687) recounts with no pleasure at all the weeks spent in a village of the Hasinai Confederacy in what is now east Texas, dwelling in detail for example on the rites after a raid on an enemy town, when a woman captive was tortured to death,

a Sacrifice to the Rage and Vengeance of the Women and Maids [in the words of the first English translation from the original French]: who having arm'd themselves with thick Stakes, sharp pointed at the End, Conducted that Wretch to a By-place, where each of these Furies began to torment her, sometimes with the Point of their Staff, and sometimes laying on her with all their Might. One tore off her Hair, another cut off her Finger, and every one of those outrageous Women endeavor'd to put her to some exquisite Torture, to revenge the Death of their Husbands and Kinsmen . . . At last, one of them gave her a Stroke with a heavy Club on the Head, and another run her Stake several times into her Body, with which she fell down Dead on the Spot. Then they cut that Miserable Victim into Morsels, and oblig'd some slaves of that Nation they had long been possess'd of to eat them.

Thus our Warriors return'd Triumphant from that Expedition. They spared none of the Prisoners they had taken, except two little Boys, and brought Home all the Skins of their Heads, with the Hair, to be kept as trophies and glorious Memorials of their Victory. . . .

. . . When the [scalp] Ceremony was ended, they serv'd up the *Sagamite*, in the Nature of Hasty Pudding . . . and before any one touch'd it, the Master of the Ceremonies took some in a Vessel, which he carry'd as an Offering to those Heads of Hair. Then he lighted a Pipe of Tabacco, and blow'd the Smoke upon them. That being perform'd, they all fell to the Meat, *Bits of the Woman that had been sacrific'd were served up to the two Boys of her Nation.* [The italics are not mine.] They also serv'd up dry'd Tongues of their Enemies, and the whole concluded with Dancing and Singing after their Manner . . .

But after all this, two teen-age boys with the French party stayed behind when the others went on, "did not keep their Word with us, but
remain'd among those Barbarians, being infatuated with that Course of
Libertinism they had run themselves into."

Some such Europeans did find, or attempt at any rate, a life of literal
liberty in the New World, even, according to some accounts, unto a libertinism to surpass brute beasts. Among them were, in the Caribbean, the
filibusters and buccaneers, the pirates of the Spanish Main, recruited
from cutthroats of all nations; and in Canada the *coureurs de bois*, adventurous and often unlicensed fur traders who had turned their backs
on the strict Jesuit discipline of the colonies to follow a life of real freedom in the seemingly endless great north woods, sometimes as natural-
ized citizens of one (or more) of the Indian nations. The number of "fli-
bustiers" and "boucaniers" was considerable, their renown in Europe
enormous; and it was officially estimated in the 1680s that of the some
1500 adult Frenchmen in Canada, 800 had taken to the tall timber to join
the bands of coureurs de bois. They defied edicts pronouncing severe
penalties against doing so, and ignored rather pathetic attempts on the
part of the authorities to offer them the amnesty of the king if they would
only come into the settled habitations and accept it. "The indigenes
gladly welcomed these men who impressed them by their boldness and
vigor, who spoke fluently their languages, and, which alone would have
sufficed to assure a cordial reception, brought brandy. A better welcome
still on the part of the savagesses . . . And the mixture of races was in
operation. But not as Champlain had dreamed. It was not Europe
which, in this alliance, civilized America, it was America which re-
venged itself against the invasion by leading the invader to barbarism."
All this brought much indignant outcry from responsible persons. Governor Denonville "accused the companions of Cavelier de La Salle of
changing savagesses every week."

In 1696 (the word reached the Canadian backwoods in 1698) all li-
censed fur traders (excepting only La Salle's old lieutenant, the peerless
Henri de Tonty, and his partner) were recalled from the forests, in a
dramatic (albeit temporary) reversal of French expansionist policy,
brought about in part by Madame de Maintenon and the Abbé Fénelon
in line with his revolutionary League of the Public Good ("I love my
family better than myself, my country better than my family, humanity
better than my country"). Legal traders were ruined; the coureurs de bois
carried on, under their distant greenwood trees, as merrily as ever.

The revolt against their familiar "civilized" world by the ordinary,
sometimes overordinary, people who transformed themselves into such

as buccaneers and coureurs de bois may have resulted at least to some degree from the insistence through the years, the centuries, on the story-book freedom of life to be found in the New World, an insistence possibly even more insistent in unwritten seaport yarns than in reports of missionaries and administrators. A few such yarns found their way into official documents and preservation thereby: one such was the golden dream of Mathieu Sagean, an illiterate sailor who said he had been born in Canada and traveled all over wild America, where he and a few companions, braving lions and tigers and leopards somewhere out there west of the Mississippi, had found the land of the Aacanibas. There the royal palace of King Hagaren was walled with bricks of gold, and caravans of three thousand oxen loaded with gold departed regularly to trade with the Japanese. The people, although fierce and soldierly (the standing army of a hundred thousand men, three-fourths cavalry, was equipped with golden trumpets and golden drums), were of a joyous disposition around the house and freely gave Sagean and his companions anything they wanted, including gold and of course girls — in fact the friendly Aacanibas offered to slay on the spot any girl who refused the Frenchmen; one of Mathieu's companions couldn't resist having several killed on his false accusation, just as a boyish prank, he "being drunk with palm wine."

Although this account was not (as rumor in England had it) the foundation for John Law's Mississippi Company, the highest authorities in Paris did treat Sagean's information, revealed to them in 1700, as valuable and confidential until he was sent to Louisiana to lead the way back to Aacaniba-land, where authorities on the scene, such as Tonty and the acting governor, Bienville, a birthright frontier expert, gave him considerably shorter shrift.

The kind of people who opted for a life totally cut off from civilization — criminals on the dodge, penniless younger sons of honorable but large families, romantic rebels, malcontents and runaways of all categories — and the backgrounds from which they opted, were both no doubt influences of importance, although the number of European captives among the Indians, including all kinds of people from all kinds of backgrounds originally seized quite against their will, who opted to remain in Indian life when repatriation was available would seem to diminish somewhat the weight of such influence. When a substantial proportion of white captives had to be forcibly repatriated in the Ohio Valley at the late date of 1764 a British officer found their behavior inexplicable: "For the honour of humanity, we would suppose those persons to have been of the lowest rank . . . For easy and unconstrained as the savage life is, certainly it could never be put in competition with the blessings of improved life and the light of religion, by any persons who have had the happiness of enjoying, and the capacity of discerning, them."

The two teen-age boys who elected to stay with the Hasinai rather than go on with their European comrades could be considered in certain respects paradigms of their kind: one, young as he was, had been an accessory in the murder of La Salle, and might anticipate, regardless of promises to the contrary, an uncertain fate upon return to France; the other was of a respectable if not distinguished family — his father was said to have been a treasury official in the French government. Both were regarded as rather better educated than was usual for the time. The background from which they opted was the debacle of La Salle's ambitious expedition of the 1680s and an assortment of murders practiced upon each other by the survivors, some carried out before an audience of startled Hasinai people whose "fiercest warriors," wrote Francis Parkman, "might learn a lesson in ferocity from these heralds of civilization."

The background of all Europe at the time was saturated with ferocity, to a degree even our own violent century might view with professional respect. The carnival of plunder that was the Thirty Years' War left countless thousands butchered, starved, driven from their homes; it has been conservatively estimated that Germany and Austria suffered a loss in population of some seven million persons between 1618 and 1648.

The religious wars and right royal extravagance — Henri III's wild excesses, "turned to the charge of the poor people" — bequeathed a shattered France to Henri IV at the close of the sixteenth century: wrote the Venetian ambassador, "Destruction everywhere . . . cattle disappeared, so that plowing is no longer possible" unless, as he said he had seen them doing, the peasants buckled on the harness and pulled the plow themselves.

A hundred years later Louis XIV left France desolated anew in the wake of his century of glory — here the cost to the multitudinous poor, in poverty and famine, of maintaining at Versailles the most lavish court in Europe, and the disruption of incessant wars, also reduced the population not only by thousands but by millions. A census of France under Charles IX gave a population of 19 million while that taken under Louis XIV (a century later) gave only 17 million but "the realm was by then a large fifth" greater in extent.

"The classic land of absolute monarchy [wrote Acton] was France. Richelieu held that it would be impossible to keep the people down if they were suffered to be well off . . . With half the present [1870s] population, he [Louis XIV] maintained an army of 450,000 men, nearly twice as large as that which the late Emperor Napoleon assembled to attack Germany. Meanwhile the people starved on grass . . . French historians believe that in a single generation six millions of people died of want. It would be easy to find tyrants more violent, more malignant, more odious than Louis XIV, but there was not one who ever used his power to inflict greater suffering or greater wrong."

A portion of such gigantic population loss reflects, no doubt, a decline of birth rate in the disordered times, but a portion must also reflect mass slaughter, pestilence, starvation. Wrote Fénelon (prudently anonymously) to the king in 1694, "The cultivation of the earth is all but abandoned, the towns and the countryside depopulated . . . You have consumed a half portion of the wealth and vitality of the nation to make and defend vain conquests abroad . . . All France is now but a vast poorhouse, desolate and without provisions . . ."

Even in times of peace and prosperity the lot of ordinary people was seldom a happy one. Their masters were many — the king's officers, the clergy, the nobility — and seldom mild. Tax "farmers," in France the *fermiers généraux*, bought by a cash advance the right to collect certain taxes and were then free to bleed the people by the throat, in Mirabeau's phrase, in collecting as much more as they could get, sometimes squeezing out twice as much as their original payment. The privileged classes, nobility and clergy and principal state officers, exempted themselves from various taxes; the lion's share was paid by the most helpless and defenseless of the poorer classes, especially the peasants.

Such massive ferocity and blunt injustice naturally instilled a taste for cruelty in both oppressed and oppressor — at the epoch of the "Fête Brésilienne" at Rouen when the "savages" of the New World were being introduced to France (1550s), the good people of Dieppe "and the Bretons" were occupied in flaying alive an English admiral. The cruelty of the oppressors was as a rule more properly institutionalized, such as the serfdom established by law in a number of German states during the late sixteenth and early seventeenth centuries as a reasonable conclusion to the enormous butchery and repression following the peasant revolt of 1525. Intercessions on behalf of the peasants ("a most wretched, downtrodden existence . . . never any rest, early and late they are hard at work") were answered with the simple logic that "without a system of slavery . . . a town could not exist. . . . The State needed a system of servitude."

This particular system of servitude was introduced by imperial legislation of 1555 granting landowners "the right to reduce their tenants to the state of serfs and bondmen." A typical ordinance of the early 1600s established that the "peasants . . . are bond-servants . . . have no dominion of any sort . . . neither they nor their sons are free to leave and settle elsewhere without the consent of the rulers, their hereditary lords, and if the rulers want to take back to themselves the farms, fields, and meadows, the peasants must submit without resistance." Nor had they any "right to urge that they and their forebears have lived on the farms for 50, 60, or even 100 years . . ." The children of peasants were subject to personal service in the manor house and on the manorial lands, and were no more free than their parents to move to another place without the consent (usually a certificate of dismissal) of their overlord; these rules applied in some places also to freeholders and their children (one thinks of J. S. Bach's difficulties — including a taste of imprisonment — in moving to a better job in 1717). Under such circumstances, not surprisingly, "traffic was carried on with serfs as with horses and cows."

Roots of this sort of legalized servility were deep in feudal vassalage, a term that meant outright slavery in Merovingian times but later in the Middle Ages was applied also to persons technically free but dependent on a lord. The Formulae Turonenses, a typical oath of vassalage in the eighth century, stipulated that the vassal himself requested a servile condition because of poverty: "Dum et omnibus habetur percognitum, qualiter ego minime habeo, unde me pascere vel vestire debeam" (Inasmuch as it is known to all and sundry that I lack the wherewithal to feed and clothe myself). That these words were not regarded as merely empty formalities is indicated by the bitter shame felt by one Adam le Yep of Gloucestershire in England when he was forced by his poverty to accept such a servile state; he had often sworn he would kill himself before doing so, and it is recorded that kill himself he did, by drowning in the river Severn, in the year 1293.

Hunting rights in central Europe of the sixteenth and seventeenth centuries were reserved with the greatest strictness for the ruling classes. Hanging was established in 1584 as the standard punishment for poaching in Saxony; in Brandenberg a poacher's eyes were put out, and the same punishment was decreed in Wurtemberg for anyone found in the "princely forests with muskets, cross-bows, or any other weapons . . ." Some rulers ordered that all dogs taken by peasants into the fields must have one forefoot cut off "to prevent their damaging the game . . ." Game was incredibly plentiful; sixteenth-century game-book records of hundreds of wild boar or red deer killed in one hunt or thousands in one season ("Duke George Ernest of Henneberg, a 'furious hunter' . . . in 1581 killed no fewer than 1003 red deer . . ." the Elector of Saxony in November 1585 killed "1532 wild boars") are not uncommon. Perhaps some of the kill was customarily distributed among the peasants; or perhaps not, since we are told the poor saw such quantities of well-fed and, incidentally, crop-destructive wild game around them "cherished and preserved, while they themselves and their families had to starve . . ."

Working hours for "free" labor were likely to hover in the upper limits of human endurance, twelve hours a day, with ninety hours a week (four in the morning until seven in the evening) not unheard of. The most enlightened of spokesmen for the succeeding Age of Enlightenment, Monsieur de Voltaire, wrote in the 1740s: "The laborer, the workman, must be cut down to necessitousness in order to be willing to toil; such is man's nature . . ." The American frontiersman and Indian trader, George Croghan, on a mission to England during Pontiac's War, was shipwrecked off the coast of Normandy and "Traveld about 140 Miles in france Butt Never See So Much pride and poverty before." Wrote Thomas Jefferson of European governments (that he had come to know well during his five years in the 1780s as U.S. Minister to France), "under pretence of governing, they have divided their nation into two classes, wolves and sheep. I do not exaggerate; this is a true picture of Europe." And said Jefferson specifically of England and France, and specifically in comparison with American Indians: "As for France and England, with all their preeminence in science, the one is a den of robbers, and the other of pirates, as if science produces no better fruits than tyranny, murder, rapine and destitution of national morality. I would rather wish our country to be ignorant, honest and estimable as our neighboring savages are."

Those unfortunates in the civilized countries who aroused the masters' acute ill will — fell afoul of the law — were, men and women, whipped, tortured, imprisoned, or put to death in any of a variety of imaginative ways, from hanging, burning, crushing, beheading, to being broken on the wheel or pulled apart by horses. A favorite (and useful) sentence in France was to the royal galleys, where life would be short and suitably castigatory ("galleys can only be worked by pitiless cruelty toward the slaves, who are considered as less than beasts . . . such terrible labor has to be seen to be believed").

La Bruyère's celebrated picture of French peasants of the 1680s may have been meant as a caricature, as were most of his satires, but was doubtless founded on solid realism, as were also most of his satires: ". . . sullen animals, male and female, scattered over the countryside . . . scrabbling in the earth with an invincible persistence; they seem to have a sort of speech, and when they stand on their feet they have a human appearance; they are in fact men. At night they crawl into their dens where they live on black bread, water, and roots."

Life in the cities was, especially for the common people, chronically insecure as well as hard. Boileau's well known satire on the streets of

Paris in the 1660s (mud and traffic, robbers taking over from dark till dawn, the honest citizen double-locked in his house kept awake by screams of "Murder!" from the night-time street: "The loneliest and most forbidding forest/ is, compared to Paris, a place of safety") was only one of many such ironic comments of the time on the beauties of Paris, including a characteristically venomous sketch from the 1640s by Scarron. Voltaire wrote that in the administration of Richelieu the high-roads were neither repaired nor guarded and were infested with brigands, while "the streets of Paris, narrow, badly paved, littered with disgusting filth, were alive with thieves." (Said Tristram Shandy in the 1760s, "Paris! . . . The streets however are nasty. But it looks, I suppose, better than it smells . . .") A form of street robbery mentioned several times in Paris in the seventeenth century was to drop a heavy rock or chunk of masonry from an upper window on a passerby below, crushing his skull, and then rifle the body for coins or rings. Cyrano de Bergerac, the greatest swordsman in Europe (by theatrical tradition anyway), died (in 1655) from injuries suffered in such an attack. The "cours des miracles" in Paris, veritable slum fortresses where the city's false beggars congregated at night (miraculously cured of their daytime disabilities), were convenient centers for commerce in stolen goods, stolen children, produce of all kinds from the richly varied crime and violence.

Even for the well-to-do the city was difficult. Paris mud was notorious from the Middle Ages for its corrosive and poisonous qualities ("there is no City in the world muddier, nor as dirty . . . mud black, stinking, of an insupportable odor . . . it burns all it touches," says a guidebook written in the 1650s), but carriages did not begin to appear until the middle 1500s and were not usual until the seventeenth century. A service of lantern-bearers or torch-bearers ("porte-falots," Shakespeare's "link-boys") was established in the mid-1600s to accompany people at night, "preserving them from nocturnal attacks," and gradually became during the following century a semi-official police auxiliary. Candlelit streets appeared in Paris in the late 1600s, lanterns twenty feet high, twenty feet apart — the galleys for breaking one — that a hundred years later became oil lamps with three reflectors each, the "réverbères" of nineteenth-century French literature. People found them blinding. Theatrical productions in the seventeenth century were usually daytime only, the night streets too hazardous for going out. In 1661 Pascal helped organize a network of omnibus lines, eight-seated carriages at fifteen-minute intervals, forbidden to soldiers, pages, lackeys, manual laborers, anyone in livery or poorly dressed (as a consequence the omnibuses were stoned in the streets). They were put out of business after only a few years by carriages for hire that were installed toward the end of the seventeenth century at a house decorated with an image of Saint Fiacre, midway between Saint Merri and Saint Josse — and thus within shouting distance of both.

Traffic jams were a daily feature of Paris life by the opening of the eighteenth century, according to a work of 1713, "those blockages, which occur every day . . . files of Carriages coming from every side . . ." and thoroughly modern notions of fast travel were already in the air in the 1700s. What next? two gentlemen asked each other, the flying dragons of Medea? "What fine journeys when we shall go round the world, like the stars, in one day." You could in fact (if you were royalty with a mounted guard to clear the way) make better time in a carriage from the gates of Versailles to the gates of Paris than you're likely to do in today's traffic (twenty-three minutes for Marie Antoinette, in a special hurry one fine summer day). But for poor people the carriages and their breakneck coachmen were no blessing, and as Louis XIV's century of glory neared its end, as the king descended "in full majesty this superb Niagara of bankruptcy," their suffering only increased, perhaps in some fairly direct ratio to glory.

Press gangs filling the military drafts (the galleys for resisters), press gangs hunting down those dying of hunger who hid to avoid being taken to the frightful general hospital, press gangs at the end of 1685 enforcing "the terrible decree: all [Protestant] children from five to sixteen years of age will be collected within eight days" to be turned over to religious establishments for bringing up in the orthodox faith, were later joined by press gangs rounding up colonists for the New World to complete quotas drumbeating propaganda had not been able to achieve. By 1719 any servant out of work for as long as three days was automatically fair game for transportation to "the colonies," while the "bandouliers du Mississippi" kidnaped anyone anywhere who seemed sufficiently unprotected. John Law's implacable political enemy, the marquis d'Argenson, who controlled the police, seems to have created the squads of "bandouliers" for the express purpose of turning public opinion against both the colony and the company. They succeeded so well riots broke out in Paris in the spring of 1720 in which several bandouliers were killed by mobs, and an image (that has managed to survive ever since) was sealed on New Orleans as a penal colony, an image not at all in line with Law's intentions but quite in keeping with Argenson's "repressive nature." Argenson was credited, by at least some informed contemporary opinion, with eventually undermining public confidence in Law's bank, "which thereafter it was impossible to reestablish."

Vicious politics and resultant public distress and disorder were by no means limited to the Regency or to Paris, nor were outlaw bands in the seventeenth century limited to the distant Tortugas or the forests of Canada. Groups of displaced persons, sometimes in large numbers, of "masterless men" (and their hungry families with them), roamed several regions in Europe. Rebellious peasants in the southwest of France, descendants of those who had raised the revolt against the gabelle in 1548 that may have been at the origin of La Boétie's *Contr'un*, were involved in a disastrous sequence of uprisings during the 1600s. Known popularly as the Croquants, they left a legend of distress and disorder for the entire century in their angry, hopeless wars and the widespread desolation always following, desolation affecting entire provinces. Villages were abandoned, and "crowds of unfortunates came to beg at the gates of the cities, here by hundreds and there by thousands." Said the provost of the army in the mid-1600s, speaking of the "vagabonds" who were flooding the country, "The wheels and the gibbets are often loaded with these monsters who, refusing to obey the divine precept of working to earn their living by the sweat of their brow, fall into poverty and from this go on to commit thefts, sacrileges, and horrible murders."

Near the village in the south of France where I have written much of this book, irregular little armies of hundreds of "wild" persons lived from time to time in the eighteenth century in the caves of the mountains and in the lost lands along the River Var. They too were given a name, toward the end of that century, the Barbets, but they were much in evidence long before, especially in the bleak years after the Treaty of Utrecht (1713), when the land was seemingly covered by "this multitude of people without house or home, living from marauding over the countryside where they terrorized the inhabitants." My village was invaded several times in the seventeenth and eighteenth centuries, by Savoyards, Italians, Hungarians, Austrians, Serbs, when the people fled to a complex of fortified caves in the cliff above the village (rather like Indians of the Rocky Mountains in similar circumstances, except that for the Indians the circumstances were usually of much briefer duration). But these invasions, for which damages could sometimes be collected from the central government, were in some ways not so burdensome as the more frequent occupation by French and allied troops, with their requisitions of money, supplies, and men and women to work on fortifications anywhere in the region. The village could sometimes escape the worst of these evils by bribing someone of influence, as in 1686 the conscription of villagers was eased by a "present" from the village council to the Abbé de Thorenc of 75 livres. Such "presents" from the poor to the great were a customary feature of feudal times and persisted long thereafter (and aren't unheard of today). The neighboring town of Vence, in the midst of the winter of 1709, the worst winter in history, bringing starvation and disaster on all sides, was suddenly presented with a demand for a thousand livres from the commandant of the Swiss troops then billeted there. The mayor said the town could not possibly raise such a sum, the commandant had his troops close the town gates and prepare to pillage the houses, and the money was gathered. Vence also, after the Peace of Utrecht, was overwhelmed by the crowds of homeless beggars that seemed to appear everywhere, "the debris of all the past wars."

Peace had its special miseries, and the worse the war the worse the aftermath. Bohemia, after the Treaty of Westphalia (1648) ending the Thirty Years' War, lay in ruins, its population of three million reduced to 800,000, the survivors placed under a new and foreign nobility for an "unspeakably miserable" fate — their historian "rejoiced" three hundred years later that the limited extent of his book "relieves me from the duty of giving a detailed account of the cruelties" they then suffered.

And war or peace there was always the law. When my village is approached by the "old" road from the east (traditional direction of foreigners) its first glimpse is glimpsed at a curve bordered by a chapel on one side of the road and the ancient gibbet on the other, with, in direct line with them, the ancient chateau still standing (villainously restored) on its nearby hilltop. The three seigneuries: the nobility, the clergy, the executioner. Gibbets, standard brand of nonfreedom, dotted the countryside from feudal times onward like the big-muscled castles they represented, and marked the crossroads in cities, a noted one at the Carrefour de Buci in Paris, at the site of which began the "September massacres" of priests and royalists in 1792. Nor did the law's bloodthirstiness diminish with the onset of the Age of Reason: in 1729 a peasant near Bar-le-Duc who had stolen some sacred vessels and had repented and turned himself in, was sentenced to be burned alive — on appeal, "the Parliament of Paris added that his tongue should be torn out first."

## 3. Parallels

The New World was "regarded by the common people as a land of the lost, who would certainly never again see their own country," a feeling that "inspired more terror than the galleys," and a feeling that restricted emigration in spite of all press gangs and propaganda could do. If stories of a people free, masterless, equal, across the seas struck a spark of interest in souls such as these, bent under centuries of toil and tyranny, it was still only an interest of dreamland idea, not of a possible reality. But that reports of free societies over there in America, reports widely disseminated and continuing, as has been seen, year after year, generation after generation, did indeed exercise some real influence on the birth and movement of ideas does seem, to say the least, not unreasonable.

Scholars who have studied such reports in detail, most notably Gilbert Chinard and Geoffroy Atkinson, have become convinced of this influence. Atkinson wrote, of the earliest "geographical" literature dealing with America, "Many travelers and missionaries had mentioned, even in the 16th century, the lack of private property among primitive peoples. Early writers had called attention to the generally happy condition of a primitive society founded upon equality and liberty. The cumulative force of such expressions in accounts of voyages published before 1700 would be a fascinating study." Or again: "There exist in the libraries in France and elsewhere, more than five hundred and fifty impressions of works printed in French before 1610, of which the principal aim was to inform the French readers of the time of the countries and contemporary peoples of Asia, Africa, and America . . . It would be incredible if this enormous publication of new knowledge in the popular tongue would not have exercised some influence on the reading public." Atkinson argued repeatedly in various works that "what is important in the history of ideas is always their expression and frequency of expression by different authors, for the date of onset of ideas is impossible to find," and that, especially for the course of thought in France between 1600 and 1750 the usual "literary history" neatly arranged by "great authors" is misleading.

Chinard, also, commented again and again on the role that the multitudes of New World accounts he had examined must have played in the movement of ideas in their time. Interest in foreign lands in seventeenth-century and early eighteenth-century France was more concerned with the Orient than with America — even the sixteenth-century works totaled above by Atkinson devoted most of their titles to the Turks, Jerusalem, Malta, China, Japan, leaving however some fifty to sixty separate titles, with plentiful further editions and reimpressions, for the New World — but the oriental picture spoke not at all of freedom, "natural" law or "natural" man. The East was, on the contrary, more often drawn, from Turkey to Cathay, as a land of civilization superior to Europe, more highly civilized and in most respects more refined and cultured — including firmer monarchies — than Europe. Liberty, in this setting, breathed not a word, as it was, on the whole, subdued too for Africa, where ever since the medieval stories of Prester John most reports and folklore had spoken more often of kings and slaves (even though frequently "good" kings) than of freedom and equality.

Chinard wrote, of the sources of the Enlightenment usually sought in the influence of seventeenth-century English thought on the eighteenth-century French *philosophes*, that the ideas noted in the Jesuit Relations and other such accounts were later reprinted in atlases and geographical "dictionaires," in "all the books of travel, and influenced the movement of ideas" long before the eighteenth-century philosophes were to travel to England. "If, instead of looking for foreign origins for *L'Esprit des Lois* or the *Contrat Social,* one studied French overseas origins, it is very probably in the relations of the Jesuits they would be found."

The motive of his work being the effect of exotic reports on French literature, Chinard cites a great many secondary (or even tertiary or quaternary) works of fiction apparently sprouted from what he refers to as Americanist literature, some of these works locating their settings elsewhere — from Australia to the moon — but exhibiting characteristics typical of books dealing with New World travel. But he also notes certain fictional productions of top rank and fame, among them Fénelon's *Télémaque* (1699), that evidently borrowed key ideas from America. Fénelon, says Chinard, who meant to be showing us a picture of the golden age, transported into his pleasant land of Bétique the simplicity of the New World that he had found in books of travel. Atkinson also notices the similarity in certain respects of the people of La Bétique to American Indians "as reported by the missionaries in Brazil and Canada" but adds still other significant parallels — they had no interest in wealth or material things, and had acquired their divine wisdom by studying simple nature: a peace-loving, free-and-equal, wise and happy people "who had maintained an original perfection unknown not only in ancient Greece but also in 17th century France" and who got that way merely by following "the law of nature" — a striking conclusion, says Atkinson, to "come from an ecclesiastic and before 1700." More striking still are Fénelon's words, reminiscent of so many New World reports, in describing the ardent love of liberty of the people of La Bétique: "This people would abandon their country or give themselves up to death rather than accept servitude."

Seventeenth-century English philosophers were "obsessed" with liberty (as said Maitland); and Grotius and Pufendorf on the Continent, and Hobbes in England, among many others of their time, were equally obsessed with a "natural law" more or less based on a supposed condition of man in a state of nature. Grotius proposed that governments were above laws made by men but under the jurisdiction of *ius naturale*; Pufendorf agreed with Grotius in defining natural law as the dictate of "right reason." This subject had long occupied the meditations of philosophers (Plato, Cicero, Stoics to Augustine and Aquinas, Duns Scotus and Occam). The political "naturalism" of Aristotle as received in the late Middle Ages, pronouncing the state a product of nature, as fixed in its growth as a sunrise, was of critical influence in Europe from the fourteenth century onward into the Renaissance. It embedded deeply in European thought the idea of the State — the familiar European state founded on property — as an inexorable creation of natural law, a rock-ribbed conviction tenaciously resistant to the new values of the post-Renaissance, post-Columbian "natural law."

But in spite of resistance this new "natural law" as observable not in the State but in individual "natural man" seems to have forced the whole subject of natural law upon the thought of the seventeenth century to an extraordinary degree. Spain may have been one of the origin points of this particular development, with Las Casas and the Salamanca lectures of Francisco de Vitoria on the New World which (with later reservations noted) established fundamental lines of some eventual importance.

It is scarcely my intention to suggest that seventeenth-century political thinkers pored over the New World reports of the preceding hundred years or so to trigger thereby their "obsessions" with liberty and natural man. My point here is only to call attention to the multiplicity of parallels in subject, place, and time, and suggest thereby that one indirect factor in the birth and growth of these "obsessions" could be this vast New World literature dealing with the liberty of "natural man" in America, a literature existing not only in its own integral form but in its infinity of extracts in other works. These obsessions became even more pronounced in the hundred years following, with nature "the key to the thought of the eighteenth century . . ." Or, "That man in a state of nature was good is one of those seductive myths which seem eternally recurrent. It had roots in antiquity, but the eighteenth-century writers revived it with a vigor and expounded it with a cogent forcefulness that had not been known before . . . whatever the contributing factors, natural man was the symbol leading the age out of medieval darkness."

Any direct interest in literature on the New World was distinctly lacking in both Grotius and Pufendorf. Grotius did write, not very well, on the origins of New World peoples, and engaged in a controversy with De Laet on the subject, revealing therein that his reading on New World matters was neither very wide nor very deep. Pufendorf, after concluding a work, went back over it and added batteries of supporting citations, nearly all classical or scholastic, giving little or no attention to the New World, whether dealing with questions of liberty or natural law or anything else.

And Hobbes did make a specific point, his most famous point, of considering the New World, unconsciously acknowledging its influence in a negative sense, in denouncing the life of "the savage people in many places of America" as "solitary, poor, nasty, brutish, and short." In toto, Hobbes included in *Leviathan* two references to America and in "Philosophical Rudiments" another very similar ("they in America" lead an existence "fierce, short-lived, poor, nasty, and deprived of all that pleasure and beauty of life which peace and society are wont to bring with them"), proving with all such references that his New World reading too was short, if not nasty and brutish.

But the forcefulness of his attack on the very idea of liberty ("if a man should talk to me of . . . *a free subject; a free will*; or any *free*, but free from being hindered by opposition, I should not say he were in error, but that his words were without meaning, that is to say, absurd") and the forcefulness of his attack on a felicitous picture of natural man (Hobbes saw the "law of nature" as a "posture of war . . . every man against every man." Man's true nature "inclineth to contention, enmity, and war . . . to kill, subdue, supplant, or repel") seems to bespeak an exasperation that might have sprung from the saturation of his time with such irritating ideas.

(Wrote, for example, in the middle years of the 1600s, the English poet Thomas Traherne, ". . . you may see who are the rude and barbarous Indians; For verily there is no savage nation under the cope of Heaven, that is more absurdely barbarous than the Christian World. They that go naked and drink water and live upon roots are like Adam, or Angels in comparison of us." Or wrote in the 1670s the popular novelist and playwright Mrs. Aphra Behn, who had lived during part of her childhood in Dutch Guiana: "And these People [Indians of Surinam] represented to me an absolute *Idea* of the first State of Innocence, before Man knew how to sin: and 'tis most evident and plain, that simple Nature is the most harmless, inoffensive and vertuous Mistress. 'Tis she alone, if she were permitted, that better instructs the World, than all the Inventions of Man: Religion would here but destroy that Tranquillity they possess by Ignorance; and Laws would but teach 'em to know Offences, of which now they have no Notion . . . They have a native Justice, which knows no Fraud; and they understand no Vice, or Cunning, but when they are taught by the *White* Men.")

F. W. Maitland, in the essay on "Liberty" mentioned previously, was "inclined to think . . . that Hobbes was led to exaggerate his account of man's naturally unsocial character by a desire to bring 'the state of nature' into discredit." Was Hobbes attacking an exasperatingly rosy picture of the state of nature in order to attack the idea of liberty allied with it? Maitland says yes, for reasons that were to Hobbes of the utmost urgency, and that will be taken up later in these pages (in VI, 3, "Myth and Reality").

Hobbes's denunciation of New World natural man and that natural man's vaunted liberty became the best known example of a reaction against such ideas, a reaction against the idea of liberty that became especially widespread in the mid-seventeenth century, generously assisted by the disturbances of the Civil War in England and the Fronde in France. "Conscience was a thing appealed to [writes Acton] by the destroyers of church and State, by enthusiasts and fanatics. At the Restoration it was disparaged and denounced as a plea for revolution and regicide." And says Michelet, of this reaction, "The objective and the general sense was Death to liberty!"

Its effect on general opinion was noted at the end of the century by Fénelon's *Télémaque*, speaking of the liberty of the people of La Bétique being derided as a myth: "We are so corroded, that we can scarcely believe this simplicity might be true. We regard the ways of this people as a pretty fable, they must regard ours as a monstrous nightmare . . ."

Montaigne's *Essays* which had had more than thirty French editions between 1600 and the 1660s, plus a dozen abridged editions, were attacked in this reactionary time by spokesmen for philosophy and religion "for he had taught that dangerous thing, to think freely," and were put on the index in 1676. There were no editions in France between 1669 and 1724, although in England his star was blazingly on the rise, particularly among the architects of deism and "natural religion," who found Montaigne's skepticism very useful in building armatures of belief founded on elements common to all religions.

During this same reactionary period an always increasing number of fugitive French intellectuals found their way to other lands, notably Holland and (after 1688) England. The New World as a stick for beating the Old, especially the Old World in the image of the Sun King, was a weapon not altogether unfamiliar to these exiles. One of these dissident emigrés in Holland was Nicolas Gueudeville, an ex-Benedictine monk turned Protestant and journalist, a friend and correspondent taken seriously by the philosopher Bayle. Gueudeville translated, edited, or wrote a number of things that gained some interest at the time, such as translations of Erasmus' *In Praise of Folly* and More's *Utopia*, a three-volume critique (widely read) of *Télémaque*, and a three-volume translation of a work, written two centuries before, on the superiority of women over men — its real point, said Gueudeville in his Preface, being to decry "the value of science, art, erudition," against the simple "light of reason."

Gueudeville possessed such splendid powers of invective, combined with such splenetic hatred of Louis XIV and Louis' established church and all their friends (including Hobbes), that he attracted very personal attention from the French government, which succeeded in muzzling him whenever the diplomatic situation with Holland permitted. At other times Gueudeville wrote a sort of international newspaper, under the varying titles of *L'Esprit des Cours de l'Europe* or *Nouvelles des Cours de l'Europe*, which provides pyrotechnic reading yet today — Louis was one of "these Princes who . . . make new progress in Conquerantism" or the Pope, in Gueudeville's frequent attacks on Vatican nepotism, was not the Holy Father but the Holy Family, and the Pope's nephew, the young Abbé Albani, should be made a cardinal at once for his "genius so much superior to good sense . . ." Hobbes was a king-worshiper, an idolater of monarchy, a "Monarcholatre," whose contention that order was more important than liberty or justice (even tyranny preferable to the disorder of anarchy) brings a long passage comparing Louis XIV to Caligula, and concluding, ". . . a free Society is the Body Politic in its Natural State: This Body is subject to incommodities, to illnesses, even to death . . . but a tyrannized Society is the Body Politic in a State of violence . . . and its suffering is continual."

## 4. Curious Dialogues

There appeared in Holland in the mid-1690s a young French ex-officer of Marines who had spent some ten years in Canada and was now in trouble with the authorities. Louis Armand de Lom d'Arce, baron de Lahontan, robbed of his inheritance in Béarn by (so he claimed) crooked lawyers, had gone to Canada in 1683 at the age of seventeen as an officer with troops attached to the Navy, and, after service in the towns and on the frontier (where he commanded in 1687 an outpost near the site of present Detroit and where at Michilimackinack in 1688 he met the survivors of La Salle's last expedition), he had come out second best in a feud with the governor of Newfoundland and had become, in 1694, in some sort a fugitive from French bureaucratic punishment — which at the time could quite easily take the form of indefinite imprisonment in the Bastille.

He was at The Hague by 1698, where, in his rage against the administration in France, he would presumably have found congenial company among the expatriate French intellectuals. There he published in 1703 a book in two small volumes on Canada, the first volume consisting of letters supposedly written to an elderly relative during his years there, the second a lengthy discussion of various matters mentioned briefly in the letters.

This little work, along with a great deal of historical and ethnographical fact and fancy — and the account of a westward exploration that most historians regard as largely fictitious — repeated the usual virtues of American Indian society, although rather more trenchantly than usual. The Americans are born free; they are all equal, with no superiority and no subordination; even the women are free, even the girls, to do as they please, "mistresses of their bodies," free by their "right of liberty;" the Indians know no thine nor mine; they have no cares; they are ferocious toward their enemies in war but among themselves they never quarrel, never do each other wilful harm, the reason for this being that each is as much a noble lord as the other.

The ethnography deals mainly with Hurons but includes information from Ottawas, Sauteurs, Miami, Potawatomi, Illinois, the Five Nations Iroquois (although, says the author, speaking with good Huron patriotism, "I hate those rascals worse than horns and lawsuits"), and still others, including presumably imaginary peoples met on the presumably imaginary western exploration. The ethnography is in general (with the exception of the last category) of much value, giving numerous indications of having been reported with, as Lahontan claims, great fidelity. The fidelity may slip most noticeably in the emphasis on the number of slaves (captives taken in war), leaving an impression of an average Huron as rather similar, with his apparent retinue of slaves, to a French planter in the Caribbean islands, and in the emphasis on the perfect sexual freedom allowed Huron girls, who are, the author notes, as many a purveyor of sensational New World news had noted since Vespucci, excessively passionate, and who conveniently prefer Frenchmen to Hurons. Sexual freedom before marriage and faithfulness after marriage, exactly the opposite of the usual European model of ladylike behavior, attracted much attention in France, being also reported some years later as a most amiable marvel by Le Page du Pratz for the Natchez, on the lower reaches of the Mississippi. Lahontan's recounting of the charming custom of "courant l'allumette" — a youth who fancied a certain girl went to her bedside with a lighted torch; if she accepted him she blew out the flame, if not, he carried the torch on to another — was endlessly recounted and repictured in eighteenth-century French publications. These two points: no work, and free love with a whole population of willing girls (in addition to the spurious journey of western discovery), gild Lahontan's golden world to a point that has sometimes been felt to tarnish the veracious reporting elsewhere within it.

Also, as in so many previous works, this fine New World is used as a springboard for jumping with both feet upon the sinful Old. But here the more than customary vehemence has still something further added — the Old World is called upon directly to think of applying these new ways to its own corrupt old soul. The tyranny of "Ministers of State or of the Evangels" says Lahontan in a Préface, will last "until that Anarchy may be introduced among us that exists among the Ameriquains, of whom the least feels himself more than a Chancellor of France." And with this, explicit statement is at last given to the formidable political reality of New World ideas that was bound to emerge sooner or later.

Scarcely launched on the "Morals and Manners of the Savages" (in the *Mémoires* of Volume II), the author indulges in a long diatribe supposedly summing up various Indian criticisms of European ways. Money, they say, is the serpent of the French: for it the civilized Europeans kill, pillage, defame one another, sell themselves or their wives and daughters. Those Indians "who had been in France," says the narrator, taunt him with the wickedness they saw there perpetrated for money. "They mock at our Sciences and Arts, deride us for the servility they observe among us. They call us slaves, they say we are wretches who can't call our lives our own, that we degrade ourselves in our servitude to one sole person who rules everything, and who has no other law than his own will." They charge "that we fight and quarrel incessantly . . . that we are never in agreement; that we imprison each other and even publicly destroy each other. They esteem themselves beyond anything one can imagine, alleging that they are all equally great lords, because men being all made from the same clay they owe no distinction or subordination whatever to anyone. They claim that their contentment of spirit far surpasses our riches; that all our Sciences do not equal knowing how to live one's life in a perfect tranquility; that a man is not a man among the Europeans unless he is rich."

Lahontan speaks several times in the letters of Volume I and in the *Mémoires* of Volume II of a noted Huron chief known as the Rat, and quotes at length several of his moral and sagacious remarks. He kept a complete record, he says, of conversations with the Rat while residing for a time in his village, a manuscript that the Comte de Frontenac, then governor of New France (and no more a friend of the Jesuits than was Lahontan) was delighted to read and even assist in revising. Dialogues modeled on these alleged conversations (with the Rat's name changed to an anagrammatic Adario drawn from his Huron name of Kondiaronk) were added to the two previous volumes as a "Supplement" to the travels of the Baron Lahontan wherein one would find "Curious Dialogues between the Author and an Intelligent Savage".

This third volume gave infinitely greater scope to a thundering invasion of the Old World by the revolutionary ideas of the New. Every sacred Old World institution from Holy Writ to holy wedlock is mocked and berated by the worldly-wise Adario, shown to be not only false but oppressive; and above all the absence of liberty and equality in the Old

World is denounced as an iniquity that should be, for men, unbearable. All this always in comparison with the New World Hurons, a society blessed with the incomparable benefits that flow from liberty and equality.

All the points made in the preceding letters and Mémoires are expanded in merciless detail, even unto the oversell of slaves and sex, with Adario evidently disposing of the services of slaves innumerable, and quoting precise figures ("from the veracious testimony of our girls") on the number of times young Frenchmen make love in one night (six) as compared with three for young Hurons — although, as a consequence, the Frenchmen are "older in this commerce" at thirty-five than the Hurons at fifty.

The author, Lahontan, piously defends the Old World ways against Adario's castigation (even to a tartuffian defense of the Jesuits) and heroically loses every round to the Huron philosopher.

It is impossible for you Europeans to follow the ostensible teachings of your religion, says Adario, "as long as *Thine* and *Mine* remain among you." In spite of their apparent material poverty, the Indians "are richer than you, who are forced by the *Thine* and *Mine* to commit all sorts of Crimes." Until they can do without Thine and Mine Europeans cannot hope to live like men. Their money is the demon of demons, their true tyrant, the source of evil, the thief of souls and the sepulcher of the living dead; to hope to live in the Land of Money and conserve your soul is impossible; this money is the father of viciousness, falseness, intrigue, lying, treason, bad faith, and generally of all evils in the European world. "Why do we have no lawsuits?" demands Adario. "Because we do not accept the use of money . . . We are born free and united brothers, each as much a great lord as the other, while you are all the slaves of one sole man . . . I am the master of my body, I dispose of myself, I do what I wish, I am the first and the last of my Nation . . . subject only to the great Spirit." While the European's life and body are subject to his king and "to a thousand people who are placed above you" and he can never dream of being his own master and doing as he himself might wish. But "you would still rather be a French Slave than a free Huron; O what a fine fellow is a Frenchman . . . since he remains in slavery and subjection" while even animals are enjoying "this precious Liberty . . ." Adario does venture to hope that some day the Europeans will gradually change, "that an equality of wealth will gradually appear, and that at last you will detest this greed that causes all the evils one sees in Europe, and thus having no *thine* nor *mine* you will live with the same felicity as Hurons . . . Would one see classes and distinctions among men if there were no *Thine* and *Mine?* You would all be equal, as are the Hurons."

When Lahontan instances the comforts and luxuries of, at least, the rich in Europe as against the immaterial forest joys of the Hurons, Adario argues that the rich and great of Europe live in terror of losing the favor of their master, the king, and are embroiled in endless plots and intrigues against one another to retain this favor — living with serpents in their hearts — while the Huron lives in tranquility of soul and liberty. Lahontan points out that in Europe this tranquility of soul would be called indolence, and Adario responds, "What have we in the world dearer than life? Why not enjoy it?" He urges Lahontan to become a Huron: he will eat, drink, sleep in serenity, he will not have to make money to be happy.

Lahontan on the other hand urges Adario to become a European, to which Adario says, "How could I watch the Needy suffer, without giving them all I have? . . . Would it be possible for me to do secret evil to my friends and pretend friendship with my enemies — deride and mock the unfortunate, honor the wicked — rejoice in the woes of others, and praise a man for his rascality; imitate the envious, the traitors, the flatterers, the unfaithful, the liars, the vain, the misers, the greedy, the informers and the hypocrites? . . . Could I have the baseness to wriggle like a little snake at the feet of a Lord?"

If only he knew more of the world, Lahontan says, Adario would not hold in such contempt the superior condition of Europeans. "We have seen in France *Chinese* and *Siamese*, people from the end of the Earth, who are in all things more opposed to our manners than are Hurons, & who nevertheless can't help but admire our manner of living . . ." But Adario has heard from the Jesuits of Paris (who had been to their countries) about these distant foreigners: "They have the *thine* and the *mine* among them, like the French; they know money as well as the French do." It is therefore not surprising they find European manners acceptable. No, for Adario the distinction is a simple one between the Old World and the New: ". . . you prefer slavery to liberty."

None of these bold ideas were new, of course. All of them have been cited repeatedly in the foregoing pages. Even the airs of superiority assumed by the "Savages" had been remarked upon by previous observers, in, for example, the Jesuit Relations at the beginning of the seventeenth century: "You will see these poor barbarians, notwithstanding their great lack of government, power, letters, art and riches, yet holding their heads so high . . . regarding themselves as our superiors." Or from another missionary at the end of the century, after twelve years' acquaintance with the people of the Gaspé Peninsula, quoting an Indian as explaining that "there is no Indian who does not consider himself infinitely more happy and more powerful than the French." Lahontan merely summed up the principal strong points made by his predecessors down through the centuries — but he related them so effectively to the actuality of his own time that echoes of his hard language are discernible in numbers of landmark works by, as says Chinard, the most daring thinkers of the eighteenth century. The *Dialogues* were neither a "political treatise nor a learned dissertation, but the trumpet blast of a revolutionary journalist . . . and that ten years before the death of Louis XIV." It was also a long half century before the appearance of works generally assumed to be among the earliest in France to bring nature down out of the purely literary clouds into the actual political arena — such as Morelly's various presentations of a Utopian communism, the best known his *Code of Nature* (1755), or the brief *Testament* of the Curé Jean Meslier left in manuscript at his death in 1729 and published by Voltaire in 1762, attacking, with a style as rough and headlong as a carriage horse (said Voltaire), both society and religion (Voltaire deleted his attack on property).

In his several Prefaces addressed directly to the reader ("whom may Heaven deign to heap with prosperity") Lahontan states these principal strong points — and revolutionary points — over and over again, as directly and as forcefully as possible: ". . . persons who know my faults do as little justice to these People as to me when they say I am a Savage and this is what obliges me to speak so favorably of my confreres. Those who make this Observation do me much honor . . . For in simply saying that I am as the Savages are, they give me, without realizing it, the character of the most respectable man in the world; since it is an incontestable fact that the Nations which have not been corrupted by the presence of Europeans have neither *thine* nor *mine*, neither Laws nor Judges nor Priests." To be such a Savage is therefore to be most wise and reasonable, says Lahontan, since one needs to be blind not to see that private property "is the sole source of all the disorders that trouble the Society of Europeans."

Lahontan's three little volumes of 1703 were published by the Frères L'Honoré at The Hague, who were also publishers of Gueudeville's *Esprit des Cours de l'Europe*. Gueudeville included information from Lahontan's work in an *Atlas Historique* he compiled for the same publishers (1705), and, also in 1705, brought out a revised edition of Lahontan's *Travels* and *Dialogues* in which he shined up some of the livelier anti-French and anti-Jesuit passages and added what was, to all intents and purposes, one additional dialogue. The Amsterdam publishing house of François L'Honoré could advertise in its "Catalogue des Livres Nouveaux" for 1706 both *L'Esprit des Cours*, Tome XIV, and the new revised and enlarged edition of Lahontan. Because of a mistaken notion published by an early critic Gueudeville was for many years credited as the sole author of the *Dialogues*, a mistake corrected in an annotated American edition of 1905, and clarified by Chinard, reprinting and comparing both the original 1703 text and Gueudeville's revised version of 1705 in the edition of 1931 which I have used, in my own translations, in these preceding pages.

Changes made by Gueudeville for the second edition are fairly few and unimportant throughout most of the book, including most of the *Dialogues*, but, as mentioned, a wholly new dialogue, in effect, is added at the end. All the revisions, including this added dialogue, deal with ideas already present in Lahontan's original version.

Gueudeville's new passages lose the last grain of verisimilitude Lahontan had managed to retain, as well as Lahontan's zest and lightheartedness, but more than make up for this with a violent and virulent insistence that the Old World consider Adario's ideas as political realities.

Says his Adario, you prostrate yourselves before those who rob the people and impoverish the nation to pay for their "despicable luxuries"; you worship them as idols who, to satisfy their unbridled passions, shed "torrents of blood"; you pay court to wretches who you know could never have crawled out of the mud except by their villainies. Lahontan in this version forgets to play the devil's advocate and readily agrees that the people are always duped, they adore the hand that strikes them, and "kiss the iron with which the Tyrant holds them enchained." The Jesuits, declares this agreeable Lahontan, preach charity, and everybody in Europe pretends to plead for charity, but nobody — including the Jesuits — practices it. Otherwise, the rich would not dissipate in ornate luxuries wealth that could bring so much happiness to society as a whole, and a monarch purportedly devout would not spend "hundreds of millions for his pleasures great and small while a third of his subjects died of hunger."

Adario replies to the argument that "the force and order of a Nation are founded on the *Thine* and the *Mine*" by suggesting the possibility, "which will probably not happen soon, that Royalty is abolished in France, and that each City become Sovereign establishes a community of goods among its inhabitants; in what way has your France become less powerful?" And to the proposition that at least the rich add luster to the nation, Gueudeville's Adario pictures two women, one with a face and bust of great beauty, but her lower body a hideous monster; the other well proportioned although not a striking beauty — the first of these women is the body politic "where *Thine* and *Mine* reign: the Court and Chateau of the Monarch, the House and Equipages of this or that great Lord, the parties and luxuries of the Rich, these are the brilliant parts of that Society." But those dead of famine can be seen along the roads "while Sir Rich Man doesn't skimp himself a penny in his pleasures," and one can see "the villagers, the artisans, the little people deprived of the comforts of life, suffering hunger and nakedness . . . then what do you say, my Friend, doesn't your Society excite horror by that frightful and disgusting lower part?" But the second woman represents "a Nation which has forever banished all distinction in riches . . . all subordination to authority," where men help one another "to secure happiness," no one works only for himself, each person "consecrates his effort and industry to the general welfare."

Lahontan objects that such an airy Utopia could not come into being since the only real gainers would be the poor, and they being the weakest party how could they constrain the others — the opulent upper class and the prosperous middle class — to give up their property?

But "in your country," says Adario, "the people without capital and without fortune are the most numerous: nothing should keep them therefore from becoming the strongest . . ." Is not the French king's great army only made up of "three hundred thousand paupers who for a few pennies a day are willing to let themselves be slain, and for whom? for the Rich from first to last; for the conservation of their riches . . ." Do these poor soldiers by the sacrifice of their blood and lives "procure the least advantage for those of their Category and Class . . . for those Persons destitute of means? Not at all, except to add to their misery." Let these troops "restore to the Nation its rights, do away with private property . . . establish a Government so equitable that all members of Society would participate . . . in the common felicity." The poor man has "no other patrimony than his labor," and however hard he tries he can't supply his family's needs, having to pay first "for the ambition, the luxury, the pleasures of the Monarch . . ." He is left in want while the financiers "grow fat on his substance" without the least concern for his and his family's misery.

Adario's condemnation of the mendacity of the king and the ruling classes at last calls from this Lahontan a blustering, "Hold on there, *Huron*, I have the honor to eat the bread of the King, and if you continue in this tone it will be my duty to silence you." And Adario, triumphant: "Now is he not my vile slave? Tell me, unworthy Frenchman, are you your King's more than your country's? Is it the bread of the King you eat? Is it not that of the Nation, & consequently your own?"

Compared to all this evil, Adario concludes, the Huron society is one in which "natural Law is found in all its perfection. Nature knows no distinction or preeminence in producing individuals of the same species, thus we are all equal." The poor man who steals for hunger is, in the "barbarian" Old World, whipped and hanged, while "one of our greatest cares is to see that none of our Compatriots finds himself in need."

# IV

# The Happiness of Seeing the New World Regenerate the Old

Lahontan, with the riotous assist from Gueudeville, had at last established a sound and solid beachhead in the Old World for the ideas so long credited to the New. His *Travels* and *Dialogues*, sometimes reprinted from his original 1703 version, more often in Gueudeville's 1705 revision, were an immediate popular success (seven editions by 1705) and ran through numerous further editions and reprintings and condensations during the eighteenth century (twenty-five by 1758). The first English translation appeared in 1703, possibly even before the *Dialogues* were published in French — Lahontan said in the Preface that it was at the suggestion of English friends ("several Englishmen of distinguished merit") that he originally decided to publish "these diverse conversations that I had in that country with a certain Huron, to whom the French had given the name of the Rat." (The English is as lively as the French and a good deal more in the mode of the moment — a typical sample: "You fobb me off very prettily, truly, when you bring in your Gentlemen, your Merchants and your Priests. If you were strangers to *Meum* and *Tuum*, those distinctions of Men would be sunk.") Other English translations followed, as well as translations into German and Dutch.

Chinard, in his (1931) comparative edition of the *Dialogues*, made an effort to trace in considerable detail the book's direct influence during the eighteenth century, noting the attention from critics, warmly favorable or hotly antagonistic, at the time of the book's first appearance ("some Ecclesiastics claim I have insulted God in insulting their conduct," Lahontan wrote in the Preface to the *Dialogues*, after his first two volumes had already been published to a fiery clerical reception), and noting quotations from Lahontan, sometimes at length, in various travel books and geographical and historical compilations and even in the contemporary New World publication of Robert Beverly's *History and Present State of Virginia* (1705). Chinard finds lahontanian notions as well in Le Sage, Diderot, Swift (with Gulliver among the Houynhnms, supported by some most ingenious but, it seems to me, shaky literary detective work — the principal clue being found also elsewhere, such as in Nicolás Denys), and probably Voltaire and Rousseau, among many others.

Lahontan, who had been penniless at the time of his book's publication, now mingled with the rich and powerful his wise Huron had so harshly treated. ("The obscure adventurer of earlier days had become the celebrated author of the moment . . . well received wherever he went.") He stayed as a guest with the Elector of Hanover (soon to become George I of England), attended the great fair of Kiel with the Governor of Holstein, was accepted as a proper savant by the philosopher Leibniz. Leibniz found in Lahontan's work important evidence refuting the speculations of Hobbes and seeming to prove that man in a state of nature was not bad but good, and that it was not need of defense or desire for conquest but the "pursuit of a better and happier life, by mutual assistance, which led to the foundation of Societies and States."

An accurate assessment of Lahontan's effect on the thought of his time, says Chinard, will have to await an accurate history of the eighteenth century's infatuation with primitivism, which is a long way in the future. But regarded rather as a symptom than a cause, since so much of what he said had been said so many times before, Lahontan does seem to mark an epoch — or at least happened to publish at an epochal moment. Some French historians have for many years commented on a "fundamental" change in the public mind in regard to "considerations of freedom" occurring at or near the opening of the eighteenth century. Perhaps, as with some other notable successes, Lahontan merely put before his readers' eyes what, having been so long in the air, was already in their minds — merely set ashore on his European beachhead an invasion force of ideas long known, but heretofore known only by exotic report, regarded only as part of an incommensurable other world.

Stories of American liberty and equality would of course have constituted but one factor among many in the structure of this epochal moment, when the seventeenth century, which loved "hierarchy, discipline, order assured by authority," gave way to the eighteenth century, which detested precisely these things. Seventeenth-century Europeans were intensely Christian, their successors "anti-Christian; the former believed in divine right, the latter in natural right; the former lived comfortably in a society divided into unequal classes, the latter dreamed only of equality," to quote a historian who mentions Lahontan alone among all the reporters of the New World. But the popularity at this particular moment of Lahontan's *Mémoires* and *Dialogues* does seem to urge that those stories of American liberty and equality were indeed one such factor.

The change in the European mind toward the idea of a "natural" right to liberty can be observed, for one example among many, in the successive editions of Pufendorf over several generations, as successive editors turn more and more against his justification of authoritarianism, sometimes with footnotes (sometimes even longer-winded than Pufendorf's long-winded text) that have a markedly lahontanian ring. (Such parallels are of small account, to be sure, in demonstrating any direct literary parentage — my point is only to indicate how thick was the air of the time with such ideas.) Pufendorf, following Grotius' lead, exercised an enormous influence in seventeenth-century political thinking and was still a cornerstone classic for Rousseau and Diderot nearly a hundred years later. His work contributed to the seventeenth-century secularization of absolutism and he "pounded, bent, and snipped the radical doctrine of the 'new' natural law just as in our own age the doctrines of democracy, nationalism, and Marxism have in their turn been pounded, bent, and trimmed — until they became acceptable and respectable."

Diderot believed his time to be so indifferent to their hierarchical architecture that, "If Puffendorf and Grotius should return to the present world," he wrote in the 1760s, "they would starve to death." But the active hostility of certain of their principal eighteenth-century editors seems to bespeak more than indifference. Jean Barbeyrac, who edited both Grotius and Pufendorf, remarks in a note to his French translation (1706) of Pufendorf's *De jure naturae et gentium* that it is surprising neither Pufendorf nor Grotius "spoke of the right each person has to defend his Liberty . . ." Grotius in fact spoke specifically against such an assumption in *The Rights of War and Peace* (1625): "Nor is the taking up Arms upon the Account of Liberty, justifiable in particular Persons, or a whole Community; as if to be in such a State, or a State of Independence, was naturally, and at all Times, every one's Right."

Barbeyrac, in his editions of Pufendorf, attacks at every turn Pufendorf's position, and that of his ally, Hobbes, against "natural" liberty, as, for instance: "Hobbes, and our Author too, far exaggerate the Advantages of Civil Society over a State of Nature . . ." Foes of Hobbes were legion by the eighteenth century, so nothing is really remarkable in Barbeyrac's hostility except as it defines the distance between his position in 1705 and that of his Author in the 1670s, who in the same work found most "unworthy of Approbation" American ideals of equality as described by Montaigne.

Barbeyrac and his Author (his Author always clinging to Hobbes for support) engage in a running battle of several pages over the state of nature, with Barbeyrac's notes responding point by point to Hobbes, as quoted by his Author.

Argues Barbeyrac: "In the state of Nature we seem to enjoy, for the most part, the Fruits of our Labour with greater Security; for poor Subjects are very often flea'd by evil Princes."

Or, "If the Fear of Laws keeps the People to their Duty, it will make a like Impression upon the Great Ones, and Persons of Quality, but they easily find out ways to evade the Laws; for those in whom the Passions reign with the greatest Fury, and in a manner most prejudicial to Society, are beyond Contradiction these Persons in Authority, of which we can't find any examples in a state of Nature, nor can any there be in a Condition of doing so much Mischief."

And "in Civil Governments is there not often more reason for terrible Apprehensions from Princes and their Ministers . . ."

Or "Whence come those Monsters of Ambition, Covetousness, Pleasure, Cruelty, and Inhumanity, which ordinarily reign in the Courts of Princes, and whose contagious Examples spread almost always to their Inferiors?"

Or "The horrible Persecutions which the Subjects sometimes suffer, and the bloody Wars which often harrass the most flourishing States and Empires, prove, that Peace and Tranquillity do not more ordinarily flourish in Civil Societies than in the state of Nature."

And finally, replying to "Riches" as a benefit of "Society," "How comes it to pass that we see so many reduced to Beggary, and so many Subjects ruin'd by Extortion?"

All of these arguments are also made specifically by Adario — not at all in itself reason to suppose Barbeyrac had seen Lahontan's *Dialogues,* published while he was writing these notes, but perhaps reason enough to recognize that these ideas, present in travel books since Vespucci and Léry, Du Tertre and the Jesuit Relations, as well as in Lahontan, were by now eminent features of the landscape of Barbeyrac's eighteenth-century mind. Possibly more to the point, in estimating the truly revolutionary bent of the *Dialogues,* is the fact that Barbeyrac's conclusion (leaning upon Locke for support), that the Civil State may be superior to the Natural State if well-governed, or unhappier if ill-governed, most specifically is not a conclusion of Adario's, not so long as the Civil State contains the mine and thine of property.

The triumph in the popular mind of the idea of a "natural right" to liberty can be seen in plays such as Delisle de la Drevetière's *Arlequin Sauvage*, first presented in June, 1721, at the Théâtre Italien in Paris, a comedy which is in some respects a direct dramatic adaptation of Lahontan. It presents an American Indian visiting France, just arrived in Marseilles fresh from his great forest, a burlesque model of the long-standing image of the noble American savage, but repeating much of the political philosophy in Lahontan's pages. Arlequin Sauvage sees, like Adario, that everything in the civilized world is false — false goodness, false wisdom, false wit — but also learns (not forgetting that this is a comedy) that even the hair is false, upon scalping a merchant and getting only his wig. Lahontan's picture of woodland amour is brought in evidence when Arlequin is baffled by the pretty Violette's complex game of coquetry. "Let's make love à la Sauvage," he offers, describing in detail the previously mentioned custom of "courant l'allumette" and saying, "This method is better than yours, it cuts short useless discourse."

When Lelio, the French friend who had brought him to France, shows him some money, Arlequin first finds it uneatable before declaring it madness: "You are madmen who think you are wise, you are ignorant and believe yourselves educated, you are poor and believe you are rich, you are slaves who believe yourselves free. Mad, because you desire . . . an infinity of useless things . . . poor, because you limit your wealth to money . . . slaves of all your possessions, that you prefer to your liberty and to your brothers, whom you cause to be hanged if they take the least part of wealth useless to you . . . ignorant because your wisdom consists only in knowing the Laws. Your greatest madness is in believing yourself obliged to be mad."

That these ideas are now current in the public mind is pointedly stated in the play by a passerby saying to himself, "Happy a thousand times the Savages, who follow simply the laws of nature," an observation naturally pleasing to Arlequin, who says, "Oh ho, here is a reasonable man. You think well of the Savages." Says the passerby, explaining that he is being tormented by lawsuits, "Would to God I were among them!"

There is not a Savage, no matter how stupid, Arlequin exclaims, upon learning that it depends on one's fine clothes if one is received in society, "who would not die laughing to learn there are people in the world who judge the merit of men by their clothes."

All this is proper enough for comedy, but when liberty takes the stage the mood turns serious: "Why, false friend, have you brought me here from my country only to teach me that I am poor? . . . in my forest I knew neither riches nor poverty: I was in myself my King, my Master, and my servant; and you have cruelly brought me from that happy state to teach me I am nothing but a pauper and [for Lelio has told him he must work to get money] a slave . . . money is the devil which possesses all of you . . . I want to be a free man, nothing more. Take me back then to where you found me, so that I can forget in my forests that there are rich and poor in the world."

In the happy ending, Arlequin and his Violette depart for his native land, "where we will have no need of money to be rich, nor of laws to be wise."

This was not at all the first Paris play dealing with heroic American Indians (e.g., Louis Ferrier de la Martinière's *Montezuma*, of 1702), but it was notable for its popularity, being several times revived from the 1720s to the 1750s, while a later play presenting the other side, arguing indignantly for "civilization" as against the "miserable savage world" (which lacked "morality, agriculture, fine arts, trades, clothes, and any hint of laws human and divine") was a signal flop with the Paris public. The opposition whether in popular literature or philosophy, where the work of Hobbes remained foremost, simply could not prevail — for the time being — against the tempestuous winds incessantly winging from those fabled lands of liberté and égalité over there in the American wilderness.

The importance of the American Indian, however, as a subject for the literature (popular or otherwise) of the time, or even as a principal figure of the period's exoticism, can be easily exaggerated — 1721 was also the year of the publication of Montesquieu's *Lettres Persanes*. *Arlequin Sauvage* appeared shortly after the bursting of the Mississippi Bubble, which for some time had kept France and in fact all Europe particularly conscious of rich America as a gold and silver treasure house kept by supposedly simple and innocent natives, and this timing may have had something to do with the play's unusual success. The crash of Monsieur Law's company and the disastrous finish of the sensational speculation in the rue Quincampoix (the word *millionaire* was coined during that frenzied time) might have disposed Paris audiences to look with favor on Arlequin's morality, so gratifyingly superior to avarice. The stock Italian-comedy character of Arlequin appeared at the Théâtre des Italiens in countless guises, many of them reflecting fashions of the moment — Delisle himself wrote a number of other comedies in which Arlequin was cast as anything from an Oriental nabob to a donkey — and his simple (but sage) morality was part of his stock character. The American Indian Arlequin, though, added Adario's morality, containing matter a good deal more serious and, with the entrance of liberty, more stirring. *Arlequin Sauvage* was also a much more substantial play than the usual formless sketch or farce offered by the Comédiens Italiens. That the New World in itself may have touched some chord of popular favor might be drawn from the fact that Delisle used the same new additives to Arlequin's morality the following year, but moved them from the New World to the Old, in *Thimon le Misanthrope*, it seems with considerably less success.

The famous Canadian frontiersman Véniard de Bourgmond brought for a visit to Paris in 1725 several very real Indians from the American West, who attracted great interest both among the general populace and at Court — Bourgmond was ennobled at this time for his successes in Indian diplomacy, and some of his Indian guests demonstrated ceremonial dances on the stage of that same Théâtre des Italiens where Arlequin had so recently demonstrated his Indian virtues.

There were still other plays of the period, and masques and ballets — such as the *Indes Galantes* (1735) with its well known score by Rameau in which a "savage" named Adario leads the Indians in singing of their freedom from prisons and locks and jealous hearts — that dealt with New World peoples. The significant point for most of them, I think, is that they were generally less concerned with the picturesque aspects of their American natives than with the lahontanian ideas associated with their Hurons, or with their Aztecs or Incas or simply their "Habitans du Nouveau Monde." The tone of *Arlequin Sauvage* won out hands down over that of "civilization" in most of these plays.

A play called *Le Nouveau Monde* (1737), for example, has Mercury the teacher saying, ". . . nature teaches them still better than can I . . . Man is meant to be happy, this is the first need nature inspires . . ." And if he cannot find happiness in peace and innocence will he then some day "with the thunder in his hand, exterminate the human race?" And sings a Nymph, to the New World people, "Peace and innocence follow in your footsteps . . ." Rather the same terminology was used by the philosopher George Berkeley, writing of his plan to establish a college for Indians in America (he arrived at Newport, Rhode Island, in 1729 to stay there for several years): "In happy climes, the seat of innocence,/ Where nature guides and virtue rules,/ . . . There shall be sung another golden age."

A twenty-nine-year-old lackey-turned-tutor, the young Jean-Jacques Rousseau, wrote in 1742 an abortive operetta dealing with the discovery of the New World, in which the high priest of the Americans chants, in Alexandrines not quite racinien, of his people, "under an odious yoke," losing forever "the dearest gifts of heaven,/ Their liberty, their innocence . . ." The chorus of Spaniards sings of this new world "made to bear our chains" while Columbus, sword in one hand and the standard of Castile in the other, proclaims to this unknown world "so enriched by nature . . . Lose your liberty!"

Rousseau, a child when *Arlequin Sauvage* was first produced, speaks of its acclaim in his "Letter to d'Alembert" of 1758, thirty-seven years after the play's first Paris success, and indicates that in his own time it was still rather well known and influential. He tried writing an "arlequinade" of his own, *Arlequin Amoureux Malgre Lui,* in the 1740s. A twentieth-century student quotes La Harpe speaking of Delisle's ideas as "pernicious sophisms against society," and adds, "In 1721, under the Regency, at the date of the *Lettres Persanes* and in the mouth of a clown they were tolerated, and perhaps were still not too dangerous. But they were going to know a new fortune thanks to Jean-Jacques. And what influence would they not have? What consequences?" Says another modern study: "the conjecture that Rousseau was influenced in the composition of his writings by Delisle de la Drevetière appears justified."

Voltaire laughed at any talk of noble savages, but his fake Huron in *L'Ingénu* (1767) sometimes echoed, and not always ironically, both Lahontan and Delisle, in spite of all Voltaire's wry efforts to keep him from doing so. Voltaire mocked at himself for falling victim to such nonsense — "My muse calls to you from America . . . I needed a new world . . . But I tremble that I'll be taken for a savage," as he wrote to a friend in 1736, the year of his *Alzire*; and he spoke of another friend hearing the plot of *Alzire* ("the state of nature placed in opposition to the state of artificial man"), saying, "I understand, it's *Arlequin Sauvage.*" *Alzire* apparently found its origin more in Dryden than in French ideas then current (to be noted, though, that it was Dryden's New World man singing "I am as free as Nature first made man,/ Ere the base law of servitude began,/ When wild in woods the noble savage ran" that gave the term to English), but even so *Alzire*'s Peruvians cannot, of course, bear the thought of a "yoke of slavery" while his Spaniards, meant to be the heroes of the play, find that the natives "equal us in courage and surpass us in goodness." A parody of *Alzire* published that same year altered the Peruvians to Missouris (a group of Missouris having recently visited Paris) and has Alzire sum up the theme: ". . . simple nature lives among us."

Clearly, "tales of noble Indians did much to mould public opinion in the eighteenth century . . ." and public opinion, oversold, repaid the favor by remoulding quite other themes into the noble savage image. Richard Steele published in the *Spectator* in 1711 a story that had been floating around for years, of an English sailor cast away among North American Indians and saved from death by an Indian girl whom he brought back with him to "civilization" and promptly sold into slavery. Steele used the story as a rebuttal to "A Woman of Ephesus," the sexist classic which for some sixteen hundred years had shown how fickle and faithless is woman — the point of Steele's story of the Englishman Inkle and the Indian girl Yarico was to show that men are even worse. Yarico being an Indian, a "savage," had nothing to do with Steele's purpose — she could as easily have been a Greek girl sold to slavery among the Turks. But the eighteenth century laid hands on the tale and changed its moral to suit the century's favorite preconceptions, so that by the time it became the extremely successful Paris play, Chamfort's *La Jeune Indienne* (1764), the point was not the contrast between faithful woman and faithless man but between the innocent and faithful savage and the white man (now an American) who almost (but not quite) throws her over for a more prosperous match back home in Philadelphia.

The presentation of a savage in an act of heroism in opposition to a dastardly act on the part of a civilized man, while the savage proclaims, "There is the civilized man, and here is the savage!" was sufficient to make a Paris success of an atrociously bad play, said a contemporary critic (the play being *Le Manco*, 1763, written by a whole Hollywood-story-conference of at least four authors). Peruvian and Canadian and even Amazon heroes and heroines continued to people the French stage in fair numbers throughout the mid-eighteenth century, inspired it seems at least as much by Alzire as by Arlequin, although many of them continued to deal expressly, as did *Le Manco*, with "all that we have been reading everywhere on Kings, on liberty, on rights of man," in a comment citing in connection with this play the works of Rousseau, then recently published.

Missionaries, particularly Jesuits, had received rough treatment at Lahontan's hands, and religious critics, not surprisingly, responded in kind. And yet the most important (for ethnologists) of all the Canadian Jesuits, Lafitau, while damning Lahontan out of measure for his assertions of Indian irreligiosity, gave a picture of the natives not at all out of line in other respects with Adario's, as did the Jesuits' most important Canadian historian, Charlevoix.

Lafitau, writing of the Iroquois although claiming to speak of all American natives except those of Peru and Mexico, certainly equaled if he didn't outdo Adario's Hurons with "they have high, proud hearts, a courage of steel, an intrepid valor, a constancy under suffering that is heroic, a poise that misfortune and ill luck do not shake; among themselves they have a civility after their fashion, which observes all proper obligations, a respect for their aged, a deference for their equals which is quite surprising, and that one can scarcely reconcile with that independence and liberty of which they appear extremely jealous." And he echoes almost to the word Peter Martyr of so many generations before: "By their good fortune they know neither Code nor Digest [of laws], nor Lawyers, nor Prosecutors, nor Bailiffs; so, with all that, if only they did not have their Jongleurs [priests] who are their miserable Physicians, would they not be the most happy people in the world?"

Charlevoix, who began his travels in America with an anti-Indian prejudice, found that the better one came to know the savages "the more one discovers in them estimable qualities." He eventually described their society as one "exempt of nearly all the faults which so often trouble the smooth course of ours." He thought they may have been, before becoming acquainted with Europeans, "perhaps the only happy beings on earth." They seem at first sight, he wrote, to have no form of government, and yet "enjoy nearly all the advantages that well-regulated authority can procure for the best-administered of nations . . . Born free and independent, they have a horror of the least shadow of a despotic power, but they stray rarely from certain usages and principles founded on good sense, which take the place of Laws and supply, after a fashion, a legitimate authority . . . inequality of condition is not to them necessary for the maintenance of society. In this country all Humanity believes itself equally men, and in Man what they most esteem is Man. No distinction of birth, no prerogative of rank."

A similar, or even flowerier, salute to this same liberty and equality among this same people came from an English witness of the same epoch: "None of the greatest *Roman* Heroes have discovered a greater Love to their Country, or a greater Contempt of Death, than these People called Barbarians have done, when Liberty came in Competition . . ." And "the *Five Nations* have such absolute Notions of Liberty, that they allow of no Kind of Superiority of one over another, and banish all Servitude from their Territories. They never make any Prisoner a Slave; but it is customary among them to make a Compliment of Naturalization into the Five Nations . . ."

More or less subversive observations such as these, so insistently repeated by both the missionaries and their foes, found their way not only into standard works of travel and geography as in previous centuries, but also into such textbooks as Buffier's *Cours de Sciences* (1720), wherein a model "Dissertation" takes as its subject that "the savage peoples are at least as happy as civilized peoples." This is debated by two gentlemen, one defending the Old World, the other preaching the virtues of the New: ". . . are not the most civilized of peoples the most artificial and the savages the most natural?" The argument is rather clearly weighted in favor of the New World, whose champion at last wins the debate outright by attacking the civilized addiction to laws and lawsuits. Buffier appended to this section of his work an apology for the use of the word *savage* to denote the people of America, in answer to a complaint from a reader who "claims that these people who pass for savages are less so than are we." Buffier apologizes to the Americans as well as to the reader for his use of the term that he agrees is far from correct, but so long established he must use it for want of a better word.

The philosophes generally shared Voltaire's amused derision for purportedly noble savages — the *Encyclopédie*, in its article on "Sauvages," stated that most of North America was inhabited by ferocious cannibals, using as authority early statements of Charlevoix. Ideas of natural liberty and equality of the genre so long associated with New World reports were, however, central to much of the philosophe thinking, and in the midst of a scathing contempt for the savage state that quite out-scathed Hobbes, Voltaire could still remark that the Huron, the Algonquin, the Illinoi, the Kaffir, the Hottentot, were at least superior to the "savages of Europe," the peasants, "our rustics" — "The peoples of America and Africa are free and our savages don't even have the idea of liberty."

Diderot and friends are believed to have had a hand, maybe a fairly generous one, in the actual writing of Raynal's *Histoire Philosophique des Indes* (1770) containing these well-worn libertarian themes combined with the contention that no event in all history was so important "for mankind in general and for the people of Europe in particular" as the discovery of the New World and the route to the East Indies via the Cape of Good Hope (a contention repeated by Adam Smith in his *Wealth of Nations* (1776): that these two discoveries were "the two greatest and most important events recorded in the history of mankind") — but this contention also combined with a strongly negative view of American fauna and flora in toto, including a negative view of European colonists supposedly withering under the baleful American sky. This generalized negative view was related to a belief ascendant in the scientific community of the time that the New World suffered from a generalized degeneracy, a curious episode that will be discussed in more detail later in these pages (in VI, 3, "Myth and Reality").

Diderot and friends naturally pondered the supposed "natural" state in connection with philosophical ruminations, displaying, as had Grotius and Pufendorf and Hobbes, conscious views that were determinedly unlearned. Says Diderot's friend Rameau, nephew of the "grand" Rameau the composer, if a savage came to Europe "of course" he would want what all Europeans want — money, fine clothes, the European conception of success. But not at all, says Diderot, arguing, as argued many another Old World thinker before and after, that being a savage, with no guide for his conduct other than his own immediate appetites, what he would really want would be to kill off his father and sleep with his mother. On the other hand Diderot argues that philosophical austerity can profitably copy the savage's supposed diet of wild (and therefore free) foods; a poor menu, says Rameau, but an extensive one, says Diderot.

However, Diderot's famous "Supplement" to Bougainville of the early 1770s gives evidence of some attentive reading of New World voyages and in his expression at about the same period of his own libertarian ideas he repeats, although presumably quite unconscious of any such derivation, the "savage" litany familiar since the time of Peter Martyr: "I am convinced there cannot be nor one cannot have true happiness for the human species except in a social state in which there is neither king nor magistrate nor priest nor laws nor thine nor mine nor property moveable or real, nor vices nor virtues . . ."

Jean-Jacques Rousseau's *Discours sur l'Origine et les Fondements de l'Inégalité Parmi les Hommes* (1755) is the climax to these centuries of reports and discussions associating the ideas of liberty and equality with "natural man" and particularly with accounts of American Indian societies. Rousseau drew from a great variety of sources in this treatise, some of them, especially in connection with the alleged physical superiority of "primitive" men, from accounts of travel in Africa, some of them American, especially in connection with his key point that man is by nature good, not wicked, and placed by nature in a world of freedom, equality, and happiness.

Unlike Diderot and Diderot's typical predecessors, Rousseau was very conscious indeed of New World associations with his ideas, especially in reference to ideas of liberty and equality. He not only made use of such as Du Tertre but, what was not always the case with Jean-Jacques, gave him credit. He also used and cited the collection of travel books published in France (the early volumes were all translations from English) by the abbé Prévost, *Histoire Générale des Voyages* (1746 ff), containing, as says Chinard, an "arsenal" of accounts from all over the world, including those on America from Léry to Charlevoix, "with condemnations of the Christian religion by priests, condemnations of civilization by colonizers, and, by everyone, satires of our morals and refutations of our prejudices." But, says the researcher who identified these and other specific sources, the generic ideas were everywhere. As is evident from the Paris theatre of that day, from Lahontan of fifty years before, from the Jesuit Relations of the preceding century, the ideas — born of reports from the New World — had been a long time in the air. In various of his other works Rousseau looked to an amethyst paradise in Europe's own rural background, but the model for the good world in his political treatises, and most strikingly in the *Discourse on Inequality*, was, in the words of a recent study, "drawn from accounts of the North American Indians, the prototype noble savages."

Pufendorf and Grotius, in editions annotated by Barbeyrac, are evident in the *Discourse on Inequality*, as are Locke and Condillac, and all these were likewise of influence to the Encyclopedists; as Diderot, a "furious giver of advice," was of special influence for Rousseau in this *Discourse* ("more to the taste of Diderot than any of my other writings, and for which his counsels were to me the most useful"). But again and again, in his basic thesis that man was contented and above all free in his state of nature before the introduction of property, the ideas expressed are similar to those expressed in more than two centuries of reports on the New World.

With his enormous literary ability — perhaps no other writer in any other time had ever possessed "such gifts," said Kant — Rousseau laid hold of these ideas and literally changed the world. From the spark he bore "there rise/a thousand beacons" wrote Shelley in his unfinished last poem. Said Madame de Staël, Rousseau "invented nothing, but he set everything on fire." Lord Acton is reputed to have said, perhaps "with a touch of exaggeration," that Rousseau "produced more effect with his pen than Aristotle or Cicero or Saint Augustine or Saint Thomas Aquinas or any other man who ever lived." Wrote the modern scholar who assembled these latter quotations, "To debate Rousseau is really to debate the main issues in our contemporary life." The somewhat more than two thousand five hundred studies on Rousseau listed in a recent bibliography of French literature would seem to support such rather lavish statements.

As has been seen in these pages, Rousseau did not in the least create the "noble savage" or any of the ideas associated with that image in regard to liberty, equality, and property. What Rousseau did do was insist on liberty and equality as elements of man's natural world, going not to the ancients for citations and examples but to the people of Arlequin and Adario, to the American societies commented upon by Du Tertre and Montaigne.

From the opening lines to the conclusion with a quotation from Montaigne's "Des Cannibales," the arguments in the *Discourse on Inequality* echo a succession of New World reflections. "The first man who, having enclosed a piece of ground, thought of saying *This is mine*, and found people simple enough to believe him, was the true founder of civil society. How many crimes, wars, murders, how many miseries and horrors, might have been spared the human race by anyone who, pulling up the boundary stakes or filling in the ditch, would have cried out to his neighbors: 'do not listen to this imposter; you are lost if you forget that the fruits of the earth belong to us all and the earth itself to nobody!' "

Hobbes had credited the invention of property with the institution of order over chaos, and consequently the establishment of the mudsill foundation of civilization. Rousseau credited it with the institution of injustice, and consequently the foundation of the evils of civilization: "competition and rivalry" bringing "an infinity of disputes and quarrels." With the introduction of property the pleasant world of nature now had to be "watered with the sweat of men . . . and one soon saw slavery and misery germinate and grow with the harvests . . ." For "the vices which make social institutions a necessity are the same vices which, at a later stage, make the abuse of them inevitable." ("Society is produced by our wants" wrote Tom Paine twenty years later "and governments by our wickedness.")

That Rousseau seemed to be asking the enlightened world of civilization to learn from savagery brought a sardonic response from, among others, Voltaire, in his often quoted letter ("I have received, Monsieur, your new book against the human race, I thank you for it . . . Never has one employed so much wit in wishing to render us witless"), who said he could not embark to go join "the savages of Canada" because his doctors would not permit it. Verses were passed around Paris of "Jacques Rousseau walking on all fours" (as he was represented in a play of the time) and browsing on "lettuces" to give "a noble pleasure to the public which hoots him."

It has sometimes been supposed that Rousseau's seemingly rosy view of a "primitive" world was simply the result of ignorance, but his anthropological reading (for all that he speaks slightingly of its authors) was very good for the period, and he frequently remarks on the popular impression that "savage" life was a life of misery and poverty, indicating his awareness of the prevalence of such allegations. His "documentation was as complete as was possible for a man of his time," says the modern ethnologist Lévi-Strauss, of "Rousseau, our teacher, Rousseau, our brother . . ." Buffon (whose writings had led Rousseau to Du Tertre) and the volumes of the *Histoire Générale des Voyages* contained plenty of testimony supporting the brute beast school, and Rousseau was well aware of La Condamine's "scientific" tour of America and his disappointed report (1745) on the Indians.

But, as he makes clear in the notes to the *Discourse on Inequality*, Rousseau believed two points of view were in conflict here, rather than contradictory ethnographical evidence: Yes, the savages were "poor" in a material sense in comparison to Europeans, but not a single savage had yet been persuaded to take up European "civilization" as a way of life, while thousands of Frenchmen and other Europeans had sought "voluntary refuge among these Nations, there to spend their entire lives, and one sees even sober Missionaries looking back with longing on their calm and innocent days among this people so despised." The recognition of happiness, concluded Rousseau, setting the birth of the Romantic movement in one short line, "is less the business of reason than of feeling."

Rousseau's less formal words also sound now and then a New World refrain but with a crescendo orchestration far beyond anything in Lahontan or Gueudeville. Enlarging in a letter upon the thought in the closing lines of the *Discourse on Inequality* for example, that among all civilized peoples a handful of rich are loaded with luxuries while the famished multitude lacks necessities, "there are persons abominable enough to dare to have a superfluity of wealth, while other Men are dying of hunger . . . Before these frightful words thine and mine were invented there were none of these men cruel and brutal that we call Masters, and none of these other species of Men lying and indecent that we call Slaves . . . It can only be a blind and stupid People that will admire those Persons who pass their lives, not in defending the people's liberty, but in stealing from them and betraying them . . . I do not accuse the Men of this century of having all the Vices. They have only those vices proper to cowardly Souls, they are sneakthieves and sly. As for vices requiring firmness and courage, of these they are incapable." Or his confession of "indignation against our foolish social institutions, by which the welfare of the public and real justice are always sacrificed to I know not what appearance of order, which does nothing more than add the sanction of public authority to the oppression of the weak and the iniquity of the powerful."

New World reverberations are sometimes audible as well in the controversies touched off by Rousseau's inflammable remarks, as, with a peculiarly modern resonance, some other verses going around Paris:

We see the maxim given us by this handsome mind
That a People well policed is only good for crime . . .

And says a typical critic, "What would become of Society, if all Men thought as Mr Rousseau?"

Thomas Jefferson is said to have shared Rousseau's belief that the North American Indians "enjoy in their general mass an infinitely greater degree of happiness than those who live under European governments." Speaking of the writing of the American Declaration of Independence, Jefferson also said that of course he had read such as Aristotle, Cicero, Montesquieu, Locke, and many others, but his ambition had been to state "an expression of the American mind." The American mind may be supposed therefore to have been expressly conscious of French libertarian thought, present day historians finding the Declaration of Independence "a practical document as well as a philosophical justification for independence; its emphasis on natural rights was designed to attract French aid . . ."

Students of Rousseau have pointed out that in various other writings he appeared to contradict the fiery libertarianism of the *Discourse on Inequality*, but it was the cry of liberty that caught the ear of his time. "Divine man!" said Robespierre, and Burke wrote that for the French Revolutionary Assembly (of 1789-91), "Rousseau is their canon of Holy Writ . . . to him they erect their first statue."

If nature was the key to the thought of the eighteenth century, liberty was the key to its spirit. "Each century has its characteristic spirit," said Diderot. "Ours seems to be that of liberty."

The Declaration of the Rights of Man proclaimed by the National Assembly (August 27, 1789) promised liberty and for a few years — the tricolor banners of its armies bearing the legend *Liberty and Equality or Death* — brought liberty to much of Europe; and Tom Paine had "the Happiness of seeing the New World regenerate the Old." The Revolution was "betrayed," as Revolutions, like trusting maidens, have a weakness for being. But the liberty announced with it has remained as an idea dominant in public rhetoric ever since.

This liberty thus so resoundingly brought to life, what in fact was it? What has it been since? What is it still today?

# V

# Definitions

## 1. Liberty

It was in punishment for their selfishness, said Jeremiah, that the Lord proclaimed for the people of Judah a liberty to the sword. Equating liberty with hostility seems always to have been, and to be still, very much in the Old World tradition. I talked to a group of students several years ago at the Vincennes campus of the University of Paris, who pretty much all agreed that liberty could exist only in struggle. I was supposed to be talking about American Indian history but when the subject of liberty was mentioned history went out the window. They were all experts on liberty. They were all majoring in liberty, as one of them said. They seemed generally in agreement that liberty has nothing to do with ideas. One starts from a position of oppression and seeks liberty via a struggle with the oppressor.

Without an oppressing enemy class to overthrow there can be no liberty, said the student who did most of the talking, a freckle-faced red-haired young woman dressed in the regulation cowboy clothes — jeans and jacket — of students everywhere. There is no need of ideas. Liberty is born of the struggle to break free from the oppression, a totally natural reaction. In the agony of the struggle (and the freckle-faced student orator, who was a natural-born orator, reminded us that *agony* in the original Greek form of the word meant struggle) one longs of course, without benefit of any history or any sort of intellectualizing, to be free. There can be no state of rest, she said, for liberty. Should the struggle cease, a new oppression would instantly begin.

Somewhat the same spirit was in the air at a cocktail party given, also several years ago, for Professor Herbert Marcuse, famous in Paris as the maitre-à-penser of the May 1968 student riots. The ambiance of the party — in a rather sumptuous apartment with trays of drinks accompanied by trays of rather sumptuous amuse-gueules served by a uniformed maid — may have contributed to the sense of general enmity. A portly young man in a suede blouse and a swooping German accent burst into rage at thought of the poor appearing to enjoy life, given the desperate state of our society, although he tore into the amuse-gueules with gusto. Your enemy is this society — it has its vulnerable points but you will face a long and bitter struggle, Professor Marcuse, aged and no longer crisp, with the eyes of a kicked cat, told the guests, mostly young French academics who amused themselves, in the way of young academics, with acid comments on the guest of honor. An occasional dropped word etched holes in the Oriental rugs (and anyway, said a young lady revolutionary who taught Emily Dickinson, your politics could not be correct if you lived west of the rue Saint-Jacques). The atmosphere, in spite of the blithesome amuse-gueules, was heavy in every quarter with thunder and lightning and pointed swords.

The church of Saint-Nicolas-du-Chardonnet, a block or so from the Place Maubert, has been (at this writing) forcibly "occupied" for several years by followers of Monseigneur Marcel Lefebvre, leader of the Catholic right wing in France, best known for continuing to read the Mass in Latin in defiance of an ecumenical Vatican's order to switch to a modern language. On pleasant Sunday mornings the sidewalk in front of the church is thronged by militants of various right wing groups, from monarchists to neo-Nazis, leafleting (as the technical term seems to have it) the passersby. From time to time a "commando" from the church "makes an irruption" (as the usual newspaper phrase seems to have it) in attacking meetings of liberal Catholics, as one such commando has just done at this moment (March 1978), disrupting a Mass at the church of Saint-Merri where a nun was scheduled to read the Gospel. The commando smashed microphones and shouted, "Women are impure," and "a woman has no right to read the Gospel." A group at a table in the brasserie across the street from the church discusses a previous "irruption" of some months ago in which a liberal Catholic speaker was clubbed with iron bars and sent to the hospital. A nun in habit says it is to save their souls that their bodies must be crushed, but an excitable old gentleman in mufti says, his false teeth going clickety-clack while he raps on the table in a way to startle the waiter, "We are fighting for liberty! We are fighting for liberty! We must respect our adversary even while we force him to his knees!"

## 2. Liberties

The rue Quincampoix, since I began writing this book, has been swamped in the wash of the immense new museum of contemporary art nearby, the Centre Georges Pompidou as it is known officially, or the

Beaubourg as it is known popularly (after the old name of the quarter and the name of the street on which it faces). At the corner of the narrow, once medieval rue de Venise and the rue Quincampoix the ancient Cabaret de l'Epée de Bois, a distant ancestor of the Opera of Paris, has been replaced by an apartment complex in faceless concrete, the cribs of the ribaudes have been replaced (at least most of them) by restaurants and shops, and the ribaudes themselves (at least most of them) by processions of camera-toting tourists and groups of souvenir-toting schoolgirls. One such schoolgirl was writing in her cahier at a table next to mine on the sunlit fifth-floor terrace of the Beaubourg only the other day, and since I am a compulsive voyeur of what other people are reading or writing I sneaked a look and saw her in the act of writing, in a list of schoolwork definitions, "la liberté: l'absence de contrainte." I took this to be an augury and asked her (thinking of the Vincennes students) how one persuaded constraint to absent itself. She said, "One does nothing, M'sieur, it is just not there," and on consideration added, "or else it isn't liberty."

In 1978 the French parliamentary commission that had been holding hearings for two years on several proposed pieces of legislation dealing with questions of liberty published its report, three volumes, 844 pages, attacking broadside the problem of just what liberty might really be. The report contained advice to this end from philosophers, scientists, historians, anthropologists, economists, sociologists, political spokesmen from the left, right, and middle, religious spokesmen, judges and lawyers and labor leaders and industrialists and assorted businessmen, psychiatrists and other physicians, newspaper editors and police officials and two grandmasters of Freemasonry.

Their specific subjects ranged over liberties public and private, liberty in law, constitutional liberty, political liberty, equality, racism, liberty of conscience; liberty in the administration of justice, liberty and bureaucracy, detention and internment, liberty and the supreme court, wiretapping and invasion of privacy, extradition and expulsion, liberty for foreigners, liberty and non-violence; labor and strikes, labor jurisdiction, shop committees, liberty and unemployment, liberty and job security and wages and labor conditions, liberty and public demonstrations; property and nationalizations and a planned society; liberty and the family, liberty and the condition of women and children, liberty and old age, liberty and divorce; liberty and medicine, public health, medications, liberty and the physically handicapped, surgical transplants, euthanasia, abortion; liberty and education, liberty and professional training, students and teaching; liberty of the press, radio, television and cinema; liberty and the police and the military; liberty and housing and urban planning; liberty and taxes; and still several dozen other categories, not counting duplications that appear to be the oversights of weary clerks.

It is evident from this roll call of expert witnesses and their specific areas of expertise that special interest was assumed to play a pronounced part in the proceedings, and that thus the old idea of liberty as privilege was not out of business. Indeed most of the concrete proposals, when disentangled from their rhetoric, called for not liberties but constraints — against somebody else. However, much if not most of the general discussion did turn on serious efforts to define liberty in reality and in theory, in history and in the present, and to identify (from various points of view) its actual friends and foes.

The whole production may have been staged, as some of the political opposition charged, merely as a political maneuver, but the testimony and debate were nonetheless real. The hearings were therefore, in some wise, a fashion show of all the principal trends and issues with which the idea of liberty is currently bedecked.

There was debate as to whether the subject should be Liberty or liberties; as to the distinction between "real" liberties and "formal" liberties (where, as in many of the questions raised, division fell for the most part along strictly partisan political lines), a distinction sometimes referred to as "bourgeois" liberties versus "democratic" liberties or even "English" liberties versus "French" liberties; as to liberty's history and extent; as to the definition of forces of oppression, especially the two major opposing forces of our time, the oppressive force of accumulations of capital or the oppressive force of the state; as to means of rendering liberty concrete, rather than merely an expression of pious sentiment.

Real liberties, said many witnesses, must offer not only choice but "the means of making the choice." Simply to "enunciate liberties does not suffice, if one is not capable of distributing to each the quantity of social power which will permit him to exercise these fundamental liberties."

The notion of some liberties as merely formal, only empty form, only empty words to those people lacking the means to enjoy them, derives, explained a historian, from "a certain Marxist Vulgate which holds that the liberties bequeathed by the Declaration of the Rights of Man and the Citizen of 1789 were bourgeois, reserved for the benefit of a dominant class, the bourgeoisie." But it "would be easy to show, today, to what point this doctrine of 'formal liberties' has served as a pretext, in many of the regimes of the twentieth century that have welcomed revolutionary ideas, for the quasi-total strangulation of concrete liberties."

However, said another historian, when the Declaration of 1789 was voted the political liberties it defined were "real for the epoch because they touched the fundamental source of oppression which came from the authoritarian state . . ." The following century, though, saw "the development of forms of economic oppression" through a burgeoning capitalism that became "the principal obstacle to the development of liberties . . . Each ideology calls real the liberty that corresponds to its own conception of oppression, and formal that which corresponds to the conception of the adversary."

The problem of turning certain of these alleged "formal" liberties into "real" liberties, theoretical liberties into concrete liberties, is, said some of the savants, so difficult as to become impossible: for example, the projects of legislation under examination called for (among other things) the right to a decent job of one's own choice, decent housing, equal education for all, including professional training for all those qualified to receive it, and for persons ill or handicapped the right to the medical care "that his state required" or to the medical care "permitted by scientific and technical progress." But France was in fact far from able to provide these material assurances, as chronic shortages of medical and educational facilities and housing, and the presence of more than a million unemployed, made clear, exposing in all too harsh a light "the vanity of the attribution of a right that could not be exercised." Genuine efforts to realize these objectives could be made, as was pointed out in some of the testimony, only in the context of a thoroughly planned society, but in such a society the individual must needs be assigned his task and place, and his individual liberties must needs suffer accordingly, and thus in a thoroughly planned economy there could be liberty "only for the planners."

Even for a freer society of "liberal planning, a planned liberalism," several witnesses warned against the growing danger to individual liberties from the amassment of computerized information on the citizenry, information available for the use or misuse of a bureaucratic government, the dangers from a whole range of sophisticated new techniques in the manipulation of the public, especially the menace of television, which must be restrained from "transforming a nation of citizens into a people of idiots."

Dispute in the hearings over liberty's origin and past history was divergent in the extreme. Man's freedom was, on the authority of Karl Marx, "his generic character." Two of the proposed projects of law, from widely differing political positions, found liberty the "distinctive character of the human will" and the "combat for a life always more free an essential aspect of the history of humanity." Various other witnesses found liberty not at all "a fact of nature" but the product of "a historical evolution" which some restricted within the borders of its European manifestation except among other societies acculturated "to the European model."

Some found the origin of liberty in Stoic philosophy (with its tenet that real freedom consists in absolute mastery of desire), but a general distinction seemed usually acknowledged for liberty in the sense in which it has been understood since the eighteenth century, concerning liberty of thought, speech, the press, the vote, "pluralist participation in public affairs, security of the person," and so on, in effect liberty "as it exists in western societies . . . a compromise between a radically individualistic conception born of the eighteenth century and a conception . . . collective or social such as has been developed in the nineteenth and twentieth centuries."

Jean-Jacques Rousseau is often cited (running third in total number of citations, behind Marx and Montesquieu), sometimes in approval, sometimes as dead wrong: " . . . a striking counter-truth. Man is not born free. In most primitive societies, most men were slaves." For other witnesses, "a certain degree of liberty has always existed in most known societies" although for a long while "these liberties were allied to privileges . . ." Or, for ethnology, "the notion of liberty, as we understand it, appeared late in history . . . to it are attached a relatively restricted number of societies among those which exist or have existed . . . Liberty is a historical product, and the conception we make of it is thus limited to a fraction of humanity." Or, full circle back to the schoolgirl's notebook, the reality at the base of liberty "is constraint . . . each great political ideology is the denunciation of a fundamental constraint and the organization of a struggle against it . . . Determining the constraints is thus the only means of determining liberties . . ."

The question of whether private property should be considered a constraint or a liberty received much attention, as well as the question of exactly what property is, in law and in ethics. The question of up to what point your constraint is justified by my liberty arose with the great majority of specific proposals: should employers be legally restrained for the benefit of labor unions, should unions be legally restrained for the benefit of employers, should advertisers be restrained from an abusive use of the female body that contributes to the cultural oppression of women — does not the liberty of the oppressed reside in a limitation of the liberty of the oppressor?

But the definition of oppressor proves most slippery and disputatious — everyone becomes at some point an adversary. Criteria of oppression in the Report go far afield, including public opinion polls as a menace to the institutions of democracy, including both abortion and its prohibition as attacks on the very basis of any liberty; and is not a proposed requirement that one's blood group be noted on a driver's license a violation of privacy?

Schoolroom catechism and public disquisition on the nature of God having fallen somewhat out of fashion, it would seem that their late subject's place has been taken, in part at least, by the nature of liberty. Learned debate on the number of angels that might dance on the head of a pin has been transmogrified into exhaustive inquiry such as these hearings or, among specialists, into even lengthier polemic on such erudite minutiae as the number of meanings accessible to the word *can*. The change is perhaps no improvement but has produced an apotheosis most marvelously diffuse, the godhead of liberty revealed in an infinity of identities as various as one man one vote or one-party rule with no vote at all, or noncompulsory automobile seat belts or unisex public toilets.

My purpose in this book is not to attempt the articulation of any part of this vast sheaf of definitions but to consider whether or not the New World added something new to them and what, if so, this may have been.

The widespread general interest in the subject itself (or at least a dutiful simulation of interest) may presumably owe something, as has been hereinbefore so much asserted, to liberty's prevalence over so many centuries in the New World reports and their subsequent echoes hereinbefore so much cited. It is not easy to imagine (unless one reverts to a boethian liberty in theological costume) two years of public deliberations on the subject of popular liberty, under the auspices of the highest officials in the land, in the Paris of the Middle Ages, or in fact anywhere else in pre-Columbian Europe.

## 3. Property and Power

Movement of ideas back and forth across the Atlantic during the time of the American and French revolutions has been much discussed by historians — I am proposing that this movement began well before the usual dates ascribed to it, and that it included ideas leading to alterations in the Old World model of liberty.

Lord Acton, Isaiah Berlin, and others have been quoted in these pages on the existence of a fundamental difference between ancient and modern (post-Renaissance, post-Columbian) notions of liberty: if Columbus, Martyr, Vespucci, Léry, Ronsard, Montaigne, Acosta, Lejeune, Sagard, Du Tertre, Lahontan, Delisle, Lafitau, and the many such others leading to Rousseau played some part in the creation of this new and different conception of liberty, what exactly was it, how was it fundamentally different? In what way does it contribute to Berlin's opening of doors and leveling of obstacles, to the "practical" liberty of Acton?

Here once more attitudes toward property may be of significance. Acton dwells on the meaning of property in those of his notes which deal with the tragedy of the Gracchi (the Kennedy brothers of their time, tribunes of the plebs in Rome of the second century B.C., done to death, one after the other, by reactionary opponents of their efforts to relieve the oppressed poor by agrarian reform). Acton's notes emphasize the especially English article of faith (especially after Harrington and Locke) that property is power, even though hedged a bit by Francis Hutcheson's moral warning that "it gives not any just right to power."

"Power goes with property" (several times repeated), becomes, in Acton's notes on the Gracchi, "The struggle for power" equated with "a struggle for property."

Rome's deterioration followed, in Acton's view, the disappearance of the yeoman-farmer with his four or five acres ("backbone of the Republic") to be replaced by the great landowners "with their herds of slaves." It was this state of things, immense landholdings of the wealthy, cultivated only by slaves, that the Gracchi opposed.

Property in the ancient world was readily transformed into political power, political authority; liberty also was to be achieved only with power, in a conflict not at all for equal rights but for supremacy, the subjection of the antagonist. The idea of liberty was merely a tactic of attack in the struggle to gain power over others. Liberty was achieved when the "bad" ruler (your adversary) was thrown out and a "good" ruler (your choice) put in his place. Liberty was achieved, that is, by gaining political power. Those in power possessed liberty, their adversaries did not — obviously the adversaries to power did not possess liberty, or they would not have been fighting to attain it.

Liberty was attained with power, and power went with property. Anything at all worth having became, in typical Old World attitudes, property — including liberty itself ("A sort of property," wrote Shaftesbury in speaking of our "original native liberty," which, "methinks, is as material to us to the full, as that which secures us our lands and our revenues").

It was not until late in the seventeenth century, at some point following Grotius, wrote Acton, that "Indeed liberty became more sacred than property. No prescription availed against it."

# 4. Dominium

The Old World idea of property was well expressed by the Latin *dominium*: from "dominus" which derived from Sanskrit "domanas" —"he who subdues." "Dominus" in the Latin carried the same principal meaning, "one who has subdued," extending naturally to signify "master, possessor, lord, proprietor, owner." "Dominium" takes from "dominus" the sense of "absolute ownership," with a special legal meaning of "property, right of ownership" (so says Lewis and Short, *A Latin Dictionary*, 1969 edition). "Dominatio" extends the word into "rule, dominium," and — we're still with Lewis and Short — "among Republican Romans with an odious secondary meaning, unrestricted power, absolute dominium, lordship, tyranny, despotism." Political power grown from property — dominium — was, in effect, domination. (What good is power if you can't abuse it, runs a Sicilian proverb.)

Liberty, perforce, under these circumstances, was at its best a diffusion of dominium through the party in power, and thus partisan. At its best, in Ramsay's words, a narrow oligarchy.

The antagonist to be subjugated, the adversary to be dominated, the opponent to be crushed, was certainly to be excluded from liberty. Would you give liberty to a ravening tiger? (Best keep no lion in your house, said the Athenians, in denying freedom of action to Alcibiades and his party — but treat him like a lion if you do.)

Crucial, then, to Old World attitudes: liberty as power.

The question of the actual realization of liberty in the Periclean world — experiential understanding as compared to abstract Aristotelian theory of political liberty — has been debated for a long while. Benjamin Constant's dictum of 1819 that the concept of individual freedom was little known in ancient Greece still has the support of many specialists, and so does the opposing view, that "in Athens, and in many another Greek city too, the citizen was possessed of freedom, and knew that he was . . ." Berlin offers the qualification, "I do not say that the ancient Greeks did not in fact enjoy a great measure of what we should today call individual liberty. My thesis is only that the notion had not explicitly emerged, and was therefore not central to Greek culture, or, perhaps, any other ancient civilization known to us."

Acton finds this same point of particular interest — that at the time when the Greeks were most concerned with keeping their liberty, they had only an imperfect notion of free and uncoerced opinion, of the "libre arbitre." But it is in the "exercise" of the libre arbitre, as says Montesquieu among many others, that "philosophical liberty consists."

Apart from marsilian abstractions previously discussed, real notions of such liberty remained still unemerged throughout the Middle Ages; no words recur oftener in medieval public documents, says a twentieth-century authority, "than the words 'liberties,' 'rights,' 'privileges.' But the liberties, rights, privileges were reserved for certain classes, not for the people in the larger sense of the term . . . Serfdom was the lot of the masses . . . Religious and intellectual liberty, even personal liberty in the case of the masses, were practically unknown . . . The Renascence and the Reformation mark a superlatively important stage in the evolution of modern history. It was . . . by means of these movements that the aspiration after intellectual and religious liberty became a mighty factor in modern history."

It simply seems that the word and idea of liberty meant to the Ancients and Medievals something other than it means in modern times.

# 5. Communitas

In the New World an overriding political tradition — whether among the towering temples of Anahuac or the skin tents of Apacheria — seems to have been rooted in attitudes better expressed by the Latin *communitas*.

Although in fact few New World peoples, locked as so many were in group identity, could represent paradigms of individual liberty, still, the prevailing impression born in the Old World of reports from the New seems to have been that of a brand of liberty less concerned with dominium, as witness the innumerable references to masterlessness in New World accounts. Thus a concept less predicated upon liberty as power, less concerned with the subjugation of the antagonist, with adversarianism, with the crushing of the opponent, than with the tolerance that might spring from some such sense of communitas, some such sense of the ruling idea of community, of masterless cooperation requiring each to be as free as the other: the idea of liberty for others as well as for one's self a basic philosophy of living.

The reciprocating social machinery apparently common in Indian communities would presumably have operated well on some such basic attitude. "Symbiosis of all kinds of cultural activity obtained between segments of the population," in the words of a recent archaeological study dealing with ancient Mexico, "giving the city-state much integration and stability."

The right of property so sacred to the Old World was reported, century after century, to be a far less sacred matter in the New, as power over others was not usually reported as motivation for contentions. The fearful longing for security which (said Hobbes) is the source of the desire for power over other men seemed in the New World less than universal. From Vespucci onward, Europeans remarked on the motives, so seldom "serious" from a European standpoint, for so many Indian versus Indian conflicts. Violence triggered by profit, property, or conquest politics seems to have been less than typical; seemingly frivolous or puzzling motivations noted by early observers are explained by present day anthropologists in terms of "emotional" and "social equilibrium," or functions of kin group equilibrium. Even territorial confrontation seems to have resulted, as often as not, in the supine withdrawal of one side or the other; "the history of Indian America is riddled with instances of inexplicable (to us) pacifism."

A difference in attitude toward real property has been recognized for a long time as basic, in consideration of New World societies. Early nineteenth-century thinking quite often concentrated on property as the first giant step for the Indians toward "civilization." Thomas Jefferson, in a Washington speech to Indian leaders: ". . . temperance, peace, and agriculture . . . will prepare you to possess property . . ."

An American pamphleteer of the 1790s found "the establishment and management of private property" one of the principles "which distinguishes social from savage manners," a view usually extended to define all "primitive" societies. A traveler at the same period wrote of the Australians and Tasmanians, ". . . if the right of property excited in them a happy emulation" their social state would improve and their "temperament become more robust." A missionary of 1820, making a speaking tour to Indian communities across the United States, urged his listeners to divide their tribal lands, "each man to have a farm of his own, with a title which he can transmit to his posterity," and by this means prepare themselves for "all the blessings" which white people enjoyed. And an early anthropologist, speculating (in 1800) on the New World people and their alleged indifference toward money and possessions: "Trade would create in the savages new 'needs' and new 'desires' and these would lead them on to higher stages . . . witness of our happiness, our riches, and at the same time of our superiority, perhaps they will call us to their midst to show them the route which will conduct them to our state. What joy! What conquest!"

The distinctive New World liberty seemed to depend in part on a relative equality of condition; how this could appear to exist in conjunction with an actual social stratification has been examined previously (II. The New World: Vision and Reality). Such a relative equality would seem unlikely in conjunction with the fundamental sense of dominium expressed so clearly in the Old World by property.

An ominous side to the dominium of property was recognized in the Old World from earliest times. "Latifundia [great estates] would be the death of Italy," said Pliny, of the huge properties on which Acton blamed Rome's decline. The same illness has been modern Mexico's "most grievous" malady and is endemic over Latin America generally, passed on as an element of Spain's Roman heritage — latifundismo, even the name barely changed. Spain, the home of so many quintessential Romans (e.g. both Senecas, Martial), seems to have clung with singular tenaciousness to certain flavors of its Roman past — in Spain today (as Henry de Montherlant notices in his novel *The Chaos and the Night*) one man meeting another customarily seeks the "dominio" — one tries to stare the other down. But among the Pueblo Indians of the American Southwest (although long subject to Spanish influence) as among some other American Indian societies still today, it is not good manners to look directly into your interlocutor's eyes while talking to him. One looks down, or aside. The dominio is not valued in communitas.

Present day students have suggested, however, several instances of something similar to latifundia in Indian America, as in one of the categories of land tenure among the Aztecs seemingly approaching the nature of personal estates, even described in some instances as worked by serfs (mentioned above in II, 2, "Reality").

The Aztecs have been characterized by more than one writer as the "Romans of the New World." But the similarities, metaphorical rather than literal, tend to dissolve upon close examination: the Aztec "empire" was impermanent and volatile and the Aztecs' conquests motivated at least in conspicuous part by religion (to capture victims for sacrifice); the counterpart of personal "estates" becomes something rather closer to usufruct from portions of conquered territories, with no indication of rights residing in the "owner" to sell or convey real property to whomever he might wish.

The much earlier (and longer lasting) Toltec society may have approached more nearly some aspects of a Roman model (although lacking evidence of personal estates ), with a more extensive and apparently more permanent "empire" exercising a truly impressive range of influence both in space and time.

Inca empire was evidently more genuinely empire still, as has been previously described, but too thoroughly devoted to the sole interest of the central administration for much likelihood of pre-Columbian latifundismo; and in the Andes also, earlier peoples seem to have produced rather more influence of a sort of Roman stamp than the late-coming and comparatively shallow Inca, and with evidence here and there of exceedingly sharp class distinctions (or kin group distinctions or religious distinctions), although again without the noticeable presence of personal estates.

Other New World societies offer as a rule markedly fewer examples of real property as a possible expression of dominium, with certain exceptions noted (II, 2, above).

Most reports on the New World, as has been seen, placed great emphasis on this basic New World oddity of no private lands, no boundaries, no hedges, no dividing walls.

Investigators generally agree that truly primitive societies were all based on group ownership of real property. In the Old World that basis was altering to one of private ownership as early as the second millennium B.C., the Code of Hammurabi revealing "the rise of this new legal entity" defined by "detailed laws dealing with private property, its transfer, its loan, its bequest."

But the great civilizations and the considerable variety of other complex social structures in the New World seem to have remained pretty much untouched by this conception of private property so fundamental to the developing Old World.

What could have been at the root of such a basic divergence?

One possibility might lie in the keeping of flocks, an activity so ancient and widespread in the Old World but unknown in the New. Could a pastoral foundation of society, by its practical operation, tend to develop a persistent conception of private property? The thought seems not unreasonable.

# 6. Foundations

The matter is one of differences in attitude that are perhaps truly fundamental, at the very foundations of the two opposing worlds.

Dominium equals adversarianism equals overthrowing the enemy, the oppressor (I can be free only if he is not free).

Communitas equals reciprocity equals symbiosis equals acting with one another rather than against one another (I can not be free if he is not free).

"The doctrine of mutual respect, which is liberty . . ." says Acton.

The dualism so often encountered in studies of the prehistoric and historic structures of American Indian societies, the reciprocative arrangements by which various factions of more or less comparable power kept the society in operation, the religious color given to so many acts of life so that so many duties — even unto common ordinary toil — seemed rather participation in a sacred eternity, the significance given to activities that the businesslike Old World regarded as trivial if not downright play: all these appear to contribute to a cluster of attitudes basically different from the Old World's typical competitiveness, acquisitiveness, adversarianism.

Such variations may be absolutely fundamental, may date back to different turnings many long ages ago, in the mists of a very distant prehistory. Each of these basically different sets of attitudes may then have developed quite naturally along its own lines — the Old World devoted to a religion of property leading to preoccupation with business and dominium, thus authoritarianism, kingship, absolutism, and the ultimate act of dominium, full-scale war; the New World developing along lines more proper to a religion of communitas, leading to the world of reciprocating relationships outlined above.

It is not easy to recall, in our present world as saturated with protestations of love of liberty as was the medieval world with protestations of Christian piety, that in earlier Old World times absolutism had its chorus of enthusiastic supporters to match liberty's today. "What a beautiful institution, monarchy founded on Divinity!" exclaimed the seventh-century poet and historian Georgius Pisides, matching, from a thousand years' distance, Lichtenberg's rhapsodic view of the other side of the libertarian coin. Loys le Roy (among numerous others) devoted a book (1575) to the "Excellence du gouvernment royal." Jean Bodin reports sixteenth-century Europeans dazzled with admiration for the majesty of the monarch of Ethiopia who had even such a lordly official as his Grand Chancellor stripped naked and publicly whipped like any common slave.

Hobbes drew on this deep-rooted love of absolutism in his declaration that to attempt to limit the sovereign's power "was not only a crime but a sin; it was the sin of rebellion, which sums up in itself all sins . . ." Acton had much to say in his notes of the "theory of the outlaw" related to this assertion of absolutist infallibility. The wickedness of the outlaw was beyond the pale of persuasion. His guilt was moral and therefore mortal. He was fit only for eradication. The "conflict was with wickedness, not with another opinion." The State (or, in Acton's examples, the Papacy or the Holy Office) "committed the execution of its sentence to everybody who would carry it out. It invited society to fall upon those it had outlawed, and cut their throats wherever they could." A moral question became less a matter of feeling one was right than of questioning whether or not one had the right even to raise the question. "A man might be quite right; but he had no right to be right against authority."

Martin Luther wrote of the rebellious peasants of 1525 that in setting themselves against the governing authorities they had forfeited body and soul, "for God wants people to be loyal and to do their duty. . . . anyone who can be proved to be a seditious person is an outlaw before God and the emperor; and whoever is the first to put him to death does right and well. For if a man is in open rebellion, everyone is both his judge and his executioner . . . Therefore let everyone who can, smite, slay, and stab, secretly or openly, remembering that nothing can be more poisonous, hurtful, or devilish than a rebel."

Absolutist states in the present day have been likewise accused of a tendency to regard political dissension as sin. Police inquisitions sent thousands of dissenters or suspected dissenters to concentration camps and death under the Nazi and Fascist and Stalinist regimes, while the later "Chinese administration considers any opposition a sacrilege . . . distinction is not made between the moral and intellectual aspect . . ." Or in an official Russian statement of recent date, "Only that is moral and democratic which serves the construction of socialism."

The idea of authoritarian domination — "despotism, albeit by the best or the wisest" — has accordingly been suggested as a "central Western tradition in ethics and politics . . ."

If current notions of liberty result in some part from collision between these two religions, these two ethics, these two visions of the purpose of life, of right behavior — dominium and communitas — then our modern world, the genuinely new world born in some part of this collision, may be supposed to reflect in some ways the various lines of force therein colliding, and those most clearly of New World origin should be to some extent recognizable.

The chronic conflict between absolutism and libertarianism, between authoritarianism and liberalism, that has been at the core of Western history since the seventeenth century and seems to show signs of remaining, under other aliases, one of the central conflicts of the future, might reveal, if regarded in the light of a generalized conflict between dominium and communitas, one of the more probable areas of New World intrusion.

The differences in fundamental attitude that underlie such a basic conflict no doubt remain still so deep as to resist examination on a conscious level; no doubt we are never quite fully aware of the attitudes and beliefs most fundamental to our lives, or perhaps the disjunction is only in the language that gives halting form to our troubled perception, in the "deep disquietudes," in Wittgenstein's phrase, of perception garbled by miscarried language. The New World intrusions I speak of here are most often only visible, I think, as distorted and dreamlike echoes of the probable New World forces present at their points of origin or during their long evolution.

Some factors usually believed to be New World products and sometimes of far-reaching effect on Old World history — syphilis, for example — may not have originated in the New World at all (syphilis is still under debate, the "field is still wide open for those who wish to theorize" about its origin).

A number of New World contributions that altered the Old World in certain direct material respects are of course clearly evident and indisputable — among them tobacco, chocolate, rubber (to revolutionize among other things our world of sports, with ball games), a considerable variety of drugs medicinal and otherwise, from quinine to curare, from peyote to cocaine, and a great variety of vegetables, from maize and white potatoes to tomatoes and peanuts, that must have revised radically Old World diet. And one fairly obvious candidate as a recognizable New World element in social thought, as has been hereinbefore so amply proposed and instanced, may be simply the omnipresence today of the subject of liberty itself, and its corollary equality.

But as often as not, maybe more often than not, what seem to be possible New World strands are doubled and redoubled back upon themselves, snarled and entangled to such a degree that they may seem by now to say the opposite of what they seemed to say upon first appearance. The New World's indirect part in the rise of capitalism, for an example previously mentioned — by the flood of its wealth, particularly silver, into the Old World — has been for a long while widely recognized, but the New World's further indirect part in the worst excesses of laissez-faire capitalism — committed, from the time of Colbert's recognition of the term, in the name of liberty — has still to be analyzed.

Crucial to such an analysis, and to the entire problem of New World influences on Old World ideas of liberty, is the frequency and gravity of subsequent distortion of such influences. Most significantly, concepts of universal liberty and equality from the New World seem to have suffered profound sea-change when set ashore on the Old World's rock-ribbed mine and thine.

# 7. Property and Oppression

The apparent dilemma of liberty and equality (how attain equality without curtailing the liberty of the strong, the powerful) may well have been thrown into extraordinarily heightened relief by this unnatural mating of liberty and property.

Liberty, when imposed upon a base of property, seems forcibly related to oppression, property being originally won by force, held by force, and in our tradition usually surrendered only to a superior, i.e., richer or stronger, force.

Armed men, provided by the state, stand ready to support at any moment the rights of property, to exclude the weak from the property (and the property's profit) of the strong (assuming that it is the strong, the aggressive, the clever, who inevitably become property's majority stockholders), to support thereby the exploitation of the propertyless by the propertied, to eject trespassers and throw into prison anyone who (with a power weaker than the state's) challenges this right sacred to Old World ways. Said Locke (liberty's champion against the king-worship of Hobbes) in his *Second Treatise of Civil Government*, 1690: "Government has no other end but the preservation of property."

"There is nothing which so generally strikes the imagination, and engages the affections of mankind, as the right of property," wrote Blackstone, although "there is no foundation in nature or in natural law, why a set of words upon parchment should convey the dominion of land . . ." And yet, "Necessity begat property: and, in order to insure that property, recourse was had to civil society, which brought along with it a long train of inseparable concomitants; states, government, laws, punishments . . ."

The rise and extension of the idea of liberty attached to the tradition of property — so that a property owner became less and less restricted in the free and exclusive use of his property — inevitably strengthened property's power. Blackstone also reminds us that in England it was not until the time of Henry VIII that one could will even a portion of his holdings in land to whomever one wished, and not until after the Restoration "that the power of devising real property became so universal as at present."

Naturally the strong, so redoubtably assisted by the state in their "liberty" to exclude the weak from their property and its profit, grow always stronger with their property's irresistible increase, the tendency of property to become self-reinforcing being squarely opposed to the idea of equality of opportunity.

Said Emerson in the 1840s, "As long as our civilization is essentially one of property, of fences, of exclusiveness, it will be mocked by delusions. Our riches will leave us sick . . ."

Property has become, wrote, a hundred years ago, the pioneer anthropologist Lewis Henry Morgan, "an unmanageable power . . . The time will come, nevertheless, when human intelligence will rise to the mastery over property, and define the relations of the state to the property it protects, as well as the obligations and the limits of the rights of its owners. The interests of society are paramount to individual interests, and the two must be brought into just and harmonious relations. A mere property career is not the final destiny of mankind, if progress is to be the law of the future as it has been of the past . . . because such a career contains the elements of self-destruction. Democracy in government, brotherhood in society, equality in rights and privileges, and universal education, foreshadow the next higher plane of society . . . It will be a revival, in a higher form, of the liberty, equality and fraternity of the ancient gentes."

In the same epoch Herbert Spencer, a passionate defender of property and its total liberty, could nevertheless foresee a possible future when — comparing private property to the ownership of man by man, slavery, which had been wiped out by an advance in civilization — private ownership of land might also disappear "at a stage still more advanced," and "the primitive ownership of land by the community . . . be revived." This primitive community ownership, in Spencer's analysis, had "lapsed" with "the development of coercive institutions."

For the present our present and still propertied world seems to depend more and more upon blunt force to impose upon itself this tangled dream of liberty ensnarled with property, the Old World and the New at their most inextricable.

"In the inspired phrasing of the Declaration of Independence [writes Perry Miller] the conventional trilogy of the English eighteenth century — life, liberty, and property — was changed into life, liberty, and the pursuit of happiness. Thomas Jefferson left to posterity a conundrum, but the mass of American lawyers never doubted that his happiness was a polite genteelism for the acquisition of wealth."

And indeed conservative American lawyers stretched Blackstone inside out, quite falsely affirming him to have shown that property was a law which "nature herself has written upon the hearts of mankind . . . the notion of property is universal . . . The right of property . . . is founded in the law of nature, and is antecedent to all civil regulation . . ." The law "will not authorize the least violation of it; no, not even for the general good of the whole community." Blackstone was thusly "improved" into "an explicit denial of the contractual idea upon which the American society was supposedly founded."

American law in actual practice, from colonial times when English colonists created at least some of their law "afresh" through the nineteenth century, was not, however, so property minded as these citations might lead one to expect; perhaps its most striking difference from Old World law lay in liberalizing the "release of creative energy" of individuals and groups rather than protecting a status quo based on landed interest. This revision of the "antidevelopmental" eighteenth-century view went so far as to embrace the drastic action of permitting "destruction of older forms of property by newer agents of economic development."

But the doctrine of giving property first place at the trough of liberty continued in evidence — in the United States of the 1850s the argument was sometimes advanced that the right to make money from slavery was thus supported by the Constitution — and is still evident in the particular sort of liberty demanded by the political right in the United States, the unrestricted freedom to make money, the unrestricted liberty to profit from one's property, frequently allied to the principle of "developmental" law referred to above when that developmental law is sufficiently respectful of the rights of property, and frequently referred to therefore as the freedom of "productive capacity." This line of thought, descended from the eighteenth-century French "Physiocrats" and English radical Dissenters with their insistence on the complete freedom of economic enterprise, is remarkably prominent at this moment in American politics, apparently with the eighteenth-century thinking quite unchanged. Says a right wing American politician, ". . . individual liberty includes the individual's economic freedom and the Founding Fathers knew it. They had good reason to leave the productive activities of men as free as possible." In this respect today's American right wing regards itself as the special champion of liberty, a special liberty perhaps bearing a sinistral kinship with certain American "anarchist" ideas of a few generations ago such as those of Josiah Warren, Lysander Spooner, or Benjamin Tucker, ideas generally bent toward the interest of private property and laissez faire economics. "Libertarian" has been adopted as the name of a current American political party dedicated to "the sancity of the individual and of private property."

The radical self-interest evident in Herbert Spencer's "moral law" of an exclusive right to one's property and its "sources of gratification," and the immorality of "meddling legislation" exacting money from that property to temper the suffering of the "good-for-nothing" and the "dissolute" was in fairly direct descent, via Joseph Priestley's laissez faire influence, from the devotion to radical liberty of Paine and Godwin.

It is significant that this primacy of liberty-for-property gives short shrift to justice, as does the absolutist primacy of order. The three reference points of justice, liberty (for property), and order, seem invariably to fall, like a neatly manipulated shell game, with justice losing, whether from the propertied view of liberty (for property's profit) above all or from the absolutist view of order above all. (In the executioner reposes "all the grandeur" of society, asserted the early-nineteenth-century reactionary Joseph de Maistre: "Remove from the world this incomprehensible agent; in an instant order gives way to chaos; thrones crash and society disappears. God is the author of punishment as well as of sovereignty.")

Justice, it would seem, is no essential concomitant of liberty, nor is any other moral quality — liberty need not at all imply being virtuous, fraternal (the rambunctiously free Etienne Dolet was said to have been so hard to get along with that even his best friends couldn't stand him), or even civil. Liberty, equality, fraternity need have nothing in common but the slogan. One can be free and antisocial — one of Berlin's defining points of liberty. Individual ideas of "happiness" may easily be antisocial to a point undreamed of in authoritarian times. The last lines of the "Internationale," written by Eugène Pottier in a Montmartre garret during the "Bloody Week" of the Paris Commune in 1871, declare the earth the property of [working-] men; the idle can go live someplace else — but Paul Lafargue, Marx's son-in-law, authored a book in defense of the "Right to Laziness." A whole platoon of more or less celebrated names (Saint-Just, Metternich, Paul Valery) have been attached to the remark that happiness was (within recent times) a new idea for Europe.

Nor of course need liberty imply any commitment to order — or vice versa. In some European thinking the two are instead regarded as the opposite ends of a continuum, so that indulgence to disorder on the part of a government may be an index of its dedication to liberty — while in Maistre's view (like that of Hobbes) "even abuses of government were better than disorder" and Acton contradicted both these contradictory preferences by supposing that liberty "always supposes order . . ." Acton adds elsewhere that although there is the "Idea that Society diminishes Liberty . . . in truth it is a cond. of its existence." And from the New World comes an observation perhaps adding still another side to this many-sided disputation: it was an apparent "obedience to the unenforceable" among the Maya that indicated they "must have measured high" in the scale of civilization.

The subject of justice may have had the starring role in antiquity that the subject of liberty seems to hold today. The Stoics maintained that justice was the product of a law of nature, independent of human laws, above human laws; the Sophists argued that there was no higher law than human law, that man was the measure of all things. A principle of justice had to be subjective to at least some degree, a subjectivity that could perhaps bring it more into concert with absolutism than could be the case with any concept of the more objective principle of liberty. Says Acton on Aristotle, "He seems not to see that the exclusive predominance of any one principle is absolutism."

# 8. Totalitarians

Three Indian tourists talking to Montaigne at Rouen in the autumn of 1562 (they may have been some of the Tupi people left over from Rouen's Fête Brésilienne of 1550) marveled that the poor of Europe did not take the rich "by the throte" (in the Florio translation of Shakespeare's day) "or set fire on their house" and a violent offshoot of New World egalitarianism has perhaps been present in the creation by explosive revolution of a number of the brave new worlds bouncing about in post-Rousseauian history.

Marx and Engels were much taken by the American Indian studies of Lewis Henry Morgan, finding in them support for their theories of history, particularly Morgan's point that primitive society is organized on a basis of family relationships while modern society is based on property relationships. Marx made notes for a study on Morgan he didn't live to complete, but Engels used Morgan's ideas in several later writings, including a book (*The Origin of the Family, Private Property, and the State in the Light of the Researches of Lewis Henry Morgan*, 1884) that produced yet one more run through of the Indian rhapsody: "No soldiers, no gendarmes or police, no nobles, kings, regents, prefects, no judges, no prison, no lawsuits . . . There cannot be any poor or needy . . . All are equal and free — the women included . . . And what men and women such a society breeds is proved by the admiration inspired in all white people who have come into contact with unspoiled Indians, by the personal dignity, uprightness, strength of character and courage of these barbarians . . ." Engels added, in a note to the 1888 edition of the *Communist Manifesto*, that the significant classlessness of Indian society had been revealed by L. H. Morgan, whose "decisive discovery" led "us to understand" the true nature of the "gens."

But it is possible that with the establishment of Marxist-Leninist states the Old World has once more stubbornly adapted New World attitudes to its own purposes, present day socialist states ostensibly eradicating the bugbear of property but actually — like the absolute monarchy of old — taking all property into the hands of a single dominant and exclusive party, the ruling apparatus. Property is thereby once again transformed into power and authority, and the propertyless may make use of it only on the sufferance — revocable at any instant — of the rulers. The similarity to the absolutism of seventeenth-century Europe in the application of certain restrictions is striking — individuals if they wish to depart from the absolutist state must obtain specific permission from the ruling apparatus and must in some cases pay to the ruling apparatus the cost of anything taken with them (unto the cost of their education), while movement within the country from one place of residence to another or one job to another is likewise likely to be closely regulated (and once again hunting privileges — and sporting arms — are likely to be closely restricted); their rights, as said a seventeenth-century jurist in speaking of the common people of Bohemia, simply cease to exist in being vested with their property in the hands of their rulers.

The basic dilemma between liberty and equality — when superimposed on a foundation of property — may be even more visible here, the socialist ideal aiming less for liberty than equality, an equality forcibly imposed on all other than the exclusive and sharply defined ruling class (as the liberty of laissez faire capitalism sustains by force the inequality between propertied and propertyless). Acton remarked on this, mentioning in his notes that in 1848 there could be no alliance between republicans and socialists on the basis of liberty since that was not what the socialists were seeking — "But on the basis of equality." He also reached a conclusion (similar to some Marxist-Leninist views today) that the "Movement of 1789 toward liberty" was "not quite genuine."

It may not be too unreasonable to see Old World tendencies toward domination, adversarianism, authoritarianism, in all sorts of modern dress, from the Vincennes student orator to the pious freedom fighters of Saint-Nicolas-du-Chardonnet and to many another (such as the right wing American "Libertarians") in between. Old World resistance to the idea of liberty has adopted the wisdom, it would seem, of calling its own goal "real" liberty — but always a liberty based on force, on power, on privilege, on, in the final analysis, dominium.

Sir James Fitzjames Stephen, who used his experience in criminal law to criticize John Stuart Mill's "On Liberty," states the Old World position with clarity in writing that Hobbes (who was his idol) "saw clearly what very few people see even now, that liberty is a negative idea, and that what is usually claimed under that name is not liberty but dominion." He found the extension of the suffrage a question "not of liberty, but of the distribution of political power."

Power, said Stephen, precedes liberty — "liberty, from the very nature of things, is dependent upon power."

He saw Mill as a sentimentalist gone soft at the center, and as for Rousseau: "I know hardly anything in literature so nauseous as Rousseau's expressions of love for mankind when read in the light of his confessions." He particularly despised Mill's views on equality for women, and found the whole idea of equality, like the idea of liberty, "a big name for a small thing."

Said an acquaintance (Sir Thomas Ferrer), Stephen had "lust for dominion, pride of race, and the cult of force as the essence of life." He worshiped war as one of the formative principles which lie at the root of national existence, as "the *ultima ratio* not only of kings but of human society in all its shapes." He would have loved to be Napoleon, would have liked in 1848 to fire "grapeshot down every street in Paris till the place ran with blood." (Sir James was an uncle of Virginia Woolf, who presumably found her sensitivity elsewhere in the family.)

He wrote, "Strength, in all its forms, is life and manhood. To be less strong is to be less of a man, whatever else you may be . . . I suppose the ardent wish to be stronger than other people and to have one's own will against them is the deepest and most general of human desires." He maintained that his opinions reflected Hobbes's "great school of thought which at present has possession of the greater part of the intelligence of Europe."

So it may have had then, a hundred years ago, and so it may have had to an even greater extent somewhat later, and so it may have to some extent now. "War is to the man what maternity is to the woman," said Benito Mussolini in 1932, and offered as his response to "liberty, equality, fraternity," the Italian Fascist slogan "believe, obey, combat." Asserted Mussolini, "Mankind is tired of liberty" and echoed French Fascist intellectuals of the same epoch, "Liberty is exhausted." And wrote in the same epoch André Gide, at that time a professing Marxist, "I lack something: belief in liberty . . . The notion of liberty, as it is taught us, seems to me singularly false and pernicious. And if I approve the Soviet constraint, I must likewise approve the Fascist discipline."

One result of the dominion in modern times of these strong views on dominium: "Reliable estimates put at about seventy million the figure of those dead through war, revolution and famine in Europe and Russia between 1914 and 1945 . . . Much of the crisis of identity and society that has overshadowed twentieth-century history comes from an impulse toward totalitarian politics."

Hobbes's Old World spirit asserting that it is security men want is reaffirmed, but in the name of liberty (freedom from want), by "Real freedom means good wages, short hours, security in employment, good houses," from the British Fascist leader Oswald Mosley in 1936; and by a similar statement from Josef Stalin at the same time that real liberty exists only "where there is no unemployment, no poverty, where a person does not tremble because tomorrow he may lose his job, his home, his food."

What good is freedom on an empty stomach? demanded Buffier's spokesman for Old World skepticism in 1720 — or, as apologists for absolutism put it today, Bread before liberty! "Erst kommt das Fressen, dann kommt die Moral" (First comes feeding, then morality), said Bertolt Brecht. Economic security and material prosperity as conditions nec-essary for liberty are sometimes also used, as in testimony cited earlier before the French parliamentary commission, to define not only a basis for liberty but liberty itself. For is not liberty nonexistent unless one is able to take advantage of it?

Similar concerns, handled in a more sophisticated manner, have led to the argument that freedom is only an illusion anyway, the nature and disposition of the real world preventing, by subtle if not always sinister means, its exercise, so that after all a benevolent authoritarianism is to be preferred in its place.

Or, say others, liberty simply can not exist in our modern world, on the grounds of lack of efficiency if nothing else. That the "abnormal complexity and sophistication" of modern life has made impossible the simple virtues of old has been asserted for at least some two thousand years, and so it is today with freedom: in "a complex society" (such as today's) "the very possibility of freedom is in doubt."

Or, say still other exponents of post-Rousseauian second thoughts, at least liberty must be banished temporarily. Friedrich Engels: "As long as the proletariat *needs* the State, it needs it *not in the interests of freedom, but in order to crush its enemies, and when it becomes possible to speak of freedom, the State, as such, will cease to exist.*" (The italics are not mine.) Or Leon Trotsky: "No organization except the army has ever controlled men with such severe compulsion as does the state organiza-tion of the working class in the difficult period of transition . . . The state, before disappearing, assumes . . . the most ruthless form . . . embraces authoritatively the life of the citizens in every direction." Lenin's often stated preference for dictatorship was nevertheless based on an assumption that "the coercion, violence, executions, the total suppression of individual differences, the rule of a small, virtually self-appointed minority, were necessary only in the interim period, only so long as there was a powerful enemy to be destroyed."

Is the insistence on an enemy to be "crushed," an opponent to be destroyed, an evil foe for whose defeat all power must be granted to the rulers, an inhuman adversary upon whom can be placed all our fears and frustrations and hatreds, be he "Communist" or "Fascist" or "Jew" or "imperialist" or "hegemonist" or "revisionist" ("heretic") — is this in-sistence a stubborn persistence of typical Old World adversarianism? If so, such insistence might seem to indicate that adversarianism in itself may represent a tradition as strong, possibly as deep-rooted and sacred, as the tradition of property-authority in itself — the two separate al-though as previously noticed most straitly linked: the adversary, the op-ponent, being a rival for power, which is to say (in Acton's equation) for property. A rival, an adversary, of such importance that one's relationship to the adversary, rather than one's own relationship to life, becomes the true reason for being.

As a rule, in the ancient Old World, such adversarian sentiment was (as has been also previously noticed) associated with a struggle for an ex parte liberty frankly recognized as the liberty (or privilege) of power. Its modern expression, however, seems to appear more often in a wildly contradictory variety of modern freedoms as various as "social" liberty depending upon equality of material benefit or liberty of "enterprise" depending upon "free" exploitation of weaker elements of society, in ex parte lines of the most compliant flexibility.

# 9. Definitions

Liberty as a major issue in academic philosophy, very much as was for so many centuries the question of the nature or existence of God, seems to have become conspicuous between the time of Hobbes and the time of Mill, whose argument for freedom rested on the proposition that truth could be found only under conditions of liberty. Following this line, Acton argued (in an extension of Augustine's theory "that liberty belongs only to virtue" and that therefore "only the good are free — only the truth has a claim to freedom") that "If truth is not absolute, then liberty is the condition of truth." And that as the belief became prevalent "that absolute truth was unattainable" but only relative and approximate, this belief assured "the reign of liberty."

His optimistic forecast of a victory for liberty was pinned by Acton to a belief in the triumph of the freedom of conscience, a freedom denied in the past on the authority of Aquinas, who could not allow religious error to be a matter for free individual choice. But if the state (says Acton) can exclude conscience in matters of faith it is ultimately free to do as it likes in all matters. "Extend the domain of conscience to religious error, and then only is liberty possible." This extension was accomplished in "the golden age of conscience," for which achievement Acton credited Bishop Butler, Rousseau, Kant, Fichte, Channing, Vinet, Shaftesbury, Ramsay, Kierkegaard. "Liberalism ultimately founded on idea of conscience. Our conscience . . . exists in each of us. It is limited by the conscience of others . . . It respects the conscience of others. Therefore it tends to restrict authority and to enlarge liberty. It is the law of self government." And as such (Acton points out) precisely the law Hobbes wished to make subject to monarchical, not philosophical or ecclesiastical, authority.

This law in action, respecting the conscience of others ("faith in reason [as says Karl Popper] is not only a faith in our own reason, but also — and even more — in that of others"), provided still one more definition of liberty: "The history of liberty is the condition of minorities."

The various and contradictory definitions of liberty already mentioned could suffice, almost by themselves, to outline the major issues of our time. Many more definitions still, all but an infinity, clamor for a hearing. The vast proliferation of such definitions might hint that liberty, not as idea only but as reality, has actually been emerging here and there in our present world. One might imagine the seventeenth-century German serfs would have had less trouble in defining it. But buried in writhing serpents of words, liberty as Laocoön may be a key symbol of our age.

Wrote Montesquieu (in *The Spirit of the Laws*), "There is no word that admits of more various significations, and has made more varied impressions on the human mind, than that of Liberty." And says Berlin, the meaning of "liberty" or "freedom" (he uses both interchangeably) "is so porous that there is little interpretation that it seems able to resist" and notes that there are "more than two hundred senses of this protean word recorded by historians of ideas."

One attempt to get to bedrock in this mountain of definitions is via "reference to three items: the agents who are free, the restrictions or limitations they are free from, and what it is they are free to do or not to do . . ."

The second and third notes of this triad are extendable into two distinct sorts of liberty, sometimes spoken of as "positive" liberty and "negative" liberty, defined by Berlin as "What, or who, is the source of control or interference that can determine someone to do, or be, this rather than that?" And "What is the area within which the subject — a person or group of persons — is or should be left to do or be what he is able to do or be, without interference by other persons?"

Maybe these could be more rudely stated as the liberty of choosing your master (positive liberty) or the liberty of doing without a master (negative liberty).

This distinction was visible to Rousseau and to some others of his contemporaries, such as the Abbé Gabriel Bonnot de Mably (who rivaled Rousseau in his denunciation of property and in his eventual influence on the course of the French Revolution and who, like Rousseau, found in the New World some of his exemplary sources). Says Rousseau in *The Social Contract*: "The populace of England believes it is free; it is greatly deceived, it is only free during the election of members of parliament; as soon as they are elected it is enslaved, it is nothing." But the distinction seems not to have been visible to others (Locke, for example) perhaps more firmly rooted in Old World dominium.

A case can be made for rather more New World coloring (masterlessness) in the second of these liberties (doing without a master); and rather more Old World coloring (the adversarian tradition of overthrowing a despot to put a "good" ruler in his place) in the first (the freedom to choose one's master). The apparent common impression today of liberty in general, with its emphasis on masterlessness (as sings Walt Whitman, "I am for those that have never been master'd,/ For men and women whose tempers have never been master'd,/ . . . persons who never knew how it felt to stand in the/ presence of superiors"), seems in this fundamental respect predominantly New World oriented.

Reference to three further items: property, the individual, and the community, might be of use in a more detailed examination of differences between Old World and New World conceptions of liberty. The three-sided figure constructed from these entities seems capable of providing, by varying the relationships between its components, fairly effective models of the varying traditions of liberty in the New World and the Old. The operating factor here, it should be noted, appears to be differences in the relationships rather than differing identities of the three items themselves.

## 10. Liberty and the New World

The vision of liberty so long associated with the New World and its people was gradually transferred to European colonies in America and eventually, not surprisingly, to the new United States. Libertarian ideas that, since Lahontan, had become increasingly fashionable for Europe and its philosophes, were brought to reality in revolutionary America, most explicitly in its Declaration of Independence and Constitution and in the constitutions of the several states — documents of intense French interest and enthusiasm. America was for France of that moment "a gigantic laboratory" of freedom, sending an "electric shock" (said Condorcet) that would be felt around the world, from the "banks of the Neva to those of the Guadalquivir." The New World, a "place of hopes and dreams ever since its discovery," was summed up in three words by St. John Crèvecoeur, "Bread and liberty," the conjunction rather than the previously-mentioned preposition ("Bread before liberty") serving as the stamp of the time.

The one most notable difference between the American Declaration of Independence of 1776 and the French Declaration of the Rights of Man of 1789 dealt with property, ignored in the Declaration of Independence but underlined as a sacred and inalienable right in revolutionary France. The Americans, said Pierre-Victor Malouet, hadn't needed "this precaution: they have taken man in the bosom of nature, and present him to the universe in his primitive sovereignty. But this American society newly formed is composed, in reality, of property owners already accustomed to equality . . . not having found in the land which they cultivate any trace of feudalism. Such men were without doubt prepared to receive liberty in all its energy; because their tastes, their customs, their position called them to democracy."

The French philosophes had looked to "enlightened" monarchs to put their views in practice, but "only in America did the Philosophes have the happiness to be kings in their own right."

These "modern liberties," said Emile de Laveleye, and spelled them out: no man or group of men shall have power over conscience, no one may be prosecuted for religious opinions, legislative representatives shall be chosen by secret vote, judges elected, trials decided by juries, no one may be imprisoned for debt, taxes must be voted by those who pay them, "were first formulated in the U.S. constitutional principles."

Maitland, however, wrote of the "conventional" theory of government — i.e., the modern theory of government by consent of the governed and its alliance with the doctrine that all men are equal, thus when the governed give their consent every man is to count for one — that, although the idea appeared late in history, the "constitutions of the American states cannot be appealed to in support of the historical truth of the theory, for they were the results of a belief in the theory."

Some few years still before the birth of the United States, the "physiocrat" Dupont de Nemours predicted that in no more than one hundred and fifty years America would form "an empire more powerful than is all Europe today" (it might be worth noting, notes Victoria Ginger, that the Old World expressed even a panegyric on New World liberty in terms of "empire" and "power"), and foresaw there liberty and equality for all with no special privilege for any, be they "Virginian, Pennsylvanian, New Yorker, Marylander, Louisianan, Mexican, Savage, European, African, White, Black, Red, Bearded, Unbearded . . ."

Diderot, as impressed as were his colleagues by the program of the "insurgents of America," gave advice that became customary among European friends of the new United States: "After centuries of general oppression, may the revolution which has just taken place across the seas, in offering to all the inhabitants of Europe an asylum against fanaticism and tyranny, teach those who govern men the legitimate use of their authority! May these brave Americans who would rather have seen their wives outraged, their children slaughtered, their dwellings destroyed, their fields ravaged, their cities burned, would rather pour out their blood and die, than lose the smallest portion of their liberty, guard against a too enormous growth and unequal division of riches, guard against luxury, idleness and ease and corruption of morals, and thus succeed in maintaining their liberty and the lasting existence of their government!" Advice that was reprinted almost word for word in Raynal, the scorn for degenerate Americans of previous editions now erased, now that Americans had become liberty's heroes.

And advice still being repeated a century later by Laveleye, who however (along with such others as Tocqueville) added a suggestion that is today just beginning to find substantial support — to reduce centralized power in favor of local authorities.

A preponderance of New World coloring might seem to tend toward the open society, the plural society on the American model, with its concomitant freedoms: of opinion, of election, of behavior ("a network of values that includes such notions as personal rights, civil liberties, the sanctity of the individual personality, the importance of privacy, personal relations, and the like") — and its concomitant problems when brought into fusion with the Old World's thine and mine. This as against the rather more heavy Old World shading of a monolithic one-party system, the closed society, with its tendency toward absolutism and relentless adversarianism and its concomitant notable export of, in Gueudeville's word, conquerantism.

Conceivably one could construct a speculative picture of the present condition over the world at large of what has been called here the New World idea of liberty, where Old World resistance appears to be more than holding its own, with closed societies of one sort or another, many so fully closed as to be totalitarian (freedom of conscience totally rejected, freedom of action totally controlled), in a steadily growing majority, even though lip service to the name of liberty (rather like a kind of universal twentieth-century incantation) continues everywhere unabated.

Extending still further such speculation, one could hazard certain inferences as to separate New World elements in these two systems, open and closed: would authoritarian forms of administration indicate an Old World parentage? But might controlled economic systems be directed toward a New World brand of social equality?

It is worth repeating, again, that there is no suggestion any such distinctions or their lines of origin are in the least neat or clear. They must be presumed to result from a number of complex factors operating over considerable periods of time, factors therefore that must be by now, if not hopelessly entangled, at any rate correspondingly diffuse. My modest intention is only to bring into relief one such factor that has not heretofore been given its due: the influence of an emphasis on certain notions of liberty in reports from the New World.

The usual "great" names associated with such values as liberty, liberalism, equality, and with distinctions between these values, are themselves contradictory, more often than not, in their most representative work; Pufendorf, for example, or Rousseau or Kant, all so deeply involved in the conflicts surrounding the emergence of modern European liberalism, present thickets of contradictions upon even a cursory analysis of their thought. As Acton put it, "Theory of conscience — did not secure entire liberality in its teachers — Briller, Rousseau, Kant, Fichte, were not liberals."

Pufendorf, favoring a strong centralized but secularized authority, held that "liberty in general denotes the status of those who serve merely the state and not another fellow-citizen in addition." Kant advocated liberty and equality for all, and at the same time the necessity of a superior authority and "of a measure of inequality for human progress . . ." Some German thinkers who were influenced by Kant's politics "took him to furnish a moral basis for political obedience, some to furnish a moral basis for political liberty . . ." The particular problem of freedom in Germany grew out of the long struggle of local princes against the authority of the empire and resulted in the brittle alloy "of one conception of liberty that could be realized only within the authoritarian state and of another that could be realized only in an absolute realm beyond all states . . . It has been traced back to Luther and up to Hitler."

Rousseau's apparent inconsistencies, between the *Discourse on Inequality* and the *Encyclopédie* article on political economy published the same year, between the liberalism of the *Discourse on Inequality* and the legalism of *The Social Contract* and the proposal for a Corsican constitution that appears to contradict both of them, and parts of *Emile* that seem to gainsay them all, are notorious. Goethe, whose *Werther* is credited with introducing the furious psychological freedom of German Romanticism, nevertheless remarked, in his conversations with Eckermann (January 18, 1827), "Freedom is an odd thing, and every man has enough of it, if he can only satisfy himself . . . The citizen is as free as the nobleman, when he restrains himself within the limits which God appointed by placing him in that rank" — an all too typical statement of European reaction. But it was also Goethe who pronounced what was probably the most acute and has been probably the most quoted comparison of Voltaire and Rousseau, "Voltaire: a world that is ending; Rousseau: a world that is beginning."

## 11. Xenokresis

My point, to repeat it still once again, is simply that this all but universal modern interest, all but endlessly entangled as it is, in equality and liberty, in a "natural" right to liberty, seems to contain something new, new as of recent centuries. It seems evident that the western world's concept of liberty changed at some point following contact with the New World. Maybe as early as More's *Utopia*, maybe — Michelet's belief — with the Regency in France, maybe (the popular impression) later still, with the American and French revolutions. Such a change is of course no proof of "influence," a birth scarcely being proof of paternity. But it seems not unreasonable, in view of the considerable evidence gathered in the foregoing pages, that this altered concept owes something, perhaps quite a bit of something, to reports from the New World.

Clear and direct influence from the set of attitudes thus reported was, to emphasize this point again, not consciously recognized. Modern students of history specifically deny it: Indian influence on the history of America, said Frederick Jackson Turner, was limited to a "retardation of [white] advance, compelling society to organize and consolidate in order to hold the frontier; training it in military discipline; determining the rate of advance, particularly at the points where the mountain barriers broke down . . ." And students specializing in the history of law deny it even more specifically still: "We confronted no elaborate, deepset pattern of Indian institutions which we must overcome or assimilate, unless one counts the influence of frontier warfare upon our security measures."

While it would be much too simplistic to argue that any New World coloration produced distinct hard edged realities, might not the general view previously outlined of absolutism versus liberalism, dominium versus communitas, seem at several points evocative of Old World adversarianism — the dominium of the classic world and of feudalism, the church-and-state absolutism of the Renaissance, the secular absolutism of the seventeenth century at the entrance cue of liberalism — versus the flimsy community states of the New?

The millions dead or ravaged in Europe in the wars of religion, in the Thirty Years' War, in the wars of Louis XIV — is it any surprise millions more were smashed in the New World by this customary route of Old World power?

Might not liberalism as materialistically weak, weak both in defense and offense, weak as an integral part of its nature in permitting free penetration, free dissension, free exodus, fearfully weak in comparison with the ironclad monster of absolutism (with its climax industry of conquerantism), recall the actual collision of the New World with the conquering Old?

If for the sake of argument these points be granted, the puzzling question then arises: how can it be that from Old World conquerantism in sixteenth-century America onward this weak and flimsy communitas has not yet been utterly eradicated, absolutism still not the sole winner and absolute world champion?

Not only does the influence of communitas still live but (if any of this is correct) subtle modifications of the reciprocating New World engine have steadily contributed to the perseverance of its liberalism, a spiritual puissance, fortified by concepts of negative liberty, that has survived through the centuries — centuries during which absolutism has attacked again and again this liberalism seen as its deadliest enemy, as an enemy that must be either overthrown and totally destroyed or driven into an absolutism of its own.

It may well be, if any of this is correct, that some of the strife of our own day is indeed due to the aggressive Old World spirit still striving to contain or deflect those stealthy New World influences. A macabre dialogue of violent authoritarian repression and equally violent authoritarian revolt does seem to have established itself as very much a part of our time, much of it under very suspect banners of freedom-fighting, the fighting often seeming to take precedence over the freedom.

"I laugh at those," said Rousseau, ". . . who . . . imagine that, to be free, it is enough to be a rebel."

One could perhaps put it that the Old World drives on bristling under arms as always before, still intent upon testing which of its bellicose "powers" will be for this moment conquering landlords, which will be servile tenants, of earth's property — fiercely determined, one might even imagine (among all its other fierce determinations), upon any Armageddon necessary to smother, at last, that stubborn New World threat to its sacred way of life and death.

The Old World (in the terminology of this view of things) seems to win all the battles but always lose the peace, and so still today the war goes on.

Wrote Benjamin Lee Whorf long ago — 1940 — in speaking of the economics of primitive societies, "We may end the war that is within all wars" for since "both Marxian communism and private capitalism are based on a stereotyped materialistic formulation of economics" then revelation of "the fact that economic behavior is conditioned by culture, not by mechanistic reactions, may be the forerunner of a NEW ERA."

The insidious influences emanating from the New World toward some such new era were (if any of this is correct) influences immaterial, subtle, oblique — one could indeed say stealthy. They emanated (and still do?) as attitudes felt rather than ideas consciously recognized. They drift through all the air of post-Columbian history and still (it may be) pulse in the air of today.

# VI.

# Myth and Antimyth

## 1. The Golden Screen: Antistrophe

They have kings, wrote Peter Martyr in his Seventh Decade, speaking of the people of the Bahamas, kings who are possessed of such absolute authority that a royal command to jump off a cliff would be instantly obeyed, "but observe within what limits is enclosed the royal power; this is a thing good to know. The king's rule extends only over planting, hunting and fishing . . . He divides labor among his subjects as he sees fit. The produce of the harvest is stored in the royal granaries, then, throughout the year, portioned out to each family according to its needs."

These people had already been "exterminated" — Martyr's word — by this time of his writing, in the 1520s; 40,000 were taken as slaves to Hispaniola where many, says Martyr, died by their own hand; the rest were eradicated in their home islands "to the number of twelve hundred thousand." Thus Peter Martyr's account is their epitaph, and thus, in the pleasant life he describes, repeating still once more his favorite theme, "did these indigenes enjoy the golden world. They knew neither mine nor thine, that seed of all discord. When not planting or harvesting they played at ball, they hunted or fished. Judicial troubles, trials, cases at law, disputes between neighbors, were unknown."

A note to these passages in the French edition of 1907 says, "The indigenes had realized the ideal communist city, but are the Spanish accounts really trustworthy on this point?"

The editor does not question the veracity of the Spanish accounts on other odd matters — cannibalism, human sacrifice, strange flora and fauna, the bizarre "drinking" of tobacco smoke, the bizarre nudity and super-sex, the wretchedness, the brutishness, the bizarre filth of such unimaginable foods as raw vermin and snakes, all the other myriad bizarreries of this bizarre New World — even the report from Panama of drops of swamp water turning into frogs elicits only the gentle disclaimer that one is merely translating, not evaluating. But obviously this one point of political economy was simply too much to accept, especially in the unctuously propertied "Belle Epoque" where we have already seen La Boétie's editor informing us that of course La Boétie didn't mean what he said if indeed he had really written what he had written.

The more admirable marvels reported from the New World, later lumped together under the general rubric of the "myth of the good (or noble) savage," encountered from an early date skepticism that in due time graduated into ridicule and eventually, as in the Belle Epoque example cited above, a rather particular antagonism. Attacks on this myth of the good savage, most pointedly, as in the example above, where the alleged marvels are of a political or economic nature, are still continuing as zealously as ever, if not more so.

This particular opposition has been largely founded for some years on the explanation (previously but briefly referred to in I, 5, "The Golden Screen: Strophe") that it was the European image of a Golden Age or some other "ancient ethnological" model operating on the explorers' imaginations that accounted for the admirable marvels they said they saw, rather than actual New World facts.

This hypothesis has had wide acceptance. Said Chinard in 1913, "The sixteenth century had received from the Middle Ages the old legend of the terrestrial paradise, and had modified it by the memories of the golden age borrowed from Latin poets; from the moment of discovery, the explorers' vision had been deformed." A moderate and conservative historian, J. H. Elliott, concludes that early explorers "all too often saw what they expected to see" and asks whether the faces of Rhode Island Indians described by Verrazzano were "really as 'gentle and noble as those of classical sculptures', or was this the reaction of a man with a Florentine humanist upbringing, who had already created for himself a mental image of the New World inspired by the Golden Age of antiquity?" The general line of thought here has been given some philosophical legitimacy by the interest present day semiotics takes in the construct the "*self* makes of the *other*." The Mexican historian Edmundo O'Gorman has, as Elliott puts it, "ingeniously argued" (in *The Invention of America*, 1961) that "America was not discovered but invented by sixteenth-century Europeans." A still more recent study takes as its point of departure: "Although the social and cultural attributes of Native Americans influenced the conception of them by Whites, it is ultimately to the history of White values and ideas that we must turn . . ." In short, as in a frequently quoted work of a few years ago, "The European's images of non-European man are not primarily if at all descriptions of real people, but rather projections of his own nostalgia and feeling of inadequacy."

I think this hypothesis is to some extent in error, and specifically in error concerning the notions of liberty so prominent in New World reports.

The Old Testament story was of a garden eastward in Eden, watered by the river of the world but planted with herbs that had grown without any other rain than a mist that went up from the earth (rather as in Vespucci's report of the New World), filled with every tree that is pleasant to the sight and good for food, and man placed in it to dress it and keep it so that the Lord might walk contentedly in it in the cool of the day. The Greek and Latin tradition was of an ancient age of gold when all men were brothers and the living was really easy, with fruit dropping daily from the trees to regale the happy residents beneath (rather as Peter Martyr and Vespucci said it really did in the New World, at least in some of the better neighborhoods); or of a land of healthy, hardy, virtuous, simple, innocent people such as the nomad Scythians or the Getae or the Germans of classic times (rather as Lescarbot and various others noted for some New World regions).

Some classic writers saw such a vision of "primitivist" times — the people of the Golden Age being, for the most of the classic references, Old World examples of "primitive" peoples — as a moment of pristine perfection from which mankind had been ever since decaying, a view strengthened in Christian analysis by the proposition that the earliest people, new made by God, must have represented perfection since God's work (before corruption by human misbehavior) could only be perfect. Some authorities (Hesiod, Plato) seemed to see such an ideal vision as a summit to which toiling mankind might return in vast cycles of time. Incidental traits in the various Golden Age pictures differed enormously. The essential point pretty generally common to most was that in the Golden Age — as in the Garden of Eden before the Fall — people were "naturally" good, not bad.

("I am assured, wrote Jean-Jacques Rousseau, "that we have long since been disabused of the chimera of the golden world. Should one add then that we have long since been disabused of the chimera of virtue?")

Some (but by no means all) of the classic references mention property held in common with its implication of equality, although more frequently in relation to "justice" or contentment than to an explicitly expressed equality. "The first inhabitants of Italy were the Aborigines, whose king, Saturn, is said to have been so just that there were no slaves under him nor any private property, but all things belonged to all in common and undivided as if all men had but one patrimony."

It is also interesting to note that not all classic references to primitivist models of presumably egalitarian repute — such as the Scythians —

were favorable; thus the early Christian father, Tertullian: ". . . their life is rude, their lust is promiscuous . . . They devour the bodies of their parents slaughtered with their cattle at their feasts . . ." Or the last of the classic poets, Claudian, "shameful appearance and bodies hideous . . . Plunder is their food . . . they think it comely to swear by their slaughtered parents." Or Agatharkhides (second century B.C.) on the Ikhthuophagoi ("Fish-eaters") of the African coast of the Red Sea, "who go stark naked, both men and women, and indulge in common procreation of children. They have an instinctive knowledge of pleasure and pain, but none of moral qualities. . . . The dead are considered worthy of no further care, for their minds are not touched by pity, which is a product of thought."

Both Agatharkhides and Strabo speak specifically of the "despotic chiefs" of the Troglodytes, a people chosen by Montesquieu for a Utopian excursion ("They worked with a common solicitude for the common interest . . . The troglodyte people regarded themselves as one sole family").

Attacks on the avaricious rich, even in the ascetic air of early Christian times, were not taken (even if meant) very seriously — the "most significant fact concerning" Saint Ambrose's denunciation (in the fourth century) of the evils of riches and of property as usurpation "is that so little came of it."

References to liberty in the classical Golden Age are few and ambiguous. For example, Seneca: ". . . observe that free peoples, such as the Germans and the Scythians, are those that are most given to anger . . ." Or, in the pretended harangue of a Scythian of the sixth century B.C. but actually dating from some hundreds of years later: "You have flutes and purses; I have javelins and a bow. Therefore it is not strange that you are a slave and I a free man, and that you have many enemies, I none."

The kinglessness, the masterlessness, the all, all at liberty repeatedly underscored in the reports from America is as a rule absent here, much more typical the concept of a "good" king, ruler, lord: "Who does not know of the Golden Age, of the king who was free from care?" Or the Aeneid: "Golden is called the age in which that king [Saturn] reigned. He ruled the people in calm peace, until little by little the age grew worse, its brilliance dimmed, and the madness of war and love of possession took its place." As has been noted, Seneca related that the first men chose the wisest among them as ruler, submitting themselves to his judgment, it being the way of nature for the inferior to render obedience to the superior. But none of the kings "in that age which we call golden" used his power against his own people, nor were any of his people ill-behaved, "since a good ruler has good subjects."

Nevertheless America did present a world apparently fulfilling, in real life, certain parts of the pretty legend (such as the lack of "love of possession") previously confined to lands of myth and antique memory. This supposed discovery of an actual golden world raised in itself complications of considerable consequence, as shown in Atkinson's work discussed in I, 5, above.

But the suggestion that this picture in accounts of the New World was based less on observed facts than on the European imagination filled with golden-world preconceptions runs into several serious difficulties, especially where the new New World liberty is concerned. For one, such liberty not being, as we have just seen, a usual feature of pre-Columbian golden-world conceptions, it would seem unlikely as an invention of preconditioned imagination based on those conceptions. For another, comparisons with the golden world of classic allusion are more commonly added by classically educated commentators than by the New World explorers and travelers themselves who made the original reports, and while information in the original eyewitness accounts was often enough decorated in this way, it was not necessarily falsified so far as its hard news was concerned.

Whether Narraganset people could have been so presumptuous as to have faces "really" as gentle and noble as the faces of ancient Italians is less the issue here than the fact that the classicism alleged for Verrazzano was not typical among sea captains and soldiers of the time. Columbus, although a prodigious reader of geographical works and thus able to offer a serious opinion as to the location of the earthly paradise of medieval legend, gives little indication of being preoccupied with the golden world old poets wrote about; it is the cultured but untraveled Peter Martyr who fits the ancient golden vision to Columbus's picture of gentle and generous and classically nude New World peoples. As remarks Columbus's biographer, "Peter Martyr never missed an opportunity to point out that the Indians were still in the Golden Age." Marc Lescarbot, a most literary lawyer (he wrote his "histories" in verse as well as in prose), found classic visions all over the place during his year in Canada with Champlain, visions mostly missed by Nicolas Denys, who however waxed dithyrambic enough (quoted above, II, 2) about the free and happy native life in his account of his forty years on Acadia's Indian frontiers in the seventeenth century.

Nor do we find the Renaissance imagination giving the same qualities (liberty, equality, masterlessness) to other exotic regions such as Africa, where favorable reports dwelt on the noble Christian king of legend, Prester John, or the Orient, which enjoyed a rage of admiration in Europe reaching a peak in the eighteenth century, but an admiration for purported philosopher-kings and the exquisite civilization (by no means masterless) they were said to represent. At the end of the eighteenth century and through the nineteenth the islands of the Pacific did assume the role of a Land of Cockaigne, but with an archetypal political expression in Diderot's *Supplément au Voyage de Bougainville* in which a venerable Tahitian philosopher (bearing a strong family resemblance to all the "philosophes nus" in French accounts of the New World) praised the "state of nature" versus "civilization" in terms much more akin to previous American reports than to Bougainville's.

Another aspect of the Golden Age versus New World reality concerns the comparative importance of the two currents of thought, Old World proponents sometimes implying that even if the New World did exist, its remote and unimportant peoples could certainly have had no serious influence on "civilized" thought and ideas — an objection that might be balanced against the generally acknowledged influence on Europe for the past two thousand years of values (I refer to Christianity) emanating from a decidely minor people in the remote eastern Mediterranean who also did not wear breeches. But in any case, would not the age-old dream of a golden world surely be of more weight in Western thought than later dreams independently born in a new America?

There seems no way of testing such atomic weight in ideas, but a comparison of the extent of the literature of the two dreams might offer some crude (so crude in fact as to be quite possibly meaningless) indication. It has been remarked in preceding pages (I, 2) that the number of pre-Columbian authors usually noted in connection with the ancient Golden Age tradition is not large. John H. Rowe, writing of the Renaissance foundations of anthropology, cites nine, five from classic times, four medievals. Lovejoy and Boas, hereinbefore so much cited as the specialists in the subject, turn up, with the most diligent search, almost fifty antique authors touching on the more or less golden world of the "noble savage" of antiquity — not all of them idealizing the savages in question — and to these may be added some one hundred or so more, from Aelian to Zenobius, who speak, even in passing, of a lost Golden Age. Most of these writers are (and were) not of earth-resounding fame and influence (e.g. Aelian and Zenobius); those who, like Cicero or Seneca, Aristotle or Pliny, were (and are) familiar names add up to the customary handful usually listed. All deal with the Golden Age among multitudinous other matters. The inflexible Order of the World, a hypothetical King of the World, the mysterious Center of the World, for samples, were also subjects of occasional reference in ancient thought, and while all are transferred on rare occasion to commentaries on the New World, the occasions are rare indeed. The oedipan myth that in the Old

World gospel according to Freud has obsessed man from the start, although given expression by a speculative thinker such as Diderot, does not as a rule figure in pre-Freudian reports from the New World.

In contrast to the rather slim library of Golden Age discussion accumulated over two thousand years, writings stressing the actual existence of a Golden Age in the New World and the liberty and equality accompanying it follow almost immediately upon the earliest meetings with the American people, and proliferate with astonishing rapidity into the scores of new titles and reeditions that have been noted in these pages. French, in spite of the primacy of Paris as a center for earliest publications on the New World, came a bit late as a vernacular for such works — after Latin, Spanish, and Italian — but even so the two-thousand-year library assembled above was considerably outdistanced by French-language works alone in the first two centuries, with a considerable number of the New World works running through numerous additional editions and reimpressions.

A further argument occasionally advanced against reports of "good" Americans points out that certain authors of such New World accounts were interested in criticizing the Old World or a political or religious faction within it (as with Las Casas, Benzoni/Chauveton, Lahontan, among others) and that their testimony might thus be suspect — a pardonable suspicion, but one that should be supported by a close examination of the testimony in question, not as to its effectiveness or even its intent as an Old World critique, but as to its validity as New World reporting. Disinterest is no guarantee of accuracy, as countless disinterested inaccuracies bear witness.

But motive, conscious or unconscious, open or concealed, has been and still remains a central issue in the long New World polemic — for many students *the* central issue, any actual interest in the nature or history of New World people subordinate in interest to the moral position, the political motives, the psychological compulsions of the European commentators, the basic point of departure being "the presumptuous conceit of European civilization that in itself was realized the nature of man."

## 2. The Bull of Taugete

Jean Bodin affirmed (1576), following Gómara and Oviedo, that impalement was the standard punishment for thievery among the native people of Hispaniola, instancing this terrible punishment as a reasonable explanation of the reported unreasonable fact that "goods were not locked up."

Benzoni disputed the accuracy of this report, insisting there could not be any theft to begin with among people who knew no mine and thine; thus the Old World punishment, otherwise unreported in the New, was doubly absurd, for the New World people were truly different. And Benzoni relates the tale of the stranger who asked what the punishment for adultery was in Sparta. There was none, said the Spartans, because there was no adultery in Sparta. But if there should be any, persisted the traveler. In that case, he was finally told, the adulterer would have to furnish as sacrifice a bull so large he would reach from the mountain pass of Taugete to the river of Eurotas. Impossible, cries the stranger, there could never a bull that size. As easily as there could be adultery in Sparta, say the Spartans.

It was impossible for Benzoni to check the truth of the matter, there being "nearly none" of the Hispaniola people then (1550s) left alive; even Oviedo could not have checked its accuracy by other than quite tenuous hearsay, there being at his time of writing ("in this present year 1535") no more than "five hundred persons child or adult" left of the "million, or more," Columbus had found on the island. God had given them death for their sinfulness, said Oviedo: many by pestilence, many from overwork in Spanish mines; and many, so "lazy, melancholy and cowardly were they," had killed themselves to avoid work, when enslaved. (Many had "perished even for very anguyshe of mynde," wrote Richard Eden's Peter Martyr.) Nor did any of the disputants discuss the physical problems in this manner of execution as described by Oviedo, "spitted perfectly alive on a tree or pole and there left to die." Oviedo contented himself with saying it wasn't done any more, "Satan now being banished from this isle . . . by the death of the Indians."

If the real issue for Oviedo was the presence of the Europeans' Satan, the issue for both Benzoni and Bodin was New World morality. Could New World people truly be so different that theft among them was unknown? (Bodin would say no; Benzoni would say yes.) Was the nature of man truly realized only in terms of European customs? (Bodin would say yes; Benzoni would say no.) An issue to be determined less on the evidence than on the psychological predilections of the European disputants, and thus an issue of interest in a study of Europe of the epoch or in a study such as this present one of New World influences on the evolution of that Europe, but an issue that should scarcely be decisive for modern scholars objectively interested in the accuracy of reports on the nature and history of the Arawakan people of Hispaniola.

In sum, when a traveler "was moved by the novel customs of the New World natives (for example, by their absence of clothing, or by the friendliness of their reception) to comment that the people met lived in a 'state of nature,' or in a 'golden age,' or with 'natural virtue,' the modern historian is not entitled to jump to the conclusion . . . that the observer believed that his subjects literally and exclusively lived in terms of the hypothetical age or state speculated upon" or "that he misunderstood the facts" or that he was merely "delivering a sermon on the defects of western civilization."

The echo of an ancient Golden Age in European reports of the New World should not be neglected, nor should other prejudices in the European observers be ignored, but it would really seem they have been given more credit than they deserve. The easy assumption of a conspiracy of distortion (conscious or unconscious) in accounts of the New World extending over three to four hundred years and involving literally hundreds of witnesses writing out of a variety of backgrounds and in a variety of languages, some of whom had spent years observing the world they thought they were accurately describing, would seem to be, to put it mildly, mildly fantastic.

## 3. Myth and Antimyth

Major frontal attacks in earlier centuries on the idea of the good savage were based most often precisely on the validity of data in New World reports, rejecting information that seemed to put New World people in a favorable light and emphasizing reports of cannibalism, devil worship, and general brute-beastliness.

For a time in the eighteenth century the European scientific community as a whole tended to accept a view that not only the people but pretty much all the fauna and flora of the New World were markedly inferior, to the point that America could be questionable as a place fit for habitation by more highly developed human beings such as Europeans. This view rested on the authority of the great Buffon, who selected bits of New World reports to suit (in 1761) his picture of America as a world where natural development had been "cut short when barely begun," and a picture of the native as "feeble and small in his organs of generation; he has neither body hair nor beard, and no ardor for the female of his kind. He is much less strong in body than the European. He is also much less sensitive and yet more fearful and more cowardly; he lacks vivacity and is lifeless in his soul." Animals of the New World, though "timid and docile" (and also smaller and weaker than their Old World counterparts) had escaped domestication (had escaped being put "under the yoke" of "slavery") because the "impotent" savage had no idea of his real power and his superiority, and was himself "no more than a species of animal incapable of commanding over others . . ." Society was necessary to effect an ascendancy over animals, and even propagation itself depended upon society; thus the immensity of the New World (excepting the "half-civilized" regions of Mexico and Peru) was left with only scattered handfuls of population, wandering unorganized bands lost in the empty land: ". . . the Savage scarcely seeking the society of his female, fears or disdains that of animals . . ." New World man, Buffon concluded, was "a being without consequence, a species of impotent automaton . . . Nature had treated him less as a mother than as a cruel stepmother in refusing him even the sentiment of love and the lively desire of multiplying his kind." The great scientist found even the names for animals in the Americans' "barbaric language . . . so difficult to pronounce that it is astonishing Europeans have taken the trouble to write them down."

Buffon later partially revised his opinion, finding America immature but the American "strong and handsome"; but his thesis had been enthusiastically adopted by the "ill-informed and malignant" (as Benjamin Franklin referred to him) Corneille de Pauw who deduced not only that the American native was degenerate but that the Europeans who had migrated to America had also visibly degenerated, in accordance with the proposition that everything in the New World was "either degenerate or monstrous." This convenient proposition was picked up by Raynal (which is to say, as previously noticed, by Diderot as well) and readily convinced so many other Old World thinkers more or less disturbed by Rousseau that even Kant swallowed it whole and agreed that the Americans were "incapable of civilization. They have no motive force, for they are without affection and passion. They are not drawn to one another by love, and are thus unfruitful. They hardly speak at all, never caress one another, care about nothing, and are lazy." The position was especially well expressed by Joseph de Maistre in speaking of Rousseau, "one of the most dangerous sophists of his century" who "has constantly taken the savage for primitive man, which he is not, for he can only be the descendant of men detached from the great tree of civilization as the result of some falseness . . . In the path of the same error the languages of these savages have been taken for beginning languages, while they are and can only be the debris of antique languages, *ruined*, if one may so express it, and degraded like the men who speak them."

The thesis continued its career to Hegel, who found America "immature and impotent," surviving en route Jefferson's *Notes on Virginia* (1784) written in part to correct Buffon's misinformation, and Franklin's famous rejoinder at a Paris dinner, when he made the common sense suggestion that the Europeans present measure their height against that of their "degenerate" American guests — among the Europeans present the abbé Raynal, who had unfortunately introduced the topic and who was, said Jefferson, "a mere shrimp."

Nor is the thesis quite dead yet: one of today's better-known French historians stated recently, apparently unaware even of the existence of any counteropinion, that "the failure of Indian humanity" in its "piecemeal and chimerical world," the "feebleness of the American man in America, the irreversible degradation of the Indian, is one of the most important principles of the early human past in the New World."

The "sham natural science" of this thesis found, or claimed to find, support in the writings of friends of the Indian demanding protection for the natives — that they needed protection was taken as evidence of their weakness, and thus was born "a theory of race inferiority kept alive from then till now, with colonial advantage," the "birth of anthropology as a colonial ideology."

Attacks on de Pauw were for the most part as tiresome as de Pauw himself — with some exceptions, such as Zacharie de' Pazzi de Bonneville, writing in 1771, who set Europe chuckling with his opening gun: "Chapter one: how that, in order to be able to say that a thing has degenerated, one must first of all prove that it previously excelled." The "Savages," he wrote, "think as they wish; they eat when they're hungry; they sleep when they're sleepy; they take a walk when they want to; they don't bother their mind with the future and their work is their play. . . . A hog's life, some will say, but it must not be so bad a way of life as it might seem, since three-fourths of our great nobles live thus . . ." He asserted, as had so many, that the Americans would give up their lives rather than accept slavery — or even accept the ordinary servitude practiced by European domestics. He devoted his longest (and lightest hearted) chapter to American versus European sex, a subject the Abbé de Pauw had dealt with by very distant second hand, Vespucci prominent among his sources; Pazzi adduced his own primary evidence from both worlds, rather less dreamy than Vespucci's but markedly more extensive.

Much of the debate surrounding the Buffon and de Pauw contentions was carried on in a rarefied scientific atmosphere, dealing quite objectively with such firm data as the American native's beardlessness and the undeniable fact (that had even been ironically admitted by Montaigne) that he did not wear breeches. The American's freedom — uncivilized disorder, lack of respect for authority, savage unconstraint, to the point, on the word of the Reverend Cotton Mather, that there was "no *Family Government* among them" ("They are abominably indulgent unto their Children") — was in itself additional evidence of inferiority. Inferiority of such a degenerate weakling was presumed by many of the participating scientists to be beyond discussion, and the real core of the debate the causes of the American's retardation — climate, suggested much earlier by Bodin and exhaustively seconded, after Buffon, by platoons of eighteenth-century naturalists, was regarded as a most likely principal factor.

However, the shadow of Rousseau was now and again fairly well discernible in the proceedings; de Pauw's claim that the savages of the New World had led precarious and miserable lives that had been ameliorated since their conquest by Europeans was rather too pointedly the exact "contrary of the theory of Jean-Jacques."

Rousseau's impact on his time can be gauged as well from his foes as from his admirers. Legions of champions dedicated to his overthrow took the field in the reaction following the Enlightenment, such as Joseph de Maistre and the economist Gian Rinaldo Carli, who "made it his life's work to combat the theses of Jean-Jacques" — their reinforcements and replacements still carry on the war in the present day.

Raynal/Diderot frankly stated their opposition to Rousseau, but for motives more subtle and complex than was usual among his opponents: that the idea of the savage happy and contented in spite of material privation was a cruel and dangerous illusion, bound to give comfort to the rich of Europe, who could assume the miserable poor all about them should be equally happy, for if "the refinements of civilization are the cause of unhappiness among men, the peasants who possessed nothing, who led a life harder than that of the Indians of Canada, as close to nature and as far from civilization, should enjoy no less happiness." Even so, Raynal's *Histoire Philosophique des Indes* admitted that the New World had brought a moral revolution to Europe, revealing Old World civilization perverted by vice and greed. Such an admission was far from usual among the scientists and philosophers engaged in pondering the New World's inferiority.

One of the leading facts on which this generally accepted inferiority was based was the American native's "unfruitfulness" — the sparse population reported by some New World travelers. Here it was necessary to tread a precariously selective measure among the varying data, since large populations, in fact enormous and teeming populations well beyond those of Europe, were reported by other New World travelers. The "Savages of these countries are extremely fecund," wrote a missionary from Guiana in the mid-1600s, speaking of the "great number" of the natives, "because of the warmth of the climate, and the abundant produce of the land . . ."

The earliest and best known of these travelers reporting large American populations was Bartolomé de Las Casas, of lasting influence as a partisan of the New World peoples but under furious attack during his long lifetime (and from some quarters ever since) for his frequent references to American natives as people more guileless and decent than the Old World norm. He was attacked still more furiously for his apparent overstatement of Spanish cruelties and the numbers of American natives he claimed were done to death in the early colonial period, of which he was an endlessly critical eyewitness.

This question of the actual number of pre-Columbian Americans has received some minute attention in recent demographic studies that more than bear out Las Casas' pre-Conquest population estimates for the island of Hispaniola (present Haiti and Santo Domingo), a native population destroyed (as we have seen) by oppression and disease within only a generation or two — estimates heretofore usually deemed, even by Las Casas' apologists, fantastically overdrawn. But his figure of "more than three million" (cited above, I, 6) is now corrected to some seven to eight million, a larger population therefore for this one island than the sixteenth-century populations of Madrid, Paris, London, and a few European cities more, combined. Further recent studies projected from detailed analysis of Aztec and Spanish tribute rolls give some twenty-five million souls for the pre-Spanish population of central Mexico. The total population of Spain at the time of the conquest of Mexico has been estimated at eight to ten million, that of England four to five million, and of France at that time, before the incorporation of Brittany, fifteen to sixteen million.

Las Casas' assertion that the figures on human sacrifice in ancient Mexico were much too high ("the estimate of brigands, who wish to find an apology for their own atrocities") has been only embarrassing to most of his admirers, who are nearly all ready to grant that here also his zeal outran his veracity. But here also, as with his population estimates, recent reexaminations appear to offer Las Casas some support. Specifically, the figures usually repeated for the notorious mass sacrifice at the dedication of the temple of Huitzilopochtli in the 1480s have been shown to be obvious exaggeration.

The touchiest of the underlying issues is always that of the "natural" goodness of man, particularly New World man. Acton noted this disturbing theme as the late nineteenth century had received it, writing that missionaries to the New World "discovered with amazement that barbarians who worshipped a god scarcely to be distinguished from the Devil, were better than the men who enjoyed a Xn education."

Such insidious heresy could be granted only at terrible cost to Old World faith — for if not "naturally" wicked this "natural" New World man did not need salvation, he had not sinned in Adam, and God himself was threatened. Most naturally, Old World defenders fought most bitterly to refute any evidence leaning toward this malign conclusion, an interminable combat in which all manner of shaky evidence on sinfulness, such as the overdrawn report on human sacrifice just mentioned, was all too readily taken as proven.

Other issues only slightly, if at all, less sacred than God himself — the Old World tradition of property, for example — were also centrally involved; said Las Casas' opponent, Sepúlveda, criticizing favorable reports of the ancient Mexicans: ". . . those . . . in New Spain . . . brag of their public institutions because they have cities . . . and nonhereditary kings, elected by popular vote . . . But on the other hand they have established in such a way their republic, that nobody individually possesses anything."

Ideas concerning natural goodness or a "good" or an "inferior" savage or for that matter an ancient Golden Age are not exactly central to primitivism in the modern sense. Today's primitivism may still take its origin in speculation as to when or where "the most excellent condition of human life, or the best state of the world in general," may have existed, but as a rule in today's thinking it rests less on any judgment of a more "primitive" condition as being "better" than our own present condition than on the possible existence of values in a more "primitive" society that may nevertheless be of worth to our own more complex society. The intention is to treat "primitive" man less "as an object to be manipulated" than "as the possessor of a culture whose values need to be sympathetically considered in the process of redefining and refining our own."

Although in some instances autocriticism can go so far as to identify our own "civilization" with "barbarism" ("the second period of barbarism may well be the continued empire of civilization itself"), categories of general "superiority" or "inferiority" (i.e., a person "superior" because resident of a "superior" world, whether "primitive" or "civilized") are more often today resisted in favor of a position of relativism, finding values admirable or otherwise, worthwhile or otherwise, beneficial or destructive, good or bad, in all societies, no matter how disparate.

The study of different peoples can bring "something other than the revelation of a utopian state of nature or the discovery of a perfect society in the depths of the forests; it can aid us in building a theoretical model of human society . . . But this model — this was Rousseau's solution — is eternal and universal . . . We can thus utilize all societies in revealing principles of social life we may apply to our own . . . for it is only the society to which we belong that we are in a position to transtorm without risk of destroying it." The objective "is self-knowledge" to be attained through "the authentic understanding of others."

Throughout most of the quarrelsome history of New World primitivism there was little occasion for this sort of objectivity, even though a common ground for early attacks that did leave some room for objective argument seems to have been simply ordinary good sense revolted by a New World confection too sugary to swallow. Gentle kindly people receiving strangers without either fear or hostility (as reported by Columbus, Vespucci, Alvar Nuñez Cabeza de Vaca, Jacques Cartier, and La Salle, among numerous others) was a picture so foreign to customary Old World ways that some skepticism was, to say the least, expectable. Furtive beast-like creatures, dismal cannibals robbing and murdering, if not cutting up and devouring strangers on the spot (as reported also from other parts of the forest by various of the above), may well have been a picture more readily acceptable to hardheaded practical readers who knew the way of the world (at any rate the Old World).

But early polemic over favorable New World reports engaged at too many points — moral, material, religious — a much more sensitive Old World quick and soon passed beyond mere considerations of credibility to the passionate criticism previously described, a largely emotional criticism founded on moral and political and religious considerations.

Some firsthand witnesses (such as the friar Toribio de Benavente, known as Motolinia, a lifelong opponent of Las Casas) contributed to these strictures, but principal early objections to reports of good Americans came from fiery defenders of the Old World faith (such as Gómara and Sepúlveda) who (like most of those who confounded the New World with the Golden Age) had never seen the New and were consequently all the more intolerant of any argument. And all the more intolerant of opposition from witnesses actually on the New World scene — an intolerance not entirely dissipated even in our own gloriously enlightened moment.

Las Casas' work, for instance, finds increasing acceptance in the present day but there still remains a sector of opinion in agreement with a recent biography by the then dean of Spanish historians maintaining that Las Casas was a "simple paranoiac," and showing his "mental imbalance as disclosed by his life and works." The most important work of Las Casas, incidentally, and one of the most important in the field of American Indian history, his *Historia*, waited three hundred years for its first publication anywhere (in 1875) and has still, at this writing — after four hundred years — to be issued in its entirety in English.

It appears though that the more important later attacks, those on the order of Hobbes's onslaught in the seventeenth century, were based less on matters moral or religious than on the frankly political, on the good savage simply as a symbol of a New World found to be emitting disquieting if not dangerous new political ideas.

The state of nature (as Maitland analyzed Hobbes's actual motivation) was the state in which God has created man; it was an ideal state, one might therefore presume, toward which civil society should be directed. Hobbes (in Maitland's analysis) thought there should be no such supralegal ideal "to which political reformers could appeal when preaching disobedience and anarchy."

Protest based on this kind of motivation was clearly no mere academic or cloistered speculation, but an urgent and deadly serious argument for authoritarianism against that disruptive idea of "natural liberty" associated with the New World.

Some such motivation (perhaps more or less unconscious) may help to expiain the overinsistence of similar efforts that continue into our own day to discredit those unwelcome New World reports. The emotional quality of protesting too much, the exaggeration that often follows, may seem more understandable if regarded as instinctive defense of real and immediate political values that appear to be direly threatened.

Roundly asserting that explorers "swarmed out of the old world in the sixteenth, seventeenth, and eighteenth centuries in search of new worlds" and "projected their ideals of a lost, primitive state of happiness onto these worlds" or dismissing Rousseau's political ideas as "the wild dream of an overwrought brain" or affirming that Peter Martyr "extolled the heavenly qualities of the New World, investing its inhabitants with all the attributes of purity, brotherly love, and perfection which God had intended for mankind before the Fall" (which scarcely matches Martyr's text) or citing Chinard 1913 as stating that the Jesuit accounts of foreign parts and peoples influenced "Europe more profoundly than all other sources combined" (which scarcely matches with Chinard's text) are fairly typical instances of such exaggeration.

A presumed exact likeness between favorable New World reports and classic references to the Golden Age is sometimes accepted as so firmly established that they are cited quite interchangeably — e.g. "the shibboleth" of property "in common" is said to be, for the classic Golden Age, "continuously balanced against the acquisitive catchwords, 'mine' and 'thine' " — but in reality these catchwords are found in only a small minority of the Golden Age quotations gathered by Lovejoy and Boas; rather it is in the New World accounts themselves, as we have seen, that these particular catchwords are present.

Response to the urgency and momentousness of Hobbes's argument was, at least in some instances, equally momentous but with sometimes an unexpected twist, if Adam Smith's judgment is to be trusted that "the notion of Conscience was first analyzed in reply to Hobbes, who founded morality on human laws," and Acton's that "the sovereignty of conscience" then resulted in precisely the anti-authoritarian revolution Hobbes had been most anxious to avert — a consequence somewhat the same as that resulting from the anti-American fireworks shot into the air by Gómara that fell to earth (unfortunately for Gómara's purpose) on Montaigne.

From the seventeenth century of Hobbes to the nineteenth century of Marx and Engels the aboriginal Indian world was generally regarded as a sort of living fossil, an exhibit of the childhood of human society miraculously preserved in the deep freeze of the New World, a "primitive" (even if golden) stage through which all human societies had once passed. The assumptions, "rooted in classical tradition," that man had "developed from his earliest state in a slow, unilinear evolutionary progress whose highest present manifestation was Western European society" and that some human groups had been mysteriously retarded and from them could be reconstructed earlier epochs of our own history were an "integral part of the theorizing of Victorian ethnologists." Society as it matured then advanced to a later stage, in this view, with the development of property, authoritarianism, technical progress, and the crystalization of a permanent state of conflict — "natural" conflict in Hobbes, class conflict in Marx and Engels.

But it is not easy to feel that Shakespeare was more primitive than Edgar A. Guest because he did not possess a typewriter, nor easy to feel that Maya and Toltec remains indicate a childhood of societies less "evolved" than their contemporary societies of medieval Europe, or even (if weighing spiritual as well as material achievement) that historic Natchez, Pawnee, Pueblo, Iroquoian societies (among others) represent some such lower level of primitive development.

Some present day views thus tend more and more to see at least a certain portion of the aboriginal American world as an effectually developed world of its own, containing societies mature but mature in different ways, distinctly separate and different from those of the Old World.

The aboriginal American world as a separate and mature world of its own rather than an infant Old World opens old wounds in anthropology as to possible Old World influences in the formation of New World civilizations. If those New World civilizations were fundamentally different from Old World civilizations — were effectively developed worlds of their own — this fundamental difference would seem to weaken arguments for Old World influence in their formation and support arguments for "the integrity of Nuclear American civilizations." The prevailing opinion among American anthropologists, despite a minority of archeological interpretations to the contrary, still seems to favor the long established belief that New World culture owed little or nothing to Old World influences and "was overwhelmingly determined from within."

Such independent development bears in turn upon the principle of the universality — in effect the unity — of world history, a principle which became popular in Germany in the nineteenth century (promoted by Leopold von Ranke) and still carries some weight in historical theory. This concept of world history cannot of course survive if the aboriginal New World maintains its position as a major isolate. But the New World's position in this respect is quite strong, founded on the often repeated but inescapable realities that civilizations of the Old World were based on sown cereals, the plow, the cow (or the goat or the pig), and the wheel, none of which were in general use in aboriginal America; and that very few of the New World products that after Columbus took the Old by storm — potatoes, tobacco, maize, chocolate, all the list of more than one hundred crops that now make up three-fifths of the world's agricultural items — seem to have occurred in any part of the Old World in pre-Columbian times. Contact of any consequence between the two worlds thus seems to have been very questionable.

If the universality of human history cannot be sustained, if the New World societies were not embryonic Old Worlds but effectively mature, although profoundly different, civilizations in their own right, then theories as to the universal sameness of men and their passions and their social objectives can be placed under some doubt.

"All peoples that have a history have a paradise, a state of innocence, a golden age," said Schiller, and have said countless other Old World voices. But to many New World societies the story of the beginning of things was "diametrically opposed" to the Christian myth, not a story of a lost Garden of Eden, of a fall from grace, but of a previous less beneficent world from which the people made their way up into a lovelier world, the actual world of the present — an ascent to grace, not a fall, and Paradise not lost but attained in the here and now, and — that heretical contention that incessantly announced itself in the wake of so many New World travelers — man not fallen but risen, not the nostalgic creature of original sin of the Old World Golden Age tradition, not damned with natural badness but blessed with natural goodness.

"I notice," wrote Rousseau, of precisely this gulf of difference, "that the present world is ruled by a multitude of little maxims that seduce simple souls by a false air of philosophy . . . Such is the following: 'Men have everywhere the same passions; everywhere greed and self-interest motivate them; thus they are everywhere the same' . . . But let us consider . . . A savage is a man, and a European is a man . . ."

I speak of these grand issues with diffidence. The point I wish to make is, to repeat, much more modest: that ideas of liberty and equality associated with the New World were abstracted less from long familiar Old World literature than derived from the New World itself via reports that were for the most part seriously recorded and largely factual (their general authenticity having been herein lengthily discussed in I, 5; II, 1 and 2; and VI, 1). And it does seem the equality, the masterlessness so often spoken of in those reports, the utter liberty that became a headline item of New World news, may really have been, in a fairly concrete sense, a new idea for Europe.

## 4. New Things

Primitivism is alive and very well at present — prospering to such a degree that it has acquired a name all its own, neo-primitivism, "similar in many ways to the earlier approach to the 'noble savage' " but differing in its use of "more sophisticated analytical tools and more comprehensive anthropological and historical data. " This bodes well for the future of serious study in New World history, and the relativism stressed in this approach may even succeed, some time, in weakening the stranglehold of white supremacy on this history, the viselike conviction that Indian America had "played so passive a role" that only the actions and attitudes of Europeans had counted as determining factors. I have documented elsewhere my disagreement with this time-honored belief.

But primitivism, neo or otherwise, is not the subject here. My subject here is history. Desirable as the relativism of neo-primitivism is, with its sympathetic consideration of values in other societies that may be of use in redefining our own, it is directed toward this consideration from a point in the present moment if not above these values at any rate outside them.

My subject is rather the proposition that we have already incorporated in our own society certain of these values, they have already become part of our own present fields of thought.

It is my specific subject here, if I may repeat it one final time, that basic ideas on which most New World societies appear to have been founded were different from corresponding ideas at the base of most Old World societies, and that reports of this difference seem to have been of influence in the creation of the world, the still-emerging new world, of today.

Perhaps one might postulate further traces of this influence not only in the general course of liberal versus authoritarian conflict or in the bloodlines of various modern nations but also in certain more specific current or recent manifestations, such as various of the tenets of an "alternative" way of life followed in late years by hippiesque youths in Indian headbands, in what seems to be a growing feeling that we "need an ethics which defies success and reward," or in signs here and there, notably in France, of a revival of interest in Proudhonism — anti-authoritarian socialism, or in the "New Philosophy" latterly creating some stir in France, put forward by leftist writers beating the same anti-authoritarian drums.

Possibly in some such respects the New World's subtle influence continues to be felt, less concerned with the conventional Old World goal of revolution — transfer of power from one group to another — than with a subtly changing mode of life.

Or possibly we have altered our ways of thought still more in fighting off various aspects of these values, or admitting them in garbled form. It is all too obvious that our reactions to deep-laid issues are not always clearcut reflections of our conscious intentions. The nineteenth-century German anarchist Max Stirner, apostle of the superindividual, of the individual's freedom from "the master" rising anew "as the State," nevertheless found "an ardent reader in Mussolini" — but also an ardent disciple in the novelist B. Traven, passionate defender of the downtrodden individual but opponent of the white man's greedy individualism as opposed to the communal "happiness" of the Indians of Chiapas, among whom Traven lived. Reality may indeed be the same to all men, but perception of it may differ, from place to place as well as from time to time. "Philosophy," said Wittgenstein, "is not a doctrine but an activity."

The New World's new idea of equality, masterlessness, utter liberty, may be suspected at least of having played a part in the "new things" Leibniz saw appearing in the political world at the opening of the eighteenth century, the "new order of things commencing" (says a European historian) toward the same time, the time of the "greatest of all moral and spiritual revolutions of history" (says a modern philosopher), even bringing a change in the usual concept of primitivism itself, which "in ancient times and down to the seventeenth century" (says its chief authority) was based on the supposition "of an inevitable and progressive decline."

The Theatre of the "Italiens" where Arlequin Sauvage expressed his libertarian sentiments has been reduced to a plaque above a vacuum cleaner salesroom, and even the plinth is now long gone from the site of Dolet's statue in the Place Maubert, the clochards and their plastic bottles of gros rouge long gone with it; and the Old World, with the substantial aid of some of those garbled catchwords from the New, is indeed still more than holding its authoritarian own. But perhaps, so the lengthy evidence in these pages might also seem to indicate, the struggle, the centuries-old contest, the subtle and stealthy and marvelously involved combat, still continues.

## 5. Doctrine and Activity

If the universality of human history and the sameness everywhere of social objectives can be brought into question, if the New World societies were not in fact embryonic Old Worlds but effectively mature although profoundly different cultures in their own right, then the idea of the universality of a passion for property and the subsequent idea of an inevitable state of conflict over property as basic to the social condition is not necessarily sound.

This seemingly basic conflict (basic in such Old World thought as that of Hobbes and Locke and Marx) might spring properly enough from the idea of property so fundamental to Old World attitudes — but this is an idea not so fundamental, as we have seen, to the ancient societies of the New World. For we do find, in the New World, societies that apparently developed without that supposedly basic condition, complex and highly organized societies apparently not much affected by the principle, so deeply established in the Old World, of giving great importance to property and individual material gain.

The point is not that the New World (to plead once more also the indulgence of summing up the variety of peoples there as one in reference to certain predominant traits) was necessarily superior to the Old. Cruelty and injustice, misery and mayhem, were as prevalent in the accounts of New World societies as were liberty and equality. The point is simply that certain attitudes on which most New World societies seem to have been constructed were different, fundamentally different from corresponding attitudes at the base of most Old World societies, and that reports of this fundamental difference have affected the course of Old World thought.

We cannot know if ordinary pre-Columbian American lives were "better" or "worse" than ours today. We cannot know whether ordinary people were more or less contented, more or less free, more or less fearful, more or less fulfilled socially or culturally, in the ancient Maya center of Tikal or the Toltec city of Tula than in the Guatemala or the Mexico City of today, or in the great Mississippi River temple-center archaeologists now call Cahokia that was the metropolis of its region for many centuries than in the modern city on its site, East St. Louis, Illinois, but we can know that those ordinary lives were fundamentally different from ours, different in ways profoundly other than simply those of an "earlier stage" of our own social development.

The difference — so the examples so abundantly cited in these pages do insist — was real, and not merely a golden mote in the eye of the beholder. A difference so real as to cast serious doubt on any certainties of the universality of men's basic conflicts, on all such certainties clung to like sacred articles of faith by those who know the way of the world and would prefer to be sure that all men everywhere really want only the dollar and its dominium and that everything else is myth.

Paris
May 1985

# *Notes*

## Prologue

*page*

1   Jacques Hillairet, *Connaissance du Vieux Paris*, 3 vol. (Paris, 1957), 1:95.

"These women . . ." *ibid.*, 1:94.

2   A "sweet sojourn": Jean Buvat, *Journal de la Régence* (1715-1723), 2 vols. (Paris, 1865), 2:48. (The translation from the song is my own, as are all translations not otherwise identified throughout the book.)

Law's "experiment": Edgar Faure, *La Banqueroute de Law* (Paris, 1977), 20.

Louis Blanc, *Histoire de la Révolution Française* (Paris, 1847), 1:273; see also 272-327.

## Chapter 1

5   The New World and "modern capitalism": Earl J. Hamilton, "American Treasure and the Rise of Capitalism (1500-1700)," *Economica*, 9 (November 1929): 344.

New World "opportunities": J. H. Elliott, *The Old World and the New 1492-1650* (Cambridge, 1972), 7.

6   *The Decades of the newe worlde or West India, Conteyning the navigations and conquestes of the Spanyardes, with the particular description of the moste ryche and large landes and Ilandes lately found in the west Ocean . . . Wrytten in the Latine tounge by Peter Martyr of Angleria, and translated into Englysshe by Richarde Eden.* (London, 1555).

The lines quoted here are from the First Decade, Book 2, fol. 8, written in 1494, and from Peter Martyr's Dedication to the Emperor Charles V, 1516.

This Eden work is a collection of translations dealing with

travel and exploration, of which the translations from Peter Martyr make up the first half. They include Martyr's first four Decades only, the fourth erroneously listed as a final book of the Third Decade.

The translation seems generally accurate, with one puzzling exception — where Martyr speaks of the idyllic life of New World people, Eden often adds embellishment, sometimes considerable embellishment, emphasizing the specific idea of freedom and liberty.

The principal passage dealt with on the page here being considered, five lines of Latin giving nineteen lines of English, adds in translation phrases on liberty and on the indifference of the New World people to wealth, "for the which in other places men take infinite paynes and commit manie unlawfull actes, and yet are never satisfied, wheras many have to muche, and none inowgh."

These embellishments are by no means false to Martyr's overall picture, but they are remarkably at odds with Eden's own Preface to the Reader, which gives lavish praise to the Spaniards for their "mercyful" conquests that have freed New World natives from their "ferefull idlenesse" and from their liberty that was (borrowing the argument from Gómara and Oviedo) a "bondage of Sathans tyrannie . . ."

Since Eden's book was dedicated to Philip of Spain and Mary Tudor, and inspired by the thought that with their royal wedding England would now share in Spain's American riches, this fulsome Preface is not surprising, but the added emphasis in the text on the free and pleasant and innocent New World life thus destroyed is all the more puzzling. The importance of the work in creating an English perception of the New World may give some special significance to this curious ambivalence.

Richard Willes brought out a new and somewhat enlarged edition of Eden's translations the year following Richard Eden's death and although in his own Preface to the Reader Willes criticized certain points in Eden's work, such as his occasional use in English of words "smellying to much of the Latine" (e.g. *ponderous, portentous, antique, despicable, obsequious, homicide, imbibed, destructive*), he has no comment on these rare deviations from literal translation, that occur only when the text touches on freedom.

Edward Arber's nineteenth-century edition of Eden's text likewise has nothing to say of this peculiarity.

I have consulted the Latin texts of *De Orbe novo. Petri Martyris*

*ab Angleria Mediolanensis* . . . (eight Decades, Alcalá, 1530);
*De Insulis Nuper Inventis Ferdinandi Cortesii ad Carolus V.
Rom. Imperatorum Narrationes, cum alio quodam Petri Martyris* . . . (Cologne, 1532), this containing Martyr's Fourth Decade
as an introduction to the letters from Cortez to Charles V on the
conquest of Mexico. It was presumably this volume that gave Eden
the Fourth Decade under his title "Of the Landes and Ilandes lately
founde" (included, as mentioned, in his Third Decade);
*De Orbe novo Petri Martyris Anglerii* . . . *Decades octo, quas
scripsit ab anno 1493 ad 1526* . . . edited by Joachim Torres Asen-
sio, 2 vols. (Madrid, 1892).

Also the English editions of Richard Willes, *The History of
Travayle in the West and East Indies* . . . *Gathered in parte, and
done into Englysshe by Richarde Eden, Newly set in order, aug-
mented, and finished by Richard Willes* (London, 1577);

Edward Arber, *The first Three English books on America* . . .
*Being chiefly Translations, Compilations, &c., by Richard Eden*
(Birmingham, 1885), including *The Decades of the newe worlde* as
the third book;

Francis Augustus MacNutt, editor and translator, *De Orbe
Novo The Eight Decades of Peter Martyr D'Anghiera*, 2 vols. (New
York, 1912), a modern and authoritative translation.

I have also used the French edition by Paul Gaffarel, *De Orbe
Novo de Pierre Martyr Anghiera Les Huit Décades* (Paris, 1907).

For further information on Richard Eden's life and work see
David Gwyn, "Richard Eden Cosmographer and Alchemist," *The
Sixteenth Century Journal*, 15/1 (Spring 1984), 13-34.

*Canoa*: Eden, *Decades*, "The Indian Language."

7    The "hidden half of the globe": quoted here from a 1670 edition of
Peter Martyr's letters, *Opus Epistolarum Petri Martyris Anglerii
Mediolanensis* (Amsterdam), Liber sextus, Epist. cxxxv, 74-75.

"Myne and Thyne": Eden, *Decades*, First Decade, Book 3, fol. 17
verso.

The Latin: *Orbe Novo* (1530), Prima Decas, Caput tertium, fol. 10.

Land in common: Eden, *loc. cit.*

"Idlenes and playe": Eden, *Decades*, First Decade, Book 3, fol. 12
verso.

8    Ambition and "the desire to rule": MacNutt, *Orbe Novo*, 1:79.

A facsimile of the Barcelona edition of 1493 of Columbus's letter-report appears in John Boyd Thacher, *Christopher Columbus, His Life, His Work, His Remains,* 3 vols. (New York, 1903), 2:18.

A recent translation of this letter-report is in Samuel Eliot Morison, *Christopher Columbus Mariner* (London, 1956), Appendix One, 212-23.

Columbus Journal: Thacher, *op. cit.,* 1:625.

The "hande of the artificer": Eden, *Decades,* First Decade, Book 3, fol. 12.

"Indian pearls": Gaffarel, *Orbe Novo,* p. 86.

Eden, "scorneful giestures": *Decades,* 1, bk. 6, fol. 31.

9   "Everything in the isles": MacNutt, *Orbe Novo,* 1:75-76.

No man "able to behowlde them": Eden, *Decades,* 1, bk. 2, fol. 7.

The terrestrial paradise: Gaffarel, *Orbe Novo,* 2, bk. 9, p. 210.

Thomas More, *Utopia,* edited by Edward Surtz and J. H. Hexter (New Haven, 1965), xxxii.

Sidney Lee, "The Call of the West: America and Elizabethan England," *Scribners,* May 1907, 543.

For Saint Thomas More said to be inscribed in Red Square: *Encyclopaedia Britannica,* 15th edition, 1974, Thomas More entry — however, *The Great Soviet Encyclopedia,* 3d edition (Moscow, 1974), does not mention this particular honor in its Thomas More entry.

The Classiques du Peuple edition: *L'Utopie,* edited by Marcelle Bottigelli-Tisserand (Paris, 1974), Introduction, 52.

10  As "complicated as vicious": *ibid.,* 107.

"American tracts": D. B. Quinn, "Renaissance Influences in English Colonization," *Transactions of the Royal Historical Society,* 5th series, 26 (1976).

The supposed marginal note by Erasmus may be found in *The Utopia of Sir Thomas More in Latin from the Edition of March 1518 . . .* edited by J. H. Lupton (Oxford, 1895), p. 195.

R. H. Tawney, *Equality* (New York, 1931), cited in Surtz and Hexter, eds., *Utopia,* pages cxxiii-cxxiv.

A. W. Reed, *Early Tudor Drama* (London, 1926), establishes John Rastell's authorship of *A new interlude and a mery of the nature of the iiii elements declarynge many proper poynts of phylosophy naturall/ and of dyvers straunge lands/* . . . (*circa* 1525, reprinted by Tudor Facsimile Texts, London, 1908), which speaks of this abortive "voyage of discovery" of 1516-1517. A recent edition of this play, done as an acting version, contains a detailed study of Rastell's publishing activities: Roger Coleman, *John Rastell, The Four Elements* (Cambridge, 1971).

John Rastell, Jr., is quoted from the 1589 edition of Richard Hakluyt, *The Principall Navigations* . . . pt. 3, 517.

12    "Surely the Greeks and the Romans": José de Acosta, *Historia Natural y Moral de las Indias* (Seville, 1590), translated into Italian 1596, German, French, and Dutch in 1598, Latin 1602, English 1604. This quotation is taken from the first French edition (Paris, 1598), 1:274.

The quotation beginning "they erre in their opinion" is the title of chap. 1, bk. 6, of the English translation of Acosta's *History* (London, 1604).

Acosta on the Elysian Fields: *Histoire* (Paris, 1598), 2:72.

Geoffroy Atkinson, *Les Nouveaux Horizons de la Renaissance Française* (Paris, 1935), 142-44, 165, *et passim*.

*L'Histoire du Nouveau Monde Descouvert par les Portugaloys, Escrite par le Seigneur Pierre Bembo* (Lyon, 1556), 13.

Jodocus Hondius (or Josse Hondt), *Atlas of Gerard Mercator* (originally published *c*. 1605), quoted here from a later English edition, *Historia Mundi: or Mercator's Atlas. Containing his Cosmographicall Description of the Fabricke and Figure of the World* . . . *By the studious inquiry of Judocus Hondy. Englished by W. S. Generosus, & Coll. Regin. Oxonia.* (London, 1635), 893-94.

13    Jean Macer, *Les Trois Livres de l'Histoire des Indes* (Paris, 1555), 76.

*Lettres d'Americ Vespuce, Florentin* . . . in J. Léon, *Historiale Description de l'Afrique* (Lyon, Jean Temporal, 1556), 1:469.

"Lettres de Manuel Nobrega, de la Compagnie de Iesu Escriptes en l'Isle du Brezil . . ." in *L'Institution des Loix, Coustumes et Autre Choses Merveilleuses & Memorables Tant du Royaume de la*

*Chine que des Indes Contenues en Plusieurs Lettres Missives Envoyées aux Religieux de la Compagnie du Nom de Iesus. Traduictes d'Italien en Francoys* (Paris, 1556).

Jean de Léry, *Histoire d'un Voyage Faict en la Terre du Bresil, autrement dite Amerique* . . . (La Rochelle, 1578), 303.

Although I "love my country": Léry, *Histoire*, 2d ed. (Genève, 1580), 342.

Neither "kings nor princes": *ibid.*, 196.

Macer, *Trois Livres*, 78.

Acosta, *Histoire* (Paris, 2d ed., 1600), 1:288.

14 Early Paris "Americana" is weighed in Rudolph Hirsch, "Printed Reports of the Early Discoveries and Their Reception," *First Images of America: The Impact of The New World on the Old*, edited by Fredi Chiapelli, Michael J. B. Allen, and Robert L. Benson, 2 vols. (Berkeley, 1976), 2:548-49.

Rastell, *Interlude*, fol. cii verso.

William Hawkins: Hakluyt, *Principall Navigations*, pt. 3, 520.

15 Lady Fleming's rapture: Brantôme [Pierre de Bourdeille, seigneur de], *Les Dames Galantes*, written *c.* 1584 (Paris: Livre de Poche, 1962), 217, 296; *n*699-670, p. 474.

Ronsard, *Oeuvres Complètes*, 2 vols. (Paris: Pléiade, 1950); "Discours Contre Fortune," 2:399-409.

17 "Les Isles Fortunées," *ibid.*, 2:409-14.

Ronsard's "ferocity": *Oeuvres Complètes*, ed. Paul Laumonier (Paris, 1928), 234.

18 Montaigne's first English translation is *The Essayes of Michael Lord of Montaigne*, translated by John Florio (first published London, 1603; quoted here from the third edition, 1632); "Of the Canniballes" is chap. 30, bk. 1.

20 Eden on the earthly paradise: "A briefe description of Afrike, gathered by Richard Eden . . ." in Hakluyt, *Principall Navigations* (1589), pt. 1, 85.

"Evidently differences among barbarians": John H. Rowe, "The

Renaissance Foundations of Anthropology," *American Anthropologist*, 67/1 (February, 1965), 6.

21 The "few writers of Classical Antiquity": *ibid.*, 2.

The "Noble Savage in Antiquity" is the title of Chapter 11, Arthur Oncken Lovejoy and George Boas, *Contributions to the History of Primitivism: Primitivism and Related Ideas in Antiquity*, with supplemental essays by W. F. Albright and P. -E. Dumont (Baltimore, 1935).

Vespucci: *Lettres* (Jean Temporal, ed., 1556), 473.

Acosta: *Histoire*, 2:114.

22 Seneca: Lovejoy and Boas, *op. cit.*, 263 ff, 272-73.

A "fundamental change" in Renaissance thinking: Rowe, *op. cit.*, 12.

*Ibid.*, on Peter Martyr's "better" information.

23 Atkinson: *Nouveaux Horizons*, 165.

Antoine de Montchrestien, *Traicté de l'Oeconomie Politique* (Rouen, 1615), cited in Atkinson, *Nouveaux Horizons*, 352.

24 Gilbert Chinard, *Les Réfugiés Huguenots en Amérique* (1925), Introduction.

Plotinus, *Ennead Five*, 5.

The golden age "within us": Claude Lévi-Strauss, *Tristes Tropiques* (Paris, 1955), 354.

A "sense to history" via the golden age: Jerome Gaïth, *Nicholas Berdiaeff, Philosophe de la Liberté* (Beirut, 1968), 168.

25 Cabochian Ordinance: see *The Cambridge Medieval History*, vol. 7:385.

Frederick William Maitland, "A Historical Sketch of Liberty and Equality," *The Collected Papers*, ed. by H. A. L. Fisher (Cambridge, 1911), 1:19-20.

Acton Papers, Cambridge University Library, Add. 4870.

*Ibid.*, Add. 4938, citing William Mitchell Ramsay, *The Church in the [Roman] Empire* (London, 1893), 175.

Isaiah Berlin, *Four Essays on Liberty* (Oxford, 1969), xl, xli.

Thomas Paine, *A Letter addressed to the Abbe Raynal . . . in which the Mistakes of the Abbe's Account of the Revolution of America are corrected and cleared up* (Philadelphia Printed, Dublin Reprinted . . . M. DCC. LXXXII.), 8.

26    Acton Papers, Add. 4862.

27    "Interests": Ferdinand Schevill, *The Medici* (New York, 1949), 33.

The ciompi speaker: M. Mollat and P. Wolff, *Ongles Bleus, Jacques et Ciompi: Les Révolutions Populaires en Europe aux XIVe et XVe Siècles* (Paris, 1970), 156.

Pierre-Joseph Proudhon, *Qu'est-ce que la Propriété? Deuxième Mémoire* (Paris, 2d ed., 1848, originally 1841), 63.

"Equivocal" thirteenth-century liberties: Jacques Le Goff, *Les Intellectuels au Moyen Age* (Paris, 1957), 73, 80.

Medieval "populist" theory: Walter Ullmann, *Principles of Government and Politics in the Middle Ages* (London, 1961, 1974), 242-82 *passim*. I am indebted to Dr. Graham Maddox for calling attention to the work of Marsilius of Padua and Bartolus of Sassoferato in this connection.

28    Ulysses' comments "commonplaces": H. Hildebrand, ed., Variorum edition of *Troilus and Cressida* (1953), 389, proposing five similar contemporary sources on "Degree."

29    Renaissance free thought: P. O. Kristeller, "The Myth of Renaissance Atheism and the French Tradition of Free Thought," *Journal of the History of Philosophy*, 6 (1968), 233-43.

30    Etienne Dolet is quoted from *Le Second Enfer* (Lyon, 1544), ed. by Claude Longeon (Genève, 1978), 108.

31    Theodore Beza, *Du Droit des Magistrats* (1574), ed. by Robert M. Kingdon (Genève, 1970), 53.

Psalm 109 as a war song: Edward Gosselin, *The King's Progress to Jerusalem* (Malibu, California, 1976), 108.

32    Martin Luther, "Admonition to Peace A Reply to the Twelve Articles of the Peasants in Swabia," 1525, translated by Charles M. Jacobs, revised by Robert C. Schultz, *Luther's Works*, Helmut Lehmann and Walther Brandt, eds., vol. 45 (Philadelphia, 1962), 339.

Beza, *Droit des Magitrats*, 8.

34 Montaigne speaks of La Boétie as "the greatest man of our century" in the Dedicace (71-72) to "Les Regles de mariage de Plutarque" (73-88), in *La Mesnagerie de Xenophon . . . traduict de Grec en Francais par feu M. Etienne De La Boetie* (Paris, 1572), a volume edited and published by Montaigne.

*Contr'un* "too fragile and delicate": *ibid.,* 3b.

35 La Boétie and the "new Indies": Michel Butor, *Essai sur les Essais* (Paris, 1968), 64.

36 *Contr'un* "an isolated effort": Sidney Lee, *French Renaissance in England,* 314.

Negative reports on New World people "exceptional": Atkinson, *Nouveaux Horizons,* 149; and see 146 ff.

37 Vespucci: *Lettres* (Jean Temporal edition, 1556).
The use of "certain herbs" or venomous insects: *The Guardian* (London) reports (January 10, 1984) on the South American spider *Lactrodectus mactans* whose bite causes in men "a permanent and extremely painful erection of the penis for as long as the poison lasts (a condition which explains the colloquial Chilean expression for local Lotharios: 'Stung by a spider')."

André Thévet, *Les Singularités de la France Antarctique* (1557), chap. 27, chap. 61, chap. 40.

Villegagnon: Léry, *Histoire,* (1580), Préface.

38 *Ibid.,* 112, enslaved "wretches" and clothing.

Thévet, *Singularitiés,* chap. 29.

Villegagnon and the natives: A. Heulhard, *Villegagnon Roi d'Amérique* (Paris, 1897), quoting a letter from the Portuguese official Mem de Sá, 18 June 1560.

An indignant English pastor: H. C. Porter, *The Inconstant Savage — England and the North American Indian 1500-1660* (London, 1979), 357, quoting Robert Gray, *A Good Speed to Virginia* (London, 1609).

"They live amongst themselves": Clements Markham, ed., *The Letters of Amerigo Vespucci and Other Documents Illustrative of His Career* (London, 1894), 46, 6-7.

The Bartolozzi Letter: Samuel Eliot Morison, *The European Dis-*

*covery of America: The Southern Voyages, A.D. 1492-1616* (New York, 1974), 285-86.

39    Thévet, *Singularités*, chap. 39, chap. 58.

Urbain Chauveton, *Brief Discours et Histoire d'un Voyage de Quelques François en La Floride. . . . Reveuë & augmentée de nouveau* (1579, attached as an appendix to his translation of Benzoni, quoted here from an edition of 1662).

"This bungler of a Thévet": Heulhard, *Villegagnon, n.* 1., 198, citing Thévet's *Cosmographie*, Livre 21, chap. 2.

40    The galley slave seduction: *Copie d'une Lettre Envoyée au Gouvernor de la Rochelle par les Capitaines des Gallères de France . . . faisât le Voyage de l'Isle de Florida* (Paris, 1565).

The "roberges" and galleys: M. Basanier, *L'Histoire Notable de la Floride* (Paris, 1586), in Suzanne Lussagnet, ed., *Les Français en Amérique Pendant la Deuxième Moitié du XVIe Siècle*, vol. 2: *Les Français en Floride* (Paris, 1958), 50, 64.

Francisco López de Gómara, *Histoire Générale* (French edition, 1568, originally published in Spain 1552), bk. 5, chap. 217, f. 251.

41    Montaigne: Pierre Villey, ed., *Les Essais . . .* 3 vols. (Paris, 1930), 3:230.

*Harangue d'un Cacique Indien* (1596), a pamphlet evidently rather rare; a copy is in the Bibliothèque Nationale, Paris.

42    Benzoni/Chauveton, *Histoire Nouvelle du Nouveau Monde* (Genève, 1579), 326 ff.

Chauveton's aims are discussed in Benjamin Keen, "The Vision of America in the Writings of Urbain Chauveton," *First Images of America*, 1:111, 112.

"Vitorian" solicitude: Henry Méchoulan, "A Propos de la Notion de Barbare Chez Las Casas," *Moreana*, 12 (Angers, February, 1975), 45, quoting Angel Losada, ed., *Los Tesoros del Péru* (Madrid, 1958).

Vitoria on Indian incapability is from the same article, quoting Vitoria's *Relectio de Indis*.

43    Sepúlveda is summarized in Elliott, *Old World and the New*, p 45, drawing on *Demócrates Segundo*, ed. Angel Losada (Madrid, 1951), 36.

Indian freedom a captivity by the devil — Gómara, *op. cit.*, 252.

"Are they not men?": Las Casas, *Historia* (ed. Madrid 1957), vol. 2, bk. 2, 144, 176; bk. 3, chap. 4.

Las Casas' argument is discussed in Lewis Hanke, *Aristotle and the American Indians* (New York, 1959, quoted here from the paper edition, Bloomington, Indiana, 1970), 41, 112-13.

Of the "more than three million": Las Casas, *Tyrannies et Cruautés des Espagnols* (Anvers, 1579), 9.

Benzoni, *History of the New World* . . . translated and edited by Rear Admiral W. H. Smyth (London, 1857), 78.

44     Motolinia is quoted from Hanke, *Aristotle and the American Indians*, 22, citing Luis Nicolau d'Olwer, *Fray Toribio de Benavente*, 195 and 65.

Las Casas on epidemics, *Historia*, 3 vols. (ed. Mexico, 1965), 3: chap. 128, 270-71.

45     The "entire liberty" of the New World: Jodocus Hondius, *Thresor de Chartes, Contenant les Tableaux de Tous les Pays du Monde* (La Haye, *c.* 1619, originally published 1603), 3-4.

# Chapter 2

47     The islanders "governed by kings": MacNutt, *Orbe Novo*, vol. 1: First Decade, chaps. 1 and 2.

48     Albert Frederick Pollard, *The Evolution of Parliament* (London, 1964, originally published 1920), 183-84.

L. H. Morgan, *Montezuma's Dinner* . . . (pamphlet, New York, 1876, reprinted by the *Labor News*, New York, 1950, including a tribute by Friedrich Engels).

49     H. H. Bancroft, *The Early American Chroniclers* (San Francisco, 1883).

Bandelier supported by T. T. Waterman, *Bandelier's Contribution to Study of Ancient Mexican Social Organization* (Berkeley, 1916-1917).

Such "false conclusions": Alfonso Caso, "Land Tenure among the Ancient Mexicans," *American Anthropologist*, 65 (1963), 863.

The "Aztec state": Gordon R. Willey, *An Introduction to American Archaeology*, 2 vols. (Englewood Cliffs, N.J., 1966), 1:160.

50    The total presence of religion: Alfonso Caso, *La Religión de los Aztecas* (Mexico, 1936), 55-56.

George C. Vaillant, *The Aztecs of Mexico: Origin, Rise and Fall of the Aztec Nation* (New York, 1941; revised edition annotated by Susannah B. Vaillant, 1962), 127.

A recent study of settlement patterns: William T. Sanders, "Pre-Conquest Settlement Patterns," Robert Wauchope, ed., *Handbook of Middle American Indians*, vol. 10 (Austin, Tex., 1971), 14, 24.

51    The two functioned "as a team": Hasso von Winning, "Tlacaelel, Aztec General and Statesman," *The Masterkey*, 38/2 (Southwest Museum, Los Angeles, 1964).

A theory of reciprocity: Claude Lévi-Strauss, *Anthropologie Structurale* (Paris, 1958), 179.

Tezcatlipoca: the lines quoted here are in the adaptation for my collection of American Indian poetry, *The Magic World* (New York, 1971), 15-23, from Book 2, Fray Bernardino de Sahagun, *General History of the Things of New Spain: the Florentine Codex*, translated by Charles Dibble and Arthur J. O. Anderson (Sante Fe, 1950 ff).

53    As "all life is illusion": *The Magic World*, 24, adapted from Daniel G. Brinton, *Ancient Nahuatl Poetry* (Philadelphia, 1887).

"The riches of this world": *The Magic World*, 26, adapted from a version translated by Fanny Calderon for William H. Prescott, printed in a Note to his *History of the Conquest of Mexico* (London, 1843).

54    The caciquedom descending in specific families: Sherburne Friend Cook, *Santa Maria Ixcatlan* (Berkeley, 1958), Appendix, 2, 73-75, the "Cacicazgo of Ixcatlan."

55    "Like people possessed": Sahagun, *Florentine Codex*, bk. 2.

Post-Conquest Indian memories of Inca life: Phelipe Guaman Poma de Ayala (facsimile manuscript edited by Paul Rivet, Paris, 1936; written *c.* 1587-1615).

56    Rule by "joint government": Ralph L. Roys, *The Political Geography of the Yucatan Maya* (Washington, 1957), 1.

58 Indians "at least ten times as religious": Harold E. Driver, *Indians of North America* (Chicago, 2d ed., 1969), 396.

59 Pawnee hymn: *The Magic World*, 68, adapted from Alice C. Fletcher, "The Hako, a Pawnee Ceremony," *Twenty-second Annual BAE Report* (Washington, 1904).

Dualism of government: William H. Fenton, "Factionalism in American Indian Society," *Actes du IVe Congrès International des Sciences Anthropologiques et Ethnologiques*, vol. 2 (Vienne, 1952).

Alvar Nuñez Cabeza de Vaca: F. W. Hodge and Theodore H. Lewis, eds., *Spanish Explorers in the Southern United States 1525-1542* (New York, 1907), 56 and 54.

60 Cartier: John Pinkerton, *A General Collection of the Best and Most Interesting Voyages and Travels in All Parts of the World*, 17 vols. (London, 1808-1841), 3:650.

Francisco Vasquez de Coronado: Herbert E. Bolton, *Coronado, Knight of Pueblo and Plains* (New York, 1949), 246.

# Chapter 3

63 Dolet's execution: Richard Copley Christie, *Etienne Dolet the Martyr of the Renaissance* (2d ed., London, 1899), 470 ff.

65 The Tupinamba living "continually in joy": *Histoire de la Mission des Pères Capucins en l'Isle de Maragnon . . .* by *the Révérend Père Claude d'Abbeville* (Paris, 1614), 282.

The Hurons: *Histoire du Canada . . . faict et composé par le F. Gabriel Sagad Theodat, mineur Recollect* (Paris, 1636), 255-56.

66 No one has "superiority": R. P. Pierre Pelleprat, *Relation des Missions . . . dans les Isles et dans la Terre Ferme de l'Amérique Meridionale* (Paris, 1655), pt. 2, 55.

Marc Lescarbot, *Histoire de la Nouvelle France* and *Les Muses de la Nouvelle France* (Paris, 1609), 841-42.

Above all, "everyone could live in liberty": Gilbert Chinard, *L'Amérique et le Rêve Exotique* (Paris, 1913), 107.

Rivers "run with milk for you" is from an anonymous French propaganda poem published with a 1598 edition of *Discours du Voyage Fait par le Capitaine Jacques Cartier.*

The "Nymph" Virginia: Samuel Purchas, *Purchas his Pilgrimage* (London, 1613, quoted here from the 3rd ed., 1617), 937.

A satirical verse history of Paris: *La Muze Historique ou Recueil des Lettres en Vers Contenant les Nouvelles du Temps 1650-1665* by J. Loret; ed. by Ch.-L. Livet, 4 vols. (Paris, 1857-1878), 1:86.

Richard Hakluyt, *A Notable Historie Containing Foure Voyages Made by Certayne French Captaynes unto Florida . . . Newly Translated out of French into English by R. H.* (London, 1587), Dedication.

William Morrell, *New-England, or a Briefe Enarration of the Ayre, Earth, Water, Fish and Fowles of That Country, with a Description of the Natures, Orders, Habits, and Religion of the Natives* (London, 1625).

67      Scarron, *Oeuvres*, 7:186; cited in Chinard, *L'Amérique* (1913), 34.

Their "entire liberty": Antoine Biet, *Voyage de la France Equinoxiale en l'Isle de Cayenne* (Paris, 1664), 9 and 139 ff.

R. P. Jean-Baptiste Du Tertre, *Histoire Générale, des Isles de S. Christophe, de la Guadeloupe, de la Martinique, et Autres dans l'Amérique* (Paris, 1654), later published in an enlarged edition of four volumes, *Histoire Générale des Antilles* (Paris, 1667 and 1671); the edition of 1654 is used here, 396-97.

68      The Indians brought up "as brute beasts": *ibid.,* 417.

Indictment a "dithyramb": Chinard, *L'Amérique* (1913), 8-9.

"After having announced that they're going to make us shiver": *ibid.,* 11.

No "true virtue could exist outside the church": *ibid.,* 11.

69      *Ibid.,* 52-53, quoting Father Pelleprat, *Mission de Cayenne et de la Guyane Francaise* (Paris, 1858, one of a series of volumes entitled *Voyages et Travaux des Missionaires de la Compagnie de Jésus . . . Pour Servir de Complément aux Lettres Edifiantes,* 143.

*Ibid.,* 141, "so taken with liberty."

Lejeune: *The Jesuit Relations and Allied Documents . . . 1610-*

*1701* . . . edited by Reuben Gold Thwaites, 73 vols. (Cleveland, 1896-1901), 8:168; and 9:141.

70   The "beautiful remnants": Father Chauchetière to his brother, 1694, *Jesuit Relations*, 64:130.

Greater "measure of liberty": Cornelius J. Jaenen, "Amerindian View of French Culture in the Seventeenth Century," *Canadian Historical Review*, 55/3 (September, 1974), 288.

Not "an inkling of covetousness": Paul Boyer, *Veritable Relation de Tout ce qui s'est fait et passé au Voyage* . . . *a l'Amérique Occidentale* (Paris, 1654), 227.

Reverend Robert Gray: H. C. Porter, *Inconstant Savage*, 356-57, citing Gray's *Good Speed to Virginia*.

Samuel Purchas, *Purchas his Pilgrimes* (London, 1625), 16.

Lescarbot's argument is in his *Histoire* (1609), 21.

Nicolas Denys, *Description Geographique et Historique des Costes de l'Amerique Septentrionale* . . . *par Monsieur Denys, Gouverneur* . . . *& Proprietaire de Toutes les Terres & Isles qui sont depuis le Cap de Campseaux, jusques au Cap des Roziers* . . . 2 vols. (Paris, 1672), 1:363, 392, 393.

71   The narrative by a survivor of La Salle's last expedition: Henry Reed Stiles, ed., *Joutel's Journal of La Salle's Last Voyage* (Albany, N.Y., 1906), reprinted from the English translation, 1714, of the original French edition of 1713; quoted here from pages 158-59.

72   *Ibid.*, 161, the "libertinism" of the two teen-age boys.

The official estimate of the 1680s on coureurs de bois: Emil Salone, *La Colonisation de la Nouvelle France* (Paris, 1905), 256, and 256 *n*1 and *n*2, citing a letter from Duchesneau to Colbert, 13 October 1680; their defiance of royal edicts is mentioned on p. 254, *n*1; their welcome from the "indigènes" p. 255. Such official estimates during this period need to be used with care, however, since Duchesneau and Frontenac were engaged in political disputes in which the numbers (and political tendencies) of coureurs de bois sometimes played a part.

73   Mathieu Sagean: *The Original Manuscript Account of the Kingdom of Aacaniba, Given by the Affidavit of Matthew Sagean, a*

*Frenchman . . . which, tho' hitherto unknown to all Geographers; yet, on the Faith of that Relation, the late Regent of France erected the Mississippi, now the French East-India Company; But as that Manuscript was never before published, which relates as Facts, Matters very singular, It is Englished by Quin Mackenzie, Esq. . . .* (London, 1755) The entire Sagean report (81 pages) was published in Pierre Margry, *Découvertes et Etablissements des Français dans l'Ouest et dans le sud de l'Amérique septentrionale,* 6 vols. (Paris, 1879-88), 6:93 ff.

White captives resisting repatriation: *Historical Account of Bouquet's Expedition Against the Ohio Indians in 1764* (Cincinnati, 1868), 76-77, 80-81; quoted in Clark Wissler, *Indians of the United States* (New York, 1940), 253-54.

74    Background on the two teen-age boys: Adolph F. A. Bandelier, *The Gilded Man* (New York, 1893), 289-302.

Francis Parkman, *La Salle and the Discovery of the Great West* (paper edition, 1963, ed. by John A. Hawgood), 320-21.

Losses in the Thirty Years' War: Will and Ariel Durant, *The Age of Reason Begins* (New York, 1961), 567, citing the *Cambridge Modern History* (1910), 4:418.

Henri III's excesses: Pierre Bayle, *Dictionnaire Historique et Critique* (1697), vol. 2.

The Venetian ambassador is quoted in André Maurois, *History of France* (New York, 1948), 167.

Census comparisons between the times of Charles IX and Louis XIV: Victor de Riquetti, marquis de Mirabeau (father of the tribune), *L'Ami des Hommes ou Traité de la Population* (Avignon, 1756), chap. 5, p. 60.

Lord Acton, "The History of Freedom in Christianity" (1877), William H. McNeill, ed., *Essays in the Liberal Interpretation of History* (Chicago, 1967), 288.

75    *Lettre de Fénelon à Louis XIV* (published by Antoine-Augustin Renouard, Paris, 1825), 24.

The flaying of an English admiral: Caesar de Nostradamus, *L'Histoire et Chronique de Provence* (Lyon, 1624), 781.

The "most wretched" peasants and the State: Johannes Janssen,

*History of the German People after the Close of the Middle Ages,* 17 vols. (London, 1896-1925), 15:171, quoting the professor Sebastian Munster, 1588; and 141, quoting the Mecklenburg jurist John Frederick Husanus, 1590.

*Ibid.*, ordinances of serfdom: 141, citing Augsburg Recess of 1555, and 148-49, quoting the Peasant and Shepherd Ordinance of 1616 in Pomerania and Rugen.

76    *Ibid.*, 152, traffic with serfs "as with horses and cows."

The oath of vassalage: F. L. Ganshof, *Feudalism* (English translation of *Qu'est-ce que la Féodalité*, Brussels, 1944, New York, 1952), 170.

Adam le Yep: Mollat and Wolff, *Ongles Bleus*, 292.

Hunting: Janssen, *History*, 15:217-18, 221, 198-200, 222.

77    Voltaire, *Siècle de Louis XIV*, 2 vols. (edition of 1966), 2: chap. 30, p. 37.

A. T. Volwiler, *George Croghan and the Westward Movement, 1741-1782* (Cleveland, 1926), 170.

Jefferson: George Tucker, *The Life of Thomas Jefferson, Third President of the United States*, 2 vols. (London, 1837), 1:255.

Jefferson on France and England in comparison with "our neighboring savages": Lester J. Cappon, ed., *The Adams-Jefferson Letters* (Chapel Hill, 1959), 291, quoted in Donald A. Grinde, Jr., *The Iroquois and the Founding of the American Nation* (San Francisco, 1977), 130.

Galleys: *Galley Slave the Autobiography of Jean Marteilhe*, ed. by Kenneth Fenwick (London, 1957, originally published Rotterdam, 1757), 74, 76.

Jean de La Bruyère, *Les Caractères* (1688), XI, 128.

Nicolas Boileau, *Oeuvres Complètes* (Paris, 1966), Satire VI.

78    Voltaire, *Siècle de Louis XIV* (1966), 1:52.

Laurence Sterne, *The Life and Opinions of Tristram Shandy* (1759-1767), bk. 7, chap. 17.

Paris mud: Henri Sauval, *Histoire et Recherches de la Ville de Paris . . .* 3 vols. (Paris, 1724, written 1650s), 1:186.

Protection against "nocturnal attacks": René Héron de Villefosse, *Histoire de Paris* (Paris, 1948), 188.

79    Traffic jams of 1713: [Robert Chasles], *Les Illustres Francoises* . . . (originally published 1713, quoted here from a 2-vol. edition, La Haye, 1731), 1:1-2. Published anonymously; the author's identity was later established but the orthography of his name — Chasles, Challes, Challe, is still uncertain.

"What fine journeys": R. P. Claude Buffier, *Cours de Sciences sur des Principes Nouveaux & Simples* (Paris, 1720 ff), 981.

Marie Antoinette's fast time is from a note by one of her mounted escort, quoted in François Cali, *La Maison Neuve sur la Place* (Paris, 1978), 278.

This "Niagara of bankruptcy": Jules Michelet, *Histoire de France* (definitive edition, Paris, 1896), 13:393.

The "terrible decree": *ibid.*, 312.

Argenson's "repressive nature": Faure, *La Banqueroute de Law*, 420.

Argenson's undermining of public confidence in Law's bank: Buvat, *Journal de la Régence*, 2:103 ff.

80    Croquants: Yves-Marie Bercé, *Histoire des Croquants, Etude des Soulèvements Populaires au XVIIe Siècle dans le Sud-ouest de la France*, 2 vols. (Genève, 1974), 1:247.

The "wheels and the gibbets": *ibid.*, 1:251, and *n.* 190.

This "multitude of people without house or home": J.-E. Malaussène, *L'Evolution d'un Village-Frontière de Provence: Saint-Jeannet* (Paris, 1909), 405-6.

81    Abbé E. Tisserand, *Histoire de Vence* . . . (Paris, 1860), 233-36.

The rejoicing historian: Count Francis von Luetzow, *Bohemia: An Historical Sketch* (London, 1910, revised ed., 1939), 312.

The "Parliament of Paris": Acton Papers, Add. 4962, citing *Bulletin du Bibliophile* 1847, 570, RP, XV, 991.

A "land of the lost": *Un Colonial au Temps de Colbert, Mémoires de Robert Challes, Ecrivain de Roi*, ed. by A. Augustin-Thierry (Paris, 1931; written before 1716), 78.

82    Geoffroy Atkinson, *The Extraordinary Voyage in French Literature before 1700* (New York, 1920), 14.

"There exist in the libraries in France": Atkinson, *Nouveaux Horizons*, Préface.

What "is important in the history of ideas": G. Atkinson, *The Sen-
timental Revolution, French Writers of 1690-1740* (Seattle, 1965),
*passim*, quoting examples from such of his previous works as *Relations de Voyages du XVIIIe Siècle et l'Evolution des Idées* (1924).

83    Chinard, *L'Amérique*, 143.

*Ibid.*, 218, the New World in *Télémaque.*

A striking conclusion to "come from an ecclesiastic and before
1700": Atkinson, *Extraordinary Voyage*, 149-150.

Fénelon's words: *Télémaque*, bk. 7.

Hugo Grotius, *De iure belli et pacis* (Paris, 1625), 1:1.

Samuel von Pufendorf, *De iure naturae et gentium* (Lundon,
Sweden 1672).

The political "naturalism" of Aristotle is analyzed in Ullmann,
*Principles of . . . Politics in the Middle Ages*, 244, 250.

84    Vitoria on the New World: James Brown Scott, ed., *The Spanish
Origin of International Law: Francisco de Vitoria and his Law of
Nations* (Oxford, 1934), Introduction.

Nature "the key to the thought of the eighteenth century": A. Cob-
ham, *New Cambridge Modern History* (1957), 7:111.

That "man in a state of nature was good": Frank E. Manuel, ed.,
*The Enlightenment* (Englewood Cliffs, N.J., 1965), 5-6.

Grotius-De Laet controversy: Lee Eldridge Huddleston, *Origins of
the American Indians/ European Concepts 1492-1729* (Austin,
Tex., 1967), 120.

Pufendorf's documentation: see Jean Barbeyrac, translator and editor, Préface to Pufendorf, *Le Droit de la Nature*, (Amsterdam,
1706).

85    Thomas Hobbes, *Leviathan, or the Matter, Forme, and Power of a
Commonwealth Ecclesiasticall and Civil* (London, 1651), xiii.

Hobbes, "Philosophical Rudiments," *English Works*, W. Molesworth, ed., 2:12, cited in Porter, *The Inconstant Savage*, chap. 17, and *nn*. 92 to 95.

Hobbes on freedom and the "law of nature": *Leviathan*, 83, 123.

Thomas Traherne, *Centuries of Meditations*, ed. by Bertram Dobell (London, 1908), 3:167.

Mrs. Aphra Behn, *Oroonoko, or the History of the Royal Slave* (*Collected Works*, 7th ed., London, 1722), 1:79.

Maitland, "Historical Sketch of Liberty, " 32.

86    Acton Papers, Add. 4901.

Michelet, *Histoire*, 13:333.

*Télémaque*, cited in Chinard, *L'Amérique*, 218.

Montaigne "had taught that dangerous thing, to think freely": Villey, ed., *Essays* (1930), Preface.

Science decried against the simple "light of reason": Henri Corneille Agrippa de Nettesheim, *Sur la Nobless et Excellence du Sexe Feminin, de sa Prééminence sur l'Autre Sexe*, tr. by Nicolas Gueudeville, 3 vols. (Leyde, 1726), Préface, 1:4, 1.

87    Nicolas Gueudeville, *Les Nouvelles des Cours de L'Europe*, Tome 10 (1704), pp. 12, 662.

A "free Society": Gueudeville, *L'Esprit des Cours de l'Europe*, Tome 12 (1705), 302.

Lahontan's first two small volumes: *Nouveaux Voyages de Mr le Baron de Lahontan, dans l'Amerique Septentrionale . . .* (La Haye, 1703), and Tome 2: *Memoires de lAmerique Septentrionale; ou la Suite des Voyages de Mr le Baron de Hontan . . .* (La Haye, 1703).

89    The "Curious Dialogues": *Supplement aux Voyages du Baron de Lahontan où l'on trouve des Dialogues Curieux entre l'Auteur et un Sauvage de bon sense qui a Voyagé . . .* (La Haye, 1703).

90    The "testimony of our girls": Gilbert Chinard, ed., *Dialogues Curieux . . . et Mémoires de l'Amérique Septentrionale* (Baltimore, 1931), 218, 219.

As long as "Thine and Mine remain": *ibid.*, 174.

This money: *ibid.*, 199.

"We are born free": *ibid.*, 184-85.

An "equality of wealth": *ibid.*, 198.

"Would one see classes?" *ibid.*, 200.

91    The Huron lives in tranquility: *ibid.*, 204.

"What have we in the world dearer than life?" *ibid.*, 206.

"How could I watch the Needy suffer?" *ibid.*, 208.

"They have the *thine* and the *mine* among them:" *ibid.*, 211.

You "prefer slavery": *ibid.*, 207.

"You will see these poor barbarians": Father Pierre Biard, writing in 1613, in Thwaites, ed., *Jesuit Relations*, 3:75; quoted in C. J. Jaenan, *Friend and Foe, Aspects of French-Amerindian Cultural Contact* . . . (New York, 1976).

92    There "is no Indian": Father Christian Leclerq, *New Relation of Gaspesia, with the Customs and Religions of the Gaspesian Indians* (Paris, 1691), tr. by William P. Ganong (Toronto, 1910).

A "revolutionary journalist": Chinard, *L'Amérique*, 18; and see Chinard, ed., *Dialogues*, Introduction, 2, 70-72.

Those "who know my faults": *Dialogues*, 1703 French ed., Préface.

Gueudeville's revised and enlarged edition: *Voyages du Baron de La Hontan dans l'Amerique Septentrionale . . . Seconde edition, revuë, corrigée, & augmentée* . . . 2 vols. (Amsterdam, 1705).

93    The mistaken early critic: Jean Le Clerc, *Bibliotheque Ancienne et Moderne, pour Servir de Suite aux Bibliotheques Universelles et Choisies* (Amsterdam, 1724), 22: pt. 1, 221-22.

An example of the mistake's longevity: André Lichtenberger, *Le Socialisme au XVIIIe Siècle* (Paris, 1895), 54 — although an excellent work, and still a standard reference.

The mistake corrected: Reuben Gold Thwaites, ed., *New Voyages to North America by the Baron de Lahontan* . . . 2 vols. (Chicago), 1905).

Their "despicable luxuries": Chinard, ed., *Dialogues*, 190n.

They "kiss the iron": *ibid.*, 192n.

Spend "hundreds of millions for his pleasures": *ibid.*, 246-47.

That "Royalty is abolished in France": *ibid.*, 237.

94   The body "where *Thine* and *Mine* reign": *ibid.*, 238.

The people "without capital": ibid., 239.

With "no other patrimony than his labor": *ibid.*, 255.

"Hold on there, *Huron*": *ibid.*, 256-57.

95   A society in which "natural Law is found": *ibid.*, 257.

# Chapter 4

97   Lahontan early editions: Albert H. Greenly, "Lahontan: An Essay and Bibliography," *Papers of the Bibliographical Society of America*, (New York, 1954), 48:344-89; and from *Dictionary of Canadian Biography* (Toronto, 1969), 2:443.

The first English translation: *New Voyages to North-America . . . also a Dialogue between the Author and a General of the Savages, giving a Full View of the Religion and Strange Opinions of These People . . . Written in* French *by the Baron Lahontan . . . now in* England. *Done into English. In Two Volumes. A great part of which never printed in the original* (London, 1703).

"You fobb me off very prettily": *ibid.*, 141.

98   "The obscure adventurer of earlier days": Gustave Lanctot, ed., *New Documents by Lahontan concering Canada and Newfoundland, the Oakes Collection* (Ottawa, 1940), Introduction.

Gottfried Wilhelm von Leibniz, *Jugement sur les Oeuvres de M. le Comte de Shaftesbury, Publiées à Londres en 1711, Sous le Titre de Characteristiks. Works*, 5:40; cited in Chinard, ed., *Dialogues*, who discusses at some length Leibniz' references to Lahontan, pp 52-56.

Some French historians, e.g.: Charles Morazé, *La France Bourgeoise, XVIIIe-XXe Siècles* (Paris, 1946), 11.

Which loved "hierarchy": Paul Hazard, *La Crise de la Conscience Européène, 1680-1715* (Paris, 1935), quoted here from the 2-vol. edition of 1961, Préface, and 16-18.

99   Pufendorf "pounded, bent, and snipped": Leonard Krieger, *The Politics of Discretion, Pufendorf and the Acceptance of Natural Law* (Chicago, 1965), Introduction, 1, 3.

Denis Diderot, *Le Neveu de Rameau*, ed. by Georges Monval (Paris, 1891), 147.

Barbeyrac: *Le Droit de la Nature et des Gens . . . Traduit du Latin de feu Mr. le Baron de Pufendorf, par Jean Barbeyrac*, 2 vols. (Amsterdam, 1706), 2:5, XIX, *n*l.

Grotius's statement is from the English translation of Barbeyrac's edition of *The Rights of War and Peace* (London, 1728), bk. 2, chap. 22, p. XI.

"Hobbes, and our Author too": the Barbeyrac translation of Pufendorf's *De jure naturae* in the fifth edition of its English translation, "to which are now added all the large notes of M. Barbeyrac, translated from his fourth and last edition . . ." (London, 1749), bk. 2, chap. 2, p. 102, *n*4.

100 Pufendorf finding American ideals "unworthy of Approbation": *De jure naturae*, English edition of 1717, bk. 3, chap. 2, p. 13.

Barbeyrac's lengthy notes are from the English edition of 1749 of his translation of *De jure naturae*, bk. 2, chap. 2, 101, *n*2 to *n*8; 102, *n*1 to *n*4.

101 Love "a la Sauvage": *Arlequin Sauvage, Comedie en Trois Actes. Par le Sieur D\*\*\* Representée pour la Premiere Fois par les Comediens Italiens Ordinaires du Roi. Nouvelle edition.* (Paris, 1756), act 1, scene 4. This fairly complete edition of the play seems to be rare. It is in a collection in the Cambridge University Library: 7735. d. 273.

Madmen "who think you are wise": *ibid.*, act 2, scene 3.

"Happy a thousand times the Savages": *ibid.*, act 3, scene 2.

Who "would not die laughing": *ibid.*, act 3, scene 4.

102 "I want to be a free man, nothing more": *ibid.*, act 2, scene 3.

No "need of money to be rich": *ibid.*, act 3, scene 4.

A later play presenting the other side: Alexis Piron, *Fernand Cortez*, 1744.

103 Will he then "with the thunder in his hand": "Le Nouveau Monde," *Théatre François, ou Recueil des Meilleurs Pieces de Théatre* (Paris, 1737), vol. 12:225.

The Americans losing "Their liberty": La Découverte du Nouveau

Monde, Tragedie en Trois Actes," *Oeuvres Complètes de Jean-Jacques Rousseau* . . . 4 vols. (Paris, 1846-1852), 3:254-61. The *Confessions*, pt. 2, bk 7, 1742, speaks of the writing of this play and the composition of the music for the first act.

104  "In 1721, under the Regency": C. Fusil, "Jean-Jacques Rousseau et Delisle de la Drevetière," *Revue d'Histoire Litteraire de la France*, 33e année (1926), 234-37.

The "conjecture": Hans Grusemann, *Die Natur-Kulturantithese bei Delisle de la Drevetiere und J.-J. Rousseau.* Inaugural Dissertation . . . Universitat zu Münster 1939, 84. The translation was very kindly made for me by Mary Shields.

"My muse": Voltaire, *Correspondance*, ed. by Theodore Besterman, vol. 1, 1704-1738 (Paris, 1965), 644, and 1430*n*.

"I understand, it's *Arlequin Sauvage*": *Oeuvres Complètes* de Voltaire (Paris, 1877), 5: *Théâtre*, quoting the Préface to the Edition de Paris (1767).

Tales "of noble Indians": Lawrence Marsden Price, *Inkle and Yarico Album* (Berkeley, 1937), 2; this book looks at the sea-changes in the story from Steele to Chamfort.

105  The comment on "Le Manco": *Mémoires Secrets Pour Servir à l'Histoire de la République des Lettres en France, Depuis M.DCC.LXII Jusqu'à Nos Jours; ou Journal d'un Observateur* . . . Tome Premier (London, 1784), entry for 13 juin 1763.

R. P. Joseph-François Lafitau, *Moeurs des Sauvages Américains Comparées aux Moeurs des Premiers Temps*, 2 vols. (Paris, 1724), 1:103, 485-86.

106  The "more one discovers in them estimable qualities": R. P. F. X. Charlevoix, *Histoire et Description Générale de la Nouvelle France. Avec la Journal Historique d'un Voyage Fait par Ordre du Roi dans l'Amérique Septentrionale*, 3 vols. (Paris, 1744), 3:255, 343-44.

"None of the greatest *Roman* Heroes": Cadwallader Colden, *The History of the Five Indian Nations of Canada Which Are Dependent on the Province of New York in America* . . . (New York, 1727, and various later editions; quotations and title used here are from the third edition, 2 vols., London, 1755), 1: from the Introductory Epistle to General Oglethorpe, p. v, and 11.

Buffier, 1732 edition of his *Cours de Sciences*, 974-87.

107  *Ibid.*, Buffier's apology to the Americans for the term "savages," p 1462, cited in Chinard, *L'Amérique*, 333.

Voltaire, *Essai Sur Les Moeurs et l'Esprit des Nations*, ed. by Jacqueline Marchand (Paris, Les Classiques du Peuple, 1962), 70 *n*1, quoting Voltaire's Introduction, written 1744 ff, published 1756.

Guillaume T. F. Raynal, *Histoire Philosophique et Politique. Des Etablissements & du Commerce des Europeens dans les Deux Indes*, 7 vols. (originally published 1770, the edition quoted here is that of La Haye, 1774), 1:1-2.

Adam Smith, *An Inquiry into the Nature and Causes of the Wealth of Nations*, 2 vols. (London, 1776), 2:235.

Diderot's ideas on the state of nature are from his *Neveu de Rameau*, 153, 170.

108  Diderot's libertarian ideas: "Le Temple du Bonheur," date uncertain but probably *c.* 1770, in Denis Diderot, *Oeuvres Complètes*, ed. by Roger Lewinter (Paris, 1971), 8:168.

Prévost's "arsenal" is described in Chinard, *L'Amérique*, 339-40.

The researcher quoted on Rousseau's sources is Jean Morel, "Recherches sur les Sources du Discours de l'Inégalité," *Annales de la Société Jean Jacques Rousseau*, vol. 5, 1909, 119-98.

109  The "prototype noble savages": Geoffrey Symcox, "The Wild Man's Return: The Enclosed Vision of Rousseau's Discourses," Edward Dudley and Maximilian E. Novak, eds., *The Wild Man Within, an Image in Western Thought from the Renaissance to Romanticism* (Pittsburgh, 1972), 223-47.

Diderot "a furious giver of advice": Jean Morel, *op.cit.*, 120.

More "to the taste of Diderot": Rousseau, *Confessions*, vol. 8.

No other writer ever possessed "such gifts": Jean Ferrari, *Les Sources Françaises de la Philosophie de Kant* (Paris, 1980) 174.

The modern scholar who assembled these quotations: Irving Babbitt, *Spanish Character and Other Essays* (Boston, 1940), 225.

More "than two thousand five hundred studies on Rousseau": Alexander Cioranescu, *Bibliographie de la Littérature Française du Dix-huitième Siècle*, vol. 3 (Paris, 1969).

110    Tom Paine, *Common Sense*, January 10, 1776: *The Life and Major Writings of Thomas Paine*, ed. by Philip S. Foner (New York, 1945, paper 1961), 4.

Jacques Rousseau "walking on all fours": *Recueil des Faceties Parisiennes, Pour les Six Premiers Mois de l'An 1760.*

Lévi-Strauss, *Tristes Tropiques*, 351.

111    The Rousseauian quotations concluding with happiness being "less the business of reason than of feeling" are from the notes to the *Discours sur l'Origine et les Fondements de l'Inégalité, Oeuvres*, vol. 2 (Amsterdam, 1769), *n.* 16, 155-59.

These "frightful words thine and mine": "Réponse à Borde," *Correspondance Complète de Jean Jacques Rousseau* (Genève, 1966), vol. 3.

His confession of "indignation": *Confessions*, 1:305.

"We see the maxim given us": *Le Parisien*, quoted by Tollot in *Correspondance Complète* (1966), 3:340.

*Ibid.*, 3:338, "What would become of Society . . ."

Jefferson sharing Rousseau's belief: John Morley, *Rousseau and his Era*, 2 vols. (London, 1923), 2:273.

Jefferson wishing to express "the American mind": Gilbert Chinard, *La Déclaration des Droits de l'Homme et du Citoyen et ses Antécédents Américains* (pamphlet, Institut Français de Washington, 1945).

112    Present day historians: *The Historian's Contribution to Anglo-American Misunderstanding*, report of a committee on national bias in Anglo-American history textbooks, Ray Allen Billington chairman (New York, 1966), 53.

Robespierre's "Divine man!": Pierre M. Masson, *La Religion de Rousseau*, 3 vols. (Paris, 1916), 3:74, cited in Will and Ariel Durant, *Rousseau and Revolution* (New York, 1967), 890.

Their "canon of Holy Writ": Edmund Burke, "Letter to a Member of the National Assembly," *Reflections on the French Revolution* (London, 1790), cited in Durant and Durant, *Rousseau*, 891.

"Each century has its characteristic spirit": Diderot to Princess

Dashkov, *c.* 1771, in Arthur M. Wilson, *Diderot* (New York, 1972), 599.

The "Happiness of seeing the New World regenerate the Old": Tom Paine, *Rights of Man* (London, 1791), pt. 1, from the Dedication to George Washington.

# Chapter 5

114 The commando shouting "a woman has no right to read the Gospel": *Le Monde* (Paris), 14 mars 1978, 34.

115 The report of the French parliamentary commission on liberty: *No. 3455, Assemblée Nationale . . . Rapport fait au nom de la commission spéciale chargée d'examiner les propositions de loi sur les libertés*, 3 vols. (Paris, Imprimerie Nationale, 1978).

116 Real liberties must offer not only choice but "the means of making the choice": testimony from Georges Séguy, secretary-general, Conféderation Générale du Travail, *Rapport*, 3:141.

Enunciating liberties "does not suffice": Richard Dupuy, grand-master, Grande Loge de France of Freemasonry, *Rapport*, 3:293.

It "would be easy to show, today": Emmanuel Le Roy Ladurie, professor, Collège de France, chair of the history of modern civilization, *Rapport*, 3:31.

117 The political liberties of 1789 were "real for the epoch": Maurice Duverger, professor, political science, University of Paris, *Rapport*, 3:174.

The projects of legislation under examination: *Rapport*, 2:150, 182.

Liberty in a planned economy "only for the planners": Jacques Rueff, Académie Française, Chancellor of the Institut de France, *Rapport*, 3:43, 52.

A "planned liberalism": Edgar Faure (Commission chairman), President of the National Assembly, *Rapport*, 3:53.

Television transforming "a nation of citizens into a people of idiots": Maurice Duverger, *Rapport*, 3:178.

Marx on freedom as man's "generic character": Guy Besse, professor of philosophy, director of the Center of Marxist study and research, *Rapport*, 3:18.

Liberty the "distinctive character of the human will" and an "essential aspect of" human history: *Rapport*, 2:129, 170.

118  Liberty not at all "a fact of nature": Maurice Druon, Académie Française, quoting Jacques Rueff, *Rapport*, 3:133.

Liberty produced by "historical evolution" on the "European model": Pierre Chaunu, professor, modern history, University of Paris, *Rapport*, 3:86.

A distinction for liberty as "understood since the eighteenth century": Emmanuel Le Roy Ladurie, *Rapport*, 3:30.

Liberty "a compromise": Raymond Aron, professor, Collège de France, chair of sociology and modern civilization, *Rapport*, 3:5.

"Man is not born free": Jacques Rueff, *Rapport*, 3:40.

A "certain degree of liberty has always existed": Emmanuel Le Roy Ladurie, *Rapport*, 3:30.

The "notion of liberty . . . appeared late in history": Claude Lévi-Strauss, Académie Française, professor, Collège de France, chair of social anthropology, *Rapport*, 3:181.

The base of liberty "is constraint": André Malraux, *Rapport*, 3:161.

120  Francis Hutcheson, *System of Moral Philosophy* (1755), 2:245.

"Power goes with property": Acton Papers, Add. 4870, 4862.

Rome's yeoman-farmer replaced by "herds of slaves": Acton Papers, Add. 4862.

Shaftesbury, "The Moralists," *Works*, 2:252, cited in Acton Papers, Add. 4901.

That "liberty became more sacred than property": Acton Papers, Add. 5434.

121  Benjamin Constant, *De la Liberté des Anciens Comparées à celle des Modernes* (Paris, 1819), *passim*.

In "Athens": Arnold Wycombe Gomme, *More Essays in Greek History and Literature* (Oxford, 1962), 147.

"I do not say that the ancient Greeks": Isaiah Berlin, *Four Essays on Liberty*, Introduction, xli.

The Greeks' imperfect notion of the "libre arbitre": Acton Papers, Add. 4938.

*Pensées choisies de Montesquieu tirées du "Common-Place Book" de Thomas Jefferson*, ed. by Gilbert Chinard (Paris, 1925), 51; from *De L'Esprit des Lois*, Livre XII, chap. 2.

122   The twentieth-century authority: James Mackinnon, *A History of Modern Liberty*, 5 vols. (London, 1906-1946), Introduction, 1:x-xii.

"Symbiosis": William T. Sanders, *Handbook of Middle American Indians*, 10:16.

123   Emotional and social "equilibrium": Anthony F. C. Wallace, *The Death and Rebirth of the Seneca* (New York, 1970), 45.

Indian America and "inexplicable pacifism": Wm Brandon, *The Last Americans* (New York, 1974), 131, 128-140, 479 *n*. 132.

Jefferson's "will prepare you to possess property": Thomas L. McKenney and James Hall, *History of the Indian Tribes of North America*, 3 vols. (Philadelphia, 1838-1844), 3:52 ff.

An American pamphleteer: *Thoughts on the State of the American Indians. By a Citizen of the United States* (New York, 1974), 30.

If "the right of property": François Peron, *Voyage de Découvertes aux Terres Australien*, 2 vols. and atlas (Paris, 1807-1816), quoted in George W. Stocking, Jr., "French Anthropology in 1800," *Isis*, 55, pt. 2 (1964), 140-41.

Each "man to have a farm of his own": Jedidiah Morse, *Report to the Secretary of War of the United States, on Indian Affairs, Comprising a Narrative of a Tour Performed in the Summer of 1820, Under a Commission from the President of the United States* (New Haven, 1822), Appendix, 10-14.

Create "in the savages new 'needs' ": Joseph Marie Degérando, *The Observation of Savage Peoples* (Berkeley, 1969), 155, 177.

124   Pliny (the Elder) is quoted from his *Natural History*, bk. 18.

Mexico's "most grievous" malady: Lesley Byrd Simpson, *Many Mexicos*, third edition (Berkeley, 1959), 228.

125   Private property from the Code of Hammurabi: Lewis Mumford, *The City in History* (New York, 1961), 108.

"The doctrine of mutual respect": Acton Papers, Add. 4862.

126   Jean Bodin, *République* (1576), 192.

Rebellion a sin: Hobbes as analyzed in Maitland, "Historical Sketch of Liberty," 34.

The "conflict was with wickedness": Acton Papers, Add. 4901.

No "right to be right against authority": Acton Papers, Add. 4963.

Martin Luther, "Against the Robbing and Murdering Hordes of Peasants," 1525, *Works*, 46:46-55.

127   "Chinese administration": André Malraux, *Rapport*, 3:170.

"Only that is moral": Leonid Brejnev, at the 25th Congress of the Communist Party of the USSR, quoted by Jacques Rueff, who described this statement as a paraphrase of a text of Lenin's, *Rapport*, 3:42.

Despotism as a "central Western tradition": Berlin, *Four Essays on Liberty*, 153, 154.

128   The origin of syphilis: Alfred W. Crosby, Jr., *The Columbian Exchange; Biological and Cultural Consequences of 1492* (Westport, Conn., 1977, originally published 1972), 147.

129   Blackstone: *The Sovereignty of the Law, Selections from Blackstone's Commentaries on the Laws of England*, ed. by Gareth Jones (London, 1973), 118, 123-24; and on "devising real property," 127-28.

Ralph Waldo Emerson, *Representative Men* (published 1850 but included in a lecture series in Boston, 1845-46, and in England, 1847-48); the comment quoted is from the closing lines of "Napoleon; or The Man of the World."

Lewis Henry Morgan, *Ancient Society, or Researches in the Lines of Human Progress from Savagery through Barbarism to Civilization* (New York, 1877).

130   Herbert Spencer, *The Principles of Sociology* (London, 1882), 2:643-44.

Perry Miller, *The Life of the Mind in America from the Revolution to the Civil War* (New York, 1965), 224.

*Ibid.*, 224-25, the Blackstone commentaries, quoting Samuel Chipman and James Kent.

English colonists creating some of their law "afresh": Zechariah Chaffee, Jr., "Colonial Courts and the Common Law," read at the December, 1945, meeting of the Massachusetts Historical Society.

New World law liberalizing the "release of creative energy": James Willard Hurst, *Law and the Conditions of Freedom in the Nineteenth-century United States* (Madison, Wis., 1956), 107.

131 Destruction "of older forms of property": Morton J. Horwitz, "The Transformation in the Conception of Property in American Law, 1780-1860," *University of Chicago Law Review*, 40, 290.

The right wing American politician: William E. Simon, *A Time for Truth* (New York, 1978), 19-22.

The "Libertarian" party's statement: *San Francisco Chronicle*, news item, September 10, 1979.

The "moral law" of right to property: Herbert Spencer, *Social Statics, Abridged and Revised; Together With The Man Versus The State* (London, 1892, originally 1850 and 1884), 64, 402, 361-63.

132 Joseph de Maistre, *Les Soirees de Saint-Petersbourg . . .* 2 vols. (Lyon, 1822), 1:44.

Maistre's view, as summed up in Francis Bayle, *Les Idées Politiques de Joseph de Maistre* (Paris, 1945), 101.

Liberty "always supposes order": Acton Papers, Add. 5684.

The Maya "obedience to the unenforceable": Sylvanus Griswold Morley and George W. Brainerd, *The Ancient Maya*, third edition revised (Stanford, 1956), 58.

134 Acton Papers, Add. 4870.

James Fitzjames Stephen, *Liberty, Equality, Fraternity* (originally published 1873, reprinted, with an Introduction by R. J . White, Cambridge, 1967).

135 The Italian Fascist slogan and Mussolini's comment on war: *Enciclopedia Italiana*, 1932, entry on "Doctrina del fascismo."

"Mankind is tired of liberty": Mussolini, in the journal *Gerarchia*, of which he was founder and editor, April, 1923.

"Liberty is exhausted": Pierre Drieu La Rochelle, *Socialisme Fasciste* (Paris, 1934), 102.

*The Journals of André Gide*, translated, selected, and edited by Justin O'Brien, 2 vols. (New York, 1956), 2:137, Oct., 1931.

"Reliable estimates" of seventy million dead: George Steiner, Preface to J. S. McClelland, ed., *The French Right (from De Maistre to Maurras)* (London, 1970).

Oswald Mosley, *Fascism* (London, 1936), cited in Dorothy Fosdick, *What is Liberty?* (New York, *c.* 1938).

Stalin is quoted from John Strachey, *The Theory and Practice of Socialism* (London, 1936), also cited in Fosdick, *op.cit.*

"Erst kommt das Fressen": Bertolt Brecht, *Selected Poems*, translated by H. R. Hays (New York, 1947), Introduction, 9.

136    The "abnormal complexity" of modern life: Arthur O. Lovejoy, Foreword to Lois Whitney, *Primitivism and the Idea of Progress in English Popular Literature of the Eighteenth Century* (Baltimore, 1934), p xiv.

In "a complex society": Karl Polanyi, *The Great Transformation* (New York, 1944; Boston, paper, 1957), 254

Friedrich Engels to August Bebel, March 18-28, 1875, cited by Stalin in *Leninism*, Vol. 2:225 (1933), quoted in Fosdick, *op.cit.*

Leon Trotsky: *The Defense of Terrorism: A Reply to Karl Kautsky* (London, 1921), 157, quoted in Fosdick, *op.cit.*

The "coercion, violence, executions": Berlin, *Four Essays on Liberty*, 17.

137    Acton Papers, Add. 4870, 4901.

The "law of self government": Acton Papers, Add. 4901.

138    Karl Popper, *The Open Society and Its Enemies*, 2 vols. (London, fifth edition revised, 1966), 2:236.

"The history of liberty is the condition of minorities": Acton Papers, Add. 4870.

Montesquieu, *De L'Esprit des Lois* (1749), bk. 11, chap. 2.

More than "two hundred senses of this protean word": Berlin, *Four Essays on Liberty*, 121.

The "reference to three items": John Rawls, *A Theory of Justice* (Cambridge, Mass., 1971), 201 ff.

Berlin's definition of positive and negative liberty: "Two Concepts of Liberty," in *Four Essays on Liberty*, 121-22.

139 Walt Whitman, "By Blue Ontario's Shore" (1856, 1881).

"Bread and liberty": Chinard, *La Déclaration des Droits de l'Homme* . . . (pamphlet, 1945).

140 *Ibid.*, the Malouet quotation. Chinard thinks this the earliest use of *democracy* applied to the American government.

Only "in America": Henry Steele Commager, *The Empire of Reason / How Europe Imagined and America Realized the Enlightenment* (New York, 1977), 238.

Emile de Laveleye, Préface to Acton, *Histoire de la Liberté* (Bruxelles, 1878).

Maitland, "Historical Sketch of Liberty," 19, 20.

Victoria Ginger's note is from a personal communication.

Pierre-Samuel Dupont [de Nemours] is quoted from a letter inserted in 1769 in *Ephemérides du Citoyen*, cited in Chinard, *La Déclaration des Droits de l'Homme* (pamphlet).

Diderot, *Oeuvres Politiques*, ed. by Paul Verniere (Paris, 1965), 1:489, "Aux Insurgents d'Amerique," 1782, first published December, 1778.

141 Raynal, *Histoire Philosophique* (Genève edition, 1780), 459.

Laveleye, Préface to Acton, *Histoire de la Liberté*.

A "network of values": Berlin, *Four Essays on Liberty*, xli.

142 Acton Papers, Add. 4901.

Pufendorf, *The Law of Nature and Nations* (1749), bk. 2, chap. 2.

Kant's contradictory influence and the particular problem of freedom in Germany: Leonard Krieger, *The German Idea of Freedom* (Chicago 1957, 1972), from which all these examples are drawn — Preface and pp 56 and 86-87 in the 1972 paper edition.

143  Frederick Jackson Turner Papers, Huntington Library, San Marino, California. Ray Allen Billington, through whose kindness this quotation (from a handwritten draft for a term summary at Harvard) was provided, dated it at about 1921.

No "deepset pattern of Indian institutions": James Willard Hurst, *Law and the Conditions of Freedom* (1966), 35.

144  "I laugh at those": J.-J. Rousseau, *Considerations sur la Gouvernement de la Pologne* (1772).

*Language, Thought, and Reality, Selected Writings of Benjamin Lee Whorf*, ed. by John B. Carroll (Cambridge, Mass., 1956), Introduction, 20-21.

# Chapter 6

147  Peter Martyr: Gaffarel, *Orbe Novo*, Fourth Decade, chap. 9, 581-83.

*Ibid.*, the editor's skeptical note: *n2*, p 581.

*Ibid.*, 292*n*, the gentle note on swamp water turning into frogs.

148  An "ancient ethnological" model: Margaret T. Hodgen, "Montaigne and Shakespeare Again," *Huntington Library Quarterly*, 16 (November, 1952), 42.

Chinard, *L'Amérique*, 431.

J. H. Elliott, *Old World and New*, 21, 20, 5.

A still more recent study: Robert F. Berkhofer, Jr., *The White Man's Indian* (New York, 1978), Preface, xvi. This work is drawn from an article prepared for the Indian-White relations volume of the new *Handbook of North American Indians* being issued by the Smithsonian Institution.

A frequently quoted work of a few years ago: Franklin L. Baumer, Foreword to Henri Baudet, *Paradise on Earth, Some Thoughts on European Images of non-European Man* (Holland, 1959, English translation, New Haven, 1965), vii.

149  J.-J. Rousseau, "Dernière réponse à M. Bordes," *Oeuvres Complètes* (Paris, 1852), 1:500.

"The first inhabitants of Italy": Pompeius Trogus, selections from Justinus, *Historiarum philippicarum epitomen*, 42: i, 3-4, written in the time of Augustus; quoted in Lovejoy and Boas, *Contributions to the History of Primitivism*, 67.

150   Tertullian, *Adversus Marcionem*, 1:1, cited in Lovejoy and Boas, *op. cit.*, 343.

     *Ibid.*, 343, Claudian, from *Rufinum*, 1.

     Agatharkhides: G. W. B. Huntingford, editor and translator, *The Periplus of the Eythraean Sea* (London, 1980), 180, 183, 144.

     Strabo: *Ibid.*, 189.

     Montesquieu, *Lettres Persanes* (1721), Lettre XII.

     Saint Ambrose's denunciation: A. O. Lovejoy, *Essays in the History of Ideas* (Baltimore, 1948), 307.

     Seneca, *De ira*, 2: xv, cited in Lovejoy and Boas, *op. cit.*, 365.

     The pretended Scythian harangue: the spurious *Letters* of Anacharsis, quoted in Lovejoy and Boas, *op. cit.*, 330.

     The Golden Age king "who was free from care": the *Aetna* (attributed to Virgil), 9-16, quoted in Lovejoy and Boas, *op. cit.*, 43n.

     *Aeneid*, 8:324-27, quoted in Lovejoy and Boas, *op. cit.*, 58.

     Seneca, *Epistulae morales*, 90, quoted in Lovejoy and Boas, *op. cit.*, 269.

151   Columbus's biographer: Samuel Eliot Morison, *Admiral of the Ocean Sea* (1942), 2:153.

152   John H. Rowe, "Renaissance Foundations of Anthropology," *American Anthropologist* (1965).

153   The "presumptuous conceit of European civilization": Fulvio Papi, *Antropologia e Civilta nel Pensiero de Giordano Bruno* (Firenze, 1968), 200.

     Bodin, *République*, 727-28.

154   The bull of Taugete: Benzoni, translated by Chauveton, *Histoire* (edition of Genève, 1579), 326-29.

     Gonzalo Fernandez d'Oviedo, *L'Histoire Naturelle et Generale des Indes . . . traduicte de Castillan en Francois par Jean Poleur* (Paris, 1555), bk. 3, chap. 6; bk. 5, chap. 3.

Richard Eden's Peter Martyr: *The First Three English Books on America*, ed. by Edward Arber (Birmingham, 1885), 199.

When a traveler "was moved by the novel customs of the New World natives": Wilcomb E. Washburn, "The Clash of Morality in the American Forest," *First Images of America*, 1:336.

155 The great Buffon as summarized in Antonello Gerbi, *The Dispute of the New World*, revised and enlarged edition translated by Jeremy Moyle (Pittsburgh, 1973, originally Italy, 1955), Prologue, xvi.

156 Georges Louis Leclerc, Comte de Buffon, *Histoire Naturelle, Générale et Particulière, avec la Description du Cabinet du Roi* (Paris, 1761), 9:104, 85-86, 103, 112-13.

The American "strong and handsome": Gerbi, *op. cit.*, 154.

Abbé Corneille de Pauw, *Recherches Philosophiques sur les Américains, ou Mémoires Intéressants pour servir à l'Histoire de l'Espèce Humaine*, 3 vols. (Berlin, 1768-1770); vol. 3, published a year after the first two volumes, is a rebuttal to criticism (reprinted therein) by Dom Antoine-Joseph Pernety, Frederick II's librarian.

*Ibid.*, 1:1, the phrase, "ou dégeneré ou monstrueux."

Kant is quoted from his lectures on "Philosophical Anthropology" at Konigsberg, 1772, quoted in Gerbi, *op. cit.*, 330.

Joseph de Maistre, *Soirées de Saint-Petersbourg* (third edition, 1836), 1:75.

Hegel's "immature and impotent" America is noted in Gerbi, *op. cit.*, Prologue, xv, and 426.

157 Jefferson's description of Raynal is from his *Writings, Memorial Edition* (1903-1904), 18:170, cited in Gilbert Chinard, "Eighteenth Century Theories of America as a Human Habitat," *Proceedings of the American Philosophical Society*, Vol. 91 (Philadelphia, 1947), 41.

One of today's better-known French historians: Pierre Chaunu, *L'Amérique et les Amériques (de la Préhistoire à Nos Jours* (Paris, 1964), p 15, cited in Gerbi, *op. cit.*, 561.

The "sham natural science": Gerbi, *op. cit.*, 76.

The heading for Chapter One of *De L'Amérique et des Américains, ou Observations Curieuses du Philosophe La Douceur* [Zacharie de' Pazzi de Bonneville] (Berlin, 1771), is quoted in Gerbi, *op. cit.*, 659.

The "Savages think as they wish": closing lines to the same little (80 pages) book of Pazzi de Bonneville's, cited in Henry Ward Church, "Corneille de Pauw, and the Controversy Over His Recherches Philosophique sur les Americans," *Publications of the Modern Language Association of America*, Vol. 51 (1936), p 197.

It should perhaps be noted that De Pauw wrote similar "Philosophical Researches" on various other peoples elsewhere in the world (Egyptians, Chinese, Greeks) without exciting any controversy whatever, then or later.

The Pazzi chapter on sex is pp 38-45.

Cotton Mather, *Magnalia Christi Americana* (1702), bk. 7, vol. 108.

158    Rather too pointedly contrary to the theory "of Jean-Jacques": Chinard, *L'Amérique*, 371. Chinard discusses in this same work, p. 396, the Raynal/Diderot opposition to Rousseau and its motivation.

The "Savages of these countries are extremely fecund": Pelleprat, *Relation*, pt. 2, 53.

159    The pre-Columbian population of Hispaniola as large as seven to eight million is suggested by Sherburne Friend Cook and Woodrow Wilson Borah, *Essays in Population History*, vol. 1: *Mexico and the Caribbean* (Berkeley, 1971), 408.

The pre-Spanish population of central Mexico at some twenty-five million: Woodrow Wilson Borah and Sherburne Friend Cook, *The Aboriginal Population of Central Mexico on the Eve of the Spanish Conquest* (Berkeley, 1963).

The "estimate of brigands": Las Casas, *Oeuvres*, ed. Llorente (Paris, 1822), 1:365, quoted in W. H. Prescott, *History of The Conquest of Mexico* (1843), 1:97.

Exaggeration of the mass sacrifice figures at the dedication of the temple of Huitzilopochtli is demonstrated in Sherburne Friend Cook, "Human Sacrifice and Warfare as Factors in the Demogaphy of pre-Colonial Mexico," *Human Biology*, 18/2 (May, 1946), 81-102; and by my own calculations in *The Last Americans*, 124, and *n*124, 478.

Acton Papers, Add. 4862.

160 Juan Ginés de Sepúlveda, *Demócrates Alter*, cited in Francisco Guerra, *The pre-Columbian Mind* (London-New York, 1971).

The definition of primitivism: Lovejoy and Boas, *Contributions to the History of Primitivism*, 1, 7.

"Primitive" man less "an object to be manipulated": Washburn, "The Clash of Morality in the American Forest," 348.

The "second period of barbarism": Herbert Marcuse, *One Dimensional Man* (Boston, 1964), 200.

Something other than "a utopian state of nature": Lévi-Strauss, *Tristes Tropiques*, 353.

161 The objective "is self-knowledge": Stanley Diamond, *In Search of the Primitive, a Critique of Civilization* (New Brunswick, N.J., 1974), 101, quoted in Washburn, *loc. cit.*

A recent biography: Ramon Menendez Pidal, *El Padre Las Casas, Su Doble Personalidad* (Madrid, 1963), 352.

His "mental imbalance": Guerra, *op. cit.*, 76.

Selections from Las Casas' *Historia* were published in English as his *History of the Indies* in 1971.

162 To which "political reformers could appeal": Maitland, "Historical Sketch of Liberty," 32.

The typical instances of such exaggeration are all quoted from Henri Baudet, *Paradise on Earth*, 35, 58, 27, 36. This work is cited as a standard modern reference on its subject by the relevant specialist in the new *Handbook of North American Indians* being issued by the Smithsonian: R. F. Berkhofer, *White Man's Indian*, 216, *n*7.

Presumed shibboleths: Harry Levin, *The Myth of the Golden Age in the Renaissance* (Bloomington, Ind., 1969; London, 1970, the London edition used here), Preface, XVI.

163 The "notion of Conscience": Adam Smith, *Theory of Moral Sentiments* (1759), 2:287, quoted in Acton Papers, Add. 4901.

The "sovereignty of conscience": Acton Papers, Add. 4901.

An "integral part of the theorizing of Victorian ethnologists," Stocking, "French Anthropology in 1800," 140-41.

The "integrity of Nuclear American civilizations": Philip Phillips, "The Role of Trans-Pacific Contacts in the Development of New World Pre-Columbian Civilization," *Handbook of Middle American Indians* (1966), 4:302.

164 New World culture "overwhelmingly determined from within": A. L. Kroeber, *Anthropology*, third edition (New York, 1948), 561.

Friedrich Schiller, *Sämtliche Werke*, Horen-Ausgabe, 22 vols. (München, 1910-1924), 12:114; cited in Deric Rigen, *Freedom and Dignity; the Historical and Philosophical Thought of Schiller* (The Hague, 1965), 39.

Diametrically opposed to the Christian myth: Richard Slotkin, *Regeneration Through Violence, the Mythology of the American Frontier, 1600-1800* (Middletown, Conn., 1973), 46.

Rousseau is quoted from his Préface to *Narcisse.*

165 Similar "in many ways to the earlier approach": Washburn, *loc. cit.*

Indian America had "played so passive a role": Henry Steele Commager, *The Empire of Reason*, 77.

My disagreement with this time-honored belief was documented in "American Indians and American History," Introduction to *The Last Americans*, 1-23.

166 We "need an ethics which defies success": Karl Popper, *The Open Society*, 2:277.

Max Stirner and B. Traven: Michael L. Baumann, *B. Traven An Introduction* (Albuquerque, 1976), 63-64, 77-78, 118.

The "new order of things commencing": Paul Hazard, *La Crise de la Conscience Européène* (edition of 1961), 1:420.

The "greatest of all moral and spiritual revolutions": Karl Popper, *The Open Society* (fifth edition revised, 1966), Preface to the Second Edition, ix.

In "ancient times and down to the seventeenth century": Arthur O. Lovejoy, Foreword to Whitney, *Primitivism and the Idea of Progress*, xii.

# Index

A

Aacanibas, 73
absolutism, *ix*, 31-2, 63-4, 74-5, 126-7, 132; and justice, 131-2; arguments for, 31, 126-7, 131-2, 134-7; in New World, 55, 147; in present day, 127, 133-4, 136-7, 144; in socialist states, 133-4; opposition to, 32, 86-7, 132; *see also* adversarianism, authoritarianism, dominium, hierarchism
abundance, in Europe, 76; in golden world, 21-3, 149; in New World, 7, 14, 21, 24, 66-7, 149
Abyssinia, 20
Acadia, 151
Acosta, José de, 12, 13, 21, 44, 119
Acton, John Emerich Edward Dalberg-Acton, Lord, 119-21, 125-6, 134, 137, 159; on absolutism, 74, 132; on adversarianism, 136; on conscience, 142, 163; on latifundia, 120, 124; on liberty in antiquity, 25-6, 121; on Rousseau, 109
Adam, 85, 160
Adam le Yep, 76
Adario, 89-94, 101-3, 105, 109
adversarianism, *ix*, 33, 139, 143-4; and religion, 27, 31-2, 33; in antiquity, 25-6, 120, 121; in Middle Ages, 26-7, 122; in present day, 113-4, 134, 136-7, 144, 166; *see also* absolutism, authoritarianism, dominium, hierarchism
Aelian, 152
*Aeneid, The*, 150
Africa, 20, 82, 107-8, 151
Agatharkhides, 150
Age of Reason, *see* Enlightenment
agriculture, 19, 164; in antiquity, 22, 124; in Europe, 74-7, 164; in New

World, 54-5, 58-9, 123, 147
Albani, (Abbé, later Cardinal) Annibale, 87
Albertus Magnus ("Maitre Albert"), 64
Alcibiades, 26, 121
Alexander (of Macedonia), 18, 25
Algonquin Indians, 107
*Alzire*, 164
Amazons, 6, 22
ambition, Ronsard's denunciation, 16-17
Ambrose (Saint), 150
America, colonization of, 14-15, 23, 38-9, 40, 42, 66-70, 72-3, 79, 87-9; discovery of, 5, 148; exploration of, 6-10, 14, 21-2, 39-40, 60, 65, 69, 72-3, 87-8, 143; Indian policy, 123; libertinism in, 40, 67, 72-3; political thought, 139-41; scientific theories concerning, 106-7, 155-7; *see also* New World
American frontier, Indian influence upon, 143
American opinion of Europe, 77
American Revolution, 25, 119, 139-41
Amsterdam, 92
Anahuac, 122
*Ancient Maya, The*, 56
anarchy, 87, 89, 131, 166
Andes, 124
anthropology, and Marxism, 133; and New World isolationism, 163-4; as a colonial ideology, 157; origin of, 7; in Renaissance, 22; Rousseau's knowledge of, 110; values of, 160, 165; *see also* archaeology, ethnology, Indians
Antilles, 36, 67